D1430775

INTEL

KEN CONBOY

INTEL

INSIDE INDONESIA'S INTELLIGENCE SERVICE

EQUINOX
PUBLISHING
JAKARTA SINGAPORE

EQUINOX PUBLISHING (ASIA) PTE. LTD.
PO Box 6179 JKSGN
Jakarta 12062
Indonesia

www.EquinoxPublishing.com

ISBN 979-97964-4-X

©2004 Ken Conboy

First Equinox Edition 2004

3 5 7 9 10 8 6 4 2

All rights reserved.

CONTENTS

PREFACE

I n October 2003, an officer from Indonesia's State Intelligence Agency (*Badan Intelijen Negara*, or BIN) stared at the young, goateed Asian sitting in a bare Karachi cell. Composed and well spoken, Gun Gun Rusman Gunawan motioned with his manacled hands to emphasize a point. The younger brother of Hambali, Southeast Asia's most infamous terrorist, Gun Gun had been detained by Pakistani authorities on 1 September. Ironically, the tip that led to his arrest came from his elder sibling, who had been captured in Thailand three weeks earlier.

What Gun Gun revealed under interrogation underscored the adaptability of the latest breed of international terrorists. He had led a cell of nearly two-dozen Asians – six Indonesians, the rest Malaysians – who had ventured to Pakistan in 2001 ostensibly to study at Islamic boarding schools. Calling themselves *al-Ghuraba* – Arabic for "The Foreigners" – their curriculum was, in fact, only partially religious. During their summer break in 2002, for example, they busied themselves perfecting counter-surveillance techniques learned from an Indonesian who had earlier trained in Afghanistan. Several of the al-Ghuraba members, too, lobbied to partake in the sectarian struggle in neighboring Kashmir.

The ultimate goal of al-Ghuraba was to return to Southeast Asia and lead the next generation of regional jihadists. But prior to that, in retaliation for his brother's arrest, Gun Gun planned for his cell members to kidnap an American executive in Karachi and hand him over to al-Qaeda; that plan was thwarted by the timely arrest of the remaining cell members in late September.

Despite those arrests, BIN could hardly rest easier. After all, al-Ghuraba had been hiding in plain sight for two years without arousing attention. Worse, an estimated one hundred additional Indonesians were enrolled in Karachi boarding schools known for their radical jihadist cirricula. BIN's campaign against religious extremism was obviously not going to be concluded anytime soon.

Indonesia's intelligence service, of course, far predates the war on terrorism. Here, for the first time, the full story of BIN and its predecessor agencies is chronicled in a detailed, objective account. It is important for this story to be told for several reasons. First, it puts contemporary Indonesian history in a more nuanced and pragmatic light. The New Order regime of President Suharto took pains to portray itself as being diplomatically neutral during the Cold War. In fact, its intelligence services were exceedingly aggressive in countering communist diplomats on Indonesian soil. By understanding this, Indonesia's role in the second half of the twentieth century can be placed in better perspective.

Second, while dozens of books about the CIA and KGB are published each year, it is rare for an intelligence agency in the developing world to be documented in such rich operational detail. Indeed, this is the first time that such a book about a Southeast Asian intelligence organization is available to the public. These operational details will allow historians to better understand intelligence operations during the post-World War II era.

And lastly, BIN has been at the forefront of Indonesia's war on terrorism even before 11 September 2001. While some aspects of this clandestine campaign have been leaked to the media, this book provides far more details than previously available.

Looking ahead, BIN can only retain its prominent role in countering the legion of challenges faced by the Republic of Indonesia. Its regional branches will keep a finger on the pulse of tensions in the provinces, especially in troublespots like Aceh and Papua. Its agents will gather information on drug smugglers and currency counterfeiters. And a large number of its officers will continue playing a lead role in countering terrorists – both domestic and foreign – that continue to foster deadly attacks across the archipelago. It is hoped that this history will allow BIN's influence and capabilities in these areas to be better understood and appreciated.

This book is based upon both written sources and oral interviews. To the extent possible, oral sources have been identified in end notes; some interviews, especially among serving intelligence officers, must remain anonymous. Special thanks go out to Lieutenant General (retired) A.M. Hendropriyono, who was extremely generous with his time and extraordinarily supportive of efforts to chronicle the history of the agency he now oversees. Without exception, BIN's other senior officials also went out of their way to offer insights and comments. Strong thanks, too, go to Mark Hanusz and John Hanusz for the yeoman's effort they gave in editing and producing this volume.

Despite such support, it must be stressed that this work is an unofficial history and does not necessarily reflect opinions within BIN. As a courtesy, BIN officials were allowed to see a draft of this book for their comments. Upon review, they requested two omissions – each consisting of a single word – to protect sources and methods. In both cases (on pages 190 and 246) these items were redacted.

Although all books are a collaborative effort, the author takes responsibility for everything in these pages. Any errors in fact or interpretation are my own.

Ken Conboy
Jakarta, December 2003

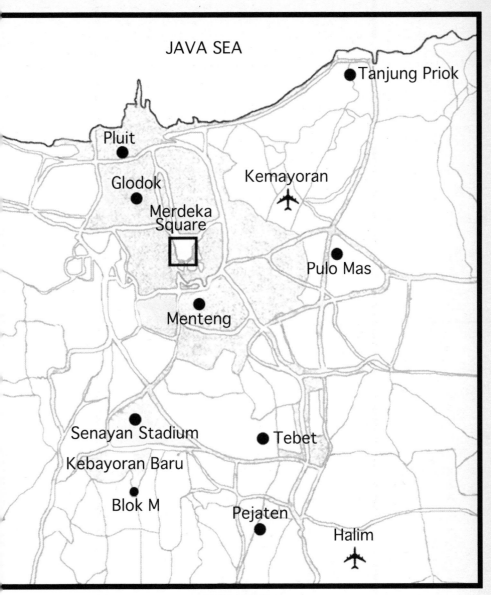

JAVA SEA

Tanjung Priok

Pluit

Glodok

Kemayoran

Merdeka
Square

Pulo Mas

Menteng

Senayan Stadium

Tebet

Kebayoran Baru

Blok M

Pejaten

Halim

JAKARTA

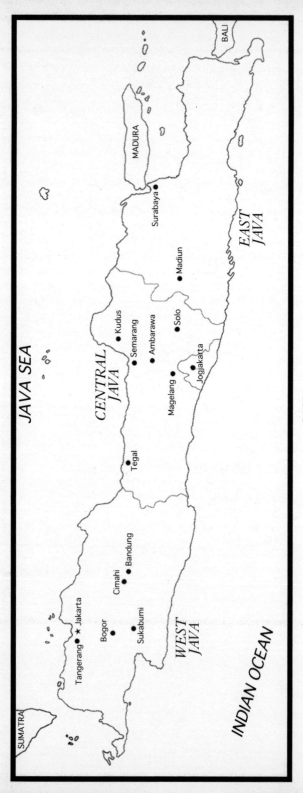

JAVA

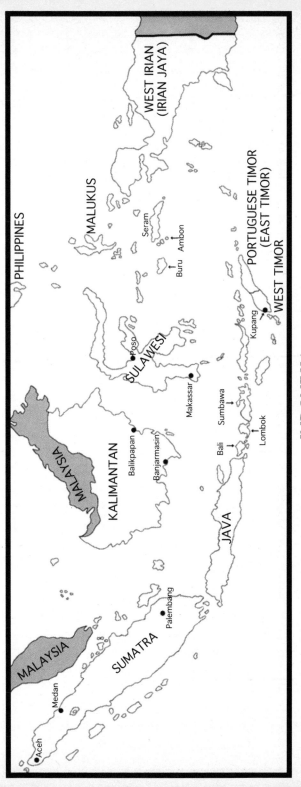

INDONESIA

INTEL

CHAPTER ONE

TIP OF THE ICEBERG

A s Indonesia's first spymaster, Zulkilfi Lubis hardly looked the role. Born in Aceh one day after Christmas 1923 as the fifth of ten children, the slight, bespectacled Lubis shunned sports as a youth. Even his complexion – soft, porcelain white – and voice – equally soft, almost effeminate – conspired against any hint of machismo. [1]

In the classroom, however, Lubis more than held his own. By the time he graduated junior high in 1941, good grades earned him a berth at a reputable senior high school in the Javanese cultural capital of Jogjakarta. The following year, when the Imperial Japanese pushed across the Indonesian archipelago, they immediately recognized his scholastic potential: not only did the 18-year old Lubis make an early cut for militia training, but in early 1943, he was among the first Indonesians selected as an officer cadet for a Japanese-controlled local auxiliary force known as Defenders of the Homeland (*Pembela Tanah Air*, or Peta).

In Peta, Lubis got his first exposure to the fundamentals of intelligence. In Tangerang, a town on the outskirts of Jakarta, the Japanese had established a local version of their famed Nakano military intelligence school; Lubis was among its first graduates.[2] Following this, he was posted in mid-1944 to Japan's regional intelligence center in Singapore. There, he absorbed not only theory, but also practical applications: among the best lessons were those drawn from a Japanese intelligence officer who recited tales of conquering the French in Indochina largely through a psychological warfare campaign, rather than force of arms.

By the time of Japanese capitulation in August 1945, Lubis could claim more wartime intelligence experience than any other Indonesian. Rushing back to Jakarta, he linked up with former Peta colleagues – most of whom were now throwing their weight behind an independent Indonesian Republic – and mused aloud about the need to create an intelligence capability for the new state. He was openly supported in this endeavor by two former Japanese officers, neither of whom was particularly anxious to surrender to the Allies or return to their homeland.

For the next month, Lubis – taking for himself the lofty rank of colonel – worked quickly to create Indonesia's first intelligence organization. Known simply as the Special Agency (*Badan Istimewa*), it reflected the urgency of the times.[3] Its initial membership was limited to about forty former Peta officers and ex-Japanese informants on hand in Jakarta, all of whom received no more than a week of lectures from Lubis in such topics as sabotage, psychological warfare, and the tenets of intelligence. With this minimal foundation, they were dispatched across Java with orders to talk up support for the Republic and report back on possible enemy designs.

The Republic of which they spoke faced a legion of challenges. Declared on 17 August, the nascent Republic's president was the charismatic, flamboyant orator Sukarno; his vice president was the pious, reserved Mohammad Hatta. But while knowledge of, and support for, Sukarno and Hatta was sufficiently high on Java, awareness was far less strong on the outer islands.

There was also the matter of schisms among the Republic's armed supporters. In theory, a unified revolutionary army was proclaimed on 5 October. But given Indonesia's island topography and myriad of ethnic groups, guerrilla bands were often divided along geographic and sectarian lines with little sense of command and control that extended beyond the district, much less the province. Further complicating matters was their disparity in training: some were skilled Peta veterans, others had once fought in the Dutch colonial military, and many others had no practical instruction at all. Thrown together, factions and prejudices took root.

Additionally, the Republic soon faced foreign opponents. While the Dutch openly declared the intent to retake their colony, they were spent from World War II and needed time to muster an expeditionary force. For the interim, the British had been selected among the Allies to accept the surrender of the Japanese in Indonesia and reassert a semblance of control. In effect, this meant frustrating republican plans.

Not surprisingly, clashes ensued. In late September 1945, the first large contingent of British troops landed on Java. Two months later, a major battle took place over control of Surabaya, with thousands of Indonesians perishing in a withering aerial bombardment. By year's end, a British contingent had stormed Semarang and was pushing its way across the center of the island.

By that time, Lubis had also shifted to Central Java and was looking to train further cycles of intelligence operatives. Scouring the Javanese heartland, there was no shortage of older teens that, due to wartime disruptions, had not completed high school. The three dozen he selected deliberately represented the archipelago: Javanese, Sundanese, Sumatrans, others from islands to the east, and even a second-generation Indonesian of Persian descent. Told to report to an overgrown coffee plantation near Ambarawa – a small hill town that hosted a sprawling Dutch fort and a key train terminus – the setting had more than a touch of the surreal. Recalls one of the trainees:

> We were sent to an abandoned Catholic church set up by Trappist monks who had taken a vow of silence. This got too hot because there was heavy fighting at Ambarawa, so we shifted to a former Japanese prisoner of war camp that once housed Dutch women.[4]

Taking up shelter in the former cells, the contingent was instructed by a diverse mix of advisors. On hand to conduct daily fitness drills were three former German submariners; crewmen on a U-boat grounded in Southeast Asia during the war, none had any yearning to go back to their defeated Nazi Germany. Running the paramilitary portion of the class were the two Japanese officers who had linked up with Lubis in Jakarta during mid-1945. Small unit tactics were taught by former Peta officers. And giving the students a weekly tutorial in intelligence was Lubis himself. His simple precept: they were to become "invisible soldiers engaged in a war of wits."[5]

By the first week of May 1946, all three dozen teens completed training and gathered in Jogjakarta. Because of wartime expediency, they were hurriedly commissioned as the Republic's first batch of second lieutenants.[6] They were also presented with identification cards signed by President Sukarno, who had shifted the republican headquarters to Jogjakarta early in the year.

According to their membership cards, the fresh lieutenants belonged to the Secret Agency of the State of Indonesia (*Badan Rahasia Negara Indonesia*, or Brani).[7] Officially formed on 7 May under the command of Lubis, Brani was an umbrella for a diverse spread of ad hoc units established by field commanders across Java. One such unit in Surabaya, known simply as Counter-Intelligence, was charged with ferreting out the large number of Dutch sympathizers in East Java. Another, known as Field Preparation, was to conduct reconnaissance and "prepare the field" by encouraging support for the Republic. No longer limiting his efforts to Java, Lubis arranged for small Field Preparation cells to travel by boat to such destinations as Bali, Kalimantan, Maluku, Nusa Tenggara, Sulawesi, and Sumatra.

A third group within Brani, built around the fresh contingent of second lieutenants, was slated for foreign operations. As the republican forces were perpetually short of ammunition and medicine, the lieutenants were to make their way to Singapore in search of these commodities. Though high on enthusiasm, these Brani operatives were short on something equally important: cash. Thinking ahead, Lubis had earlier approached some sugar cane plantation owners in the Javanese town of Tegal and negotiated a percentage of their income for export rights to Singapore. Lubis had also raided the opium reserves kept by the Dutch in Jogjakarta, marketing the opiate to Chinese merchants in Jakarta.[8] But that money could not cover the entire Brani budget. Most of the operatives dispatched to Singapore, therefore, did not have enough funds to pay for their own sustenance, let alone arrange for the procurement of critical wartime goods. To eat, many were forced to find menial labor (more than a few worked on the local British airbase).

Such hardships did not dampen enthusiasm. By 1947, several of the Brani operatives in Singapore had branched out to places like Hong Kong, Thailand, and Burma. While getting high marks for their effort, success remained fleeting. One of their few positive achievements: Lieutenant Aswis Sumarmo, who managed to reach Bangkok without a passport or financial backing, evoked just enough sympathy for the Indonesian cause to have a few boxes of medicine shipped home.

Back in Indonesia, Lubis worked hard to fulfill his role of spymaster. With Brani answerable directly to Sukarno, he was one of the few military officers able to enter the president's bedroom to give a briefing. This trust was repaid with loyalty. In July 1946, as Sukarno was having his authority challenged by Sudarsono, a senior officer in Central Java, Lubis arranged for one of his most competent Brani agents to serve as the president's aide. When a pistol-toting Sudarsono arrived at Sukarno's office for an emotional (and potentially deadly) showdown, the aide requested the general to secure his sidearm outside – only to turn it on Sudarsono, leading to the latter's immediate arrest.

But while Sukarno may have implicitly trusted Lubis, there were influential civilians within the young Republic's Ministry of Defense lobbying to have the intelligence function taken away from a military officer and placed under civilian rule. Taking the lead in this effort was the defense minister himself, Amir Sjarifuddin, a leftist independence activist since the thirties who had been a member of the underground resistance against the Japanese.

Earlier in his term as defense minister, Sjarifuddin had flirted with the creation of an intelligence organization within his ministry. Known as Defense Agency B (*Badan Pertahanan B*) and headed by a former police commissioner, the effort never made much headway. But following the results of a 12 March 1947 planning conference in Jogjakarta, Sukarno agreed on April 30 to merge all existing intelligence bodies into a new unit within Sjarifuddin's ministry. On the following day, Brani was dissolved, as was the skeletal Defense Agency B; both were now folded into a new office of the Ministry of Defense known as the Fifth Section (*Bagian V*).

From the start, political machinations were prominent within the Fifth Section. Handpicked by Sjarifuddin to lead the unit was a former navy cadet named Abdulrahman. Trained by the Allies in Australia during World War II, Abdulrahman had nothing by way of a formal intelligence background. But more important were his political sympathies: like the defense minister, he was left of center.

Under Abdulrahman, the Fifth Section remained a modest effort. Initially counting just thirteen other members in its headquarters, most were divided among desks focusing on military, political, and economic affairs. Dr. Rubijono, Sukarno's personal physician, handled coded communications.[9] Lubis, the most experienced in the group, was sidelined as one of a three-man executive staff.

It was not surprising that, given its limited numbers and underqualified human resources, what little the Fifth Section accomplished often bordered on the laughable. Remembers one field operative:

They had a former Japanese informant prepare a one-page memo on how to conduct surveillance. It included such pointers as 'keep a sufficient distance between you and the target,' and 'when peering from the corner of a building, take care not to be seen.' It was all common sense, almost a joke.[10]

Within two months of the section's creation, the Republic hit hard times. The Dutch, who had been patiently redeploying forces to Southeast Asia, launched a major offensive to retake the Indonesian archipelago. Within two weeks, they had managed to secure all of Java except for the Central Java heartland around Jogjakarta.

Though republican forces were on the ropes, a diplomatic reprieve was in the cards. Pressured from overseas – particularly by the United States – the Dutch were at the negotiating table by year's end. A subsequent truce – known as the Renville Agreement, after the U.S. warship where it was signed – was in effect by the beginning of 1948.

Renville had considerable impact on Indonesia's intelligence structure. On a superficial level, the agreement stipulated that all military officers accept reductions in rank; as a result, Lubis found himself demoted to lieutenant colonel. More substantial, the truce led to the fall of Sjarifuddin (who had been promoted to prime minister in mid-1947) in early 1948. As a result, his coddled Fifth Section was dissolved after less than a year in existence.

Seizing the opportunity, Lubis wasted little time wresting back the intelligence portfolio for himself. Because Sjarifuddin had encouraged members of the Indonesian Communist Party (*Partai Komunis Indonesia*, or PKI) to join the Fifth Section, that body was considered politically compromised. Instead of trying to resurrect a unit within the Ministry of Defense, for the next six months, Lubis worked on nurturing a tactical intelligence capability within the army.

Those efforts came none too soon. In August 1948, Sjarifuddin publicly proclaimed that he had been a secret PKI member since 1935. The following month, a PKI-controlled front seized control of the East Java town of Madiun. Incensed, the military struck back. By the end of November, the communist uprising in Madiun had been quelled. Fleeing the scene, Abdulrahman was eventually incarcerated by the Dutch. Less fortunate, Sjarifuddin was captured by the republicans and executed for his indiscretion.

While the PKI challenge had ended, the Republic had little reason for cheer. That December, the Dutch broke the peace accord and launched a major military offensive. This time, they successfully worked their way into Jogjakarta and took most of the republican leadership captive. Their gains proved Pyrrhic, however. As was the case during the first campaign, the Netherlands faced stifling diplomatic pressure. Although negotiations ran for nearly a year, it was increasingly evident that true Indonesian independence was a matter of when, not if. The end result came on 27 December 1949, at which time the Dutch agreed to transfer sovereignty for all its Southeast Asian holdings except West New Guinea.

Though Indonesia had thrown off the colonial shackles, challenges continued. Its young military – at the time, collectively known as War Forces (*Angkatan Perang*) – as of early 1950 had to contend with several rebellions flaring on outer islands. Of equal concern were the backroom intrigues within the military's upper ranks. This was to be expected: now that the war of independence was over, there were bound to be unwelcome troop cuts as the military rationalized its roster in line with a peacetime mandate and limited budget.

In the midst of this internecine fighting was Lubis. Over the previous two years, his efforts to nurture an intelligence agency had made little headway beyond lip service. Instead, Lubis had shown a special flair for picking personal fights with senior army officers. High on his hit list was the army chief of staff, Colonel Abdul Haris Nasution. Both Lubis and Nasution were Batak, the entrepreneurial and socially-blunt ethnic group from northeastern Sumatra; in fact, the two were cousins. But rather than forging close ties from their common heritage, Nasution and Lubis were among the most bitter rivals in the entire armed forces. Observed one of their contemporaries: "When you put a lion and tiger together, they fight."[11]

Lubis also had developed bad blood with the chief of staff of the War Forces, T.B. Simatupang. This seething rivalry ultimately cost Lubis (who had again risen to the rank of colonel) a tactical defeat. In early 1952, following his renewed efforts to establish an intelligence service in the capital of Jakarta, Simatupang intervened and downgraded the service to a minor staff position. This reduction was reflected in its bland, benign title: Information Bureau for the War Forces Staff (*Biro Informasi Staf Angkatan Perang*, or BISAP).[12]

From the start, BISAP languished. Part of this was due to continued limitations in budget and human resources. But much blame also fell on Lubis who, obsessed over his political sparring with Nasution and Simatupang, came to treat his intelligence post as a sideshow. Though he ultimately scored successes in the political arena (and was able to triumph over Nasution in a showdown during October 1952), BISAP as an organization withered from his lack of attention. By early the following year, it faded completely.[13]

Because of its inherent discretion, one truism of the intelligence world is that it encourages diplomatic pragmatism. In Indonesia, this became apparent in February 1952 when the latest in a series of short-lived Indonesian cabinets collapsed because of a dispute over U.S. military aid. Over the preceding months, Washington, in the midst of the Korean War, had been insistent that military assistance to Indonesia be contingent on Jakarta's public repudiation of the Communist bloc. The ill-fated Indonesian cabinet had acquiesced to the U.S. demand – only to catch a firestorm from top officials, including Mohammad Hatta, who fiercely safeguarded Indonesia's non-aligned foreign policy.

In April 1952, a new cabinet took its seat in Jakarta. Chosen for the critical role of defense minister was the Sultan of Jogjakarta, Hamengku Buwono IX. A popular public figure, the revered sultan had offered key support to Sukarno and Hatta throughout the independence struggle; for most of the revolution, in fact, he had sheltered the republican leadership in Jogjakarta.

On the political spectrum, the sultan was relatively neutral. Like Hatta, he held fast to non-alignment. Despite such neutrality, however, both the sultan and Hatta were soon being discreetly pitched by the brash U.S. ambassador to Indonesia, Merle Cochran. Renowned for his extensive contacts among Indonesia's elite, and his penchant for secrecy toward even his own embassy staff, Cochran had an intriguing offer. The U.S. government, he said, could provide clandestine training for an intelligence cadre within the sultan's Ministry of Defense. Playing on latent anti-Chinese sentiment felt by many Indonesians, Cochran noted that this cadre could act as a guerrilla force in the event of a possible communist Chinese invasion of Southeast Asia.

The offer put the sultan and Hatta in a bind. The previous cabinet, after all, had fallen precisely because of U.S. aid; advocating a strategic embrace with Washington was nothing short of political suicide. But at the same time, both figures desired a strategic intelligence capability, and BISAP was not delivering. What's more, Cochran promised that this American largesse would be offered away from the public eye. As quietly as it was offered, the two pragmatically consented.

To implement the project, Hatta turned to Sumitro Kolopaking. A former district chief from Central Java, Sumitro had earlier been appointed by Hatta as his most trusted aide in the Security Bureau (*Biro Keamanan*), a cabinet-level office that coordinated operations of the Ministry of Defense. Once Hatta and the sultan brainstormed a list of fifty capable civilians in their mid-twenties, Sumitro on 3 September 1952 sent orders for them to report to Jakarta. From there, all fifty were dispatched in early November to a quiet estate in Central Java and put through the paces of a monthlong paramilitary selection course.

Shortly before year's end, the top seventeen members from this contingent (including Sumitro's own son) were given new orders to make their way to a point along the beach due east of Semarang. There they found the cargo vessel *Maria Elisa* anchored offshore. Under cover of darkness, they shuttled out to the ship and were welcomed by its Japanese merchant crew.

Over the next three days, the *Maria Elisa* slowly steamed through the Makassar Strait between the islands of Kalimantan and Sulawesi. Heavy seas en route had left most of the trainees seriously ill, but all perked up when they saw a plane circle low overhead. The unmarked aircraft – a PBY Catalina amphibian – landed in the low swells and pulled abreast.

Though the Indonesians did not know it, the PBY was operated by Civil Air Transport (CAT), a Far East proprietary airline operated by the U.S. Central Intelligence Agency (CIA). Taking a skiff between the *Maria Elisa* and the amphibian, the recruits were soon in its cabin. Most had never seen the inside of an aircraft; as a rude baptism to flight, the pilot activated a pair of rocket booster pods during take-off. "Our stomachs," lamented one of the Indonesians, "went inside our heads."[14]

After an uneventful trip north, the PBY approached Clark Air Base in the Philippines. The hub of American airpower in Southeast Asia, Clark, 82 kilometers northwest of Manila, was the size of a small U.S. city. The Indonesians, however, saw little of it. As their plane taxied to the end of the runway, a jeep pulled in front. Hanging from the back of the vehicle was a handwritten sign reading FOLLOW ME. The pilot did as directed, steering the amphibian to a remote hanger. Assembling behind the building, the recruits were each given snacks and, in the event they needed to relieve themselves, a small shovel.

At nightfall, the Indonesians were ushered back aboard the PBY. Because of its slow speed but long loitering capability, the plane droned on well through the following dawn and did not come to rest until arriving at a tear-shaped island in the middle of the Western Pacific. Though the Indonesians were never told the location, they had arrived at the U.S. trust territory of Saipan.

Situated on the southern end of the Northern Mariana island chain, Saipan was of volcanic origin and had an equally violent history of human habitation. Its original population, coincidentally, had been seafarers from the Indonesian archipelago, but had been virtually wiped out by Spanish colonialists. Later sold to Germany and subsequently administered by Japan as part of a League of Nations mandate, the island, though no larger than the city of San Francisco, had taken on extraordinary significance by the time of World War II. This was because the Allied strategy in the Pacific hinged on the premise that the Japanese would not surrender until their homeland was invaded. According to Allied estimates, such an invasion would cost an estimated one million American lives and needed the support of a concerted air campaign. For this, Washington required a staging base where its bombers could launch and return safely; the Marianas chain, the U.S. top brass calculated, fell within the necessary range.

Before the Allies could move in, however, there remained the thorny problem of removing nearly 32,000 Japanese defenders firmly entrenched on the island. In June 1944, one week after the landings in Normandy, 535 U.S. naval vessels closed in on Saipan. In what was to become one of the most hotly-contested battles in the Pacific, they blasted the island from afar before putting ashore 71,000 troops.

The Japanese were not intimidated. Having already zeroed their heavy weapons on likely beachheads, they ravaged the landing columns. Some 3,100 U.S. servicemen died; another 13,100 were wounded or missing.

Despite such heavy Allied casualties, the Japanese had it worse. Overwhelmed by the size of the invasion force, some 29,500 defenders perished in the month-long battle to control the island. Of these, hundreds jumped to their deaths from the northern cliffs rather than face the shame of capture.

Once in Allied hands, the Marianas were quickly transformed into their intended role as a staging base for air strikes against Japan. It was from there, in fact, that a B-29 began its run to drop the atomic bomb on Hiroshima. Nine days later, Japan surrendered.

Following World War II, the United States remained on hand to administer the Northern Mariana Islands. In July 1947, this role was codified under a trusteeship agreement with the new United Nations, which specifically gave the U.S. Navy responsibility for the chain. In practice, this trusteeship translated into an exceedingly small U.S. presence. With Japan's wartime population either dead or repatriated, the chain boasted few settlements of any note; only Saipan hosted anything approaching the size of a town. Even its airfields – which had once been so critical during the war – now fell largely dormant after being vastly overshadowed by the sprawling U.S. military bases in neighboring Guam and the Philippines.

For the CIA, however, the tranquility of the Marianas held appeal. Looking for a discreet locale to build a Far East training camp to instruct agents and commandos from like-minded nations, the agency in 1950 established the Saipan Training Station. Officially known by the cover title, Naval Technical Training Unit, Saipan station took up much of the island's northern peninsula and featured numerous segregated compounds where groups of Asian trainees from various nations could spend several months in isolation.

On hand to greet Saipan's newest students was CIA instructor Gilbert Layton. A reserve cavalry officer during World War II, Layton had served in armored reconnaissance squadrons through 1946. Seconded to the CIA at the agency's inception in 1947, he conducted recruitment operations at refugee camps in Germany before switching to Saipan. He had already coached recruits from two of America's closest Asian allies, the Republic of Korea and the Republic of China on Taiwan.

As a first order of business, Layton had all the Indonesians swept for compromising pocket litter – photographs, clove cigarettes – that might link them to their home country. Next, each was given a simple American nickname to ease communication with their trainers. Sumitro's son, whose real name was Purboyo, was now dubbed Bob. Kartono Kadri, a Magelang native of small stature, was appropriately christened Shorty. Another, a former medical student from Jogjakarta, became Doc.

Over the next two months, the seventeen Indonesians were put through rigorous paces by a team of CIA advisors. Much of the training focused on paramilitary skills and Morse communication. "I fired more bullets during that short period," recalled one, "than during the entire five years of the revolution."

At that point, Shorty and Doc, both of whom showed exceptional promise, were taken aside for a month of concentrated instruction in intelligence tradecraft and analysis. The rest, meanwhile, continued their paramilitary tutorial.

In February 1953, all seventeen boarded a transport plane and headed for Clark Air Base. Once there, they transferred to a CAT amphibian and retraced their journey to the Makassar Strait. Rendezvousing with a U.S. Navy frigate, they landed on the sea and refueled. Taking off once more, they flew through the night and settled off the southern coast of Bali. There they waded ashore, then eventually made their way to Jakarta and reported to Sumitro.

The Indonesian capital, they found, had changed much during their absence. In October 1952, even before they had departed, President Sukarno had survived a tense showdown with the army leadership. The result of this had been the sacking of army chief Nasution and the elevation of Lubis to deputy army chief. Lubis's BISAP had already atrophied from a lack of attention; in its place, each of the military services was left to expand its own intelligence sections.

Within the Ministry of Defense, meanwhile, the sultan had stepped down as minister in December 1952. Still, the sultan retained close contact with Sumitro at the Biro Keamanan. Working through Sumitro, the sultan had the Saipan graduates gathered within a front organization known as *Firma Ksatria*; literally, the "Warrior Company."

Over the remainder of 1953, Ksatria members were dispatched on odd jobs around the country. Kartono Kadri – "Shorty" while on Saipan – spent time in Pontianak, West Kalimantan. Working with army auxiliaries, his task was to make a detailed survey of local Chinese inhabitants and gauge their sympathies. This was done because of lingering fears that the People's Republic of China might sweep through insular Southeast Asia. If that indeed were to take place, Kartono was pessimistic. "The Chinese were heavily represented around Pontianak, even among the peasantry," he recalls. "The army was like foreigners in the region."

Although the first Saipan contingent was perhaps not being used to its fullest potential, the U.S. in mid-1953 judged the project worthy of continuation. So, too, did the sultan and the vice president, who had Sumitro quietly ready a second cycle of nineteen trainees for Saipan. This group was exfiltrated by seaplane from a beach on North Sulawesi; after three months at the CIA base, they headed home. Rather than landing near Bali, this time, the

PBY placed them off the southern coast of Java.[15]

By the time the second Saipan cycle returned to Indonesia, the political landscape of the country was being turned on its head. With ineffectual cabinets falling on an almost annual basis, the PKI benefited from the resultant public disillusionment and made significant electoral gains in the 1955 polls. Disgusted by the political infighting, Vice President Hatta in late 1956 withdrew from public office. That same year, Colonel Lubis instigated a failed putsch, then fled Jakarta to the welcoming arms of a rebel movement gathering momentum on the islands of Sumatra and Sulawesi. On the diplomatic scene, ties to the West in general, and the U.S. in particular, degenerated due to Sukarno's caustic tongue and Washington's growing condemnation of non-alignment.

Throughout this critical period, the Indonesian government lacked a strategic intelligence body. Though the Saipan graduates still ostensibly belonged to the Ksatria front organization, their talents were being all but squandered; some returned to university, others were spread among minor government ministries. (Ironically, the rebel movements on Sumatra and Sulawesi began to receive covert CIA aid, and two cycles of Sumatran rebels were taken to Saipan in 1958 for agent training.[16]) While the army, air force, navy, and police each had their own intelligence desks, none of their product was being coordinated at the national level.

In late 1958, this was set to change. By that time, the military had already successfully swept through the main rebel base camps in Sumatra and Sulawesi. Far from turning complacent, however, Sukarno grew fixated on the persistent political opposition he was receiving from his national assembly. To sidestep the assembly, the president advocated a return to the 1945 wartime constitution; this featured a much more powerful presidency than the provisional constitution that had replaced it in 1950. The assembly, naturally, was strongly resisting efforts to curtail its power.

To coordinate his battle against the parliamentarians, Sukarno saw benefit in an intelligence body whose sole purpose would be to coordinate the push to implement the 1945 constitution. Accordingly, a government decree on 5 December 1958 authorized creation of a new organization called – appropriately – the Intelligence Coordination Agency (*Badan Koordinasi Intelijen*, or BKI).

Over the next four months, the BKI took shape. On the morning of 5 April 1959, Sukarno presided over its formal inauguration ceremony at the palace. Present were all members of the nascent agency: the heads of intelligence from the army, air force, navy, police, attorney general's office, and foreign ministry, as well as each of their deputies. Also present was a three-man BKI permanent staff, two of whom were Saipan graduates. These three, along with a navy colonel named as the overall BKI chief and a member of *Biro Keamanan* selected as his deputy, were given a modest office on Jalan Mampang I in Jakarta.[17]

Very quickly, the BKI's raison d'être wafted away. On 5 July, Sukarno dissolved the assembly and reinstituted the 1945 constitution by presidential decree. This effectively allowed the army and president to build up their power at the expense of the party system and parliamentary government, something that Sukarno was calling "Guided Democracy."

While Sukarno was obviously pleased with his expansion in authority, the BKI could hardly claim any credit in the process. The army, which was the true powerbroker, had already vowed its critical support prior to the creation of the BKI. And given that the military intelligence chiefs rarely had the time or compunction to gather at the BKI's office, even its coordinating function drew sneers. Mocked Kartono Kadri, one of the BKI's permanent staff members: "You cannot coordinate anything in Indonesia."[18]

But rather than abolishing the BKI, Sukarno elected to give it some teeth. More than a talk shop, he now wanted an intelligence unit with operational capabilities that answered directly to him. This was codified on 10 November, when the BKI was officially renamed the Central Intelligence Agency (*Badan Pusat Intelijen*, or BPI).

In some ways, little changed besides the initials. The BPI was still largely a coordinating forum that drew on voluntary intelligence contributions from the existing information networks established by the army, air force, navy, police, and attorney general's office. And its own numbers were still extremely anemic: the BPI headquarters – established in a converted house on Jalan Madiun in Jakarta's upscale Menteng neighborhood – counted just a dozen full-time officers.

There were some significant differences, however. For one thing, Sukarno made sure that the BPI got a comfortable budget for its modest size. As a result, the military intelligence chiefs began attending regular afterhours briefings – if only to get free dinners. Members of these frequent gatherings dubbed themselves the Joint Intelligence Estimates Group (JIEG).

Even more important, the BPI got an ambitious and politically connected chief. Dr. Subandrio, 44, was born in Malang, East Java, to an aristocratic family. Though he had graduated as a general medical practitioner on the eve of the Japanese invasion in 1942, diplomatic service was his calling: he served as the chief Indonesian representative in London from 1947 to 1949, ambassador to the United Kingdom for an additional four years, and ambassador to the Soviet Union for another three. In 1956, Subandrio was named secretary general of the foreign ministry; one year later, he was promoted to foreign minister.

As foreign minister, Subandrio initially impressed many in the diplomatic corps. An "articulate, skillful advocate," wrote the U.S. ambassador in 1958, "a master at creating impressions he desires to make."[19] But he also had a growing roster of detractors who lamented his undiplomatic habit of speaking over the top of others. Others derided his slavish devotion to Sukarno and political opportunism. His image was not helped by his wife, also a doctor from East Java, who was as crass as she was ambitious.

For those in the BPI, Subandrio was like an absentee landlord. Retaining his second hat as foreign minister, the doctor rarely bothered to grace the BPI's Jalan Madiun office (he did not even maintain his own room in the cramped headquarters). For daily operations, he ceded full authority to the JIEG, which in turn, exploited his coattails by browbeating full support from bureaucrats in the foreign ministry. Very quickly, diplomats around the world started satisfying intelligence requirements from the BPI. "Our headquarters looked small," said one JIEG member, "but we were only the tip of the iceberg."[20]

1   "Komandan Intelijen Pertama," *Tempo*, 29 July 1989.
2   Stephen C. Mercado, *The Shadow Warriors of Nakano* (Washington, D.C.: Brassey's, Inc., 2002), p. 239.
3   Members of the Special Agency were officially called Special Military Spies (*Penyelidik Militer Chusus*).
4   Interview with Aswis Sumarmo, 25 March 2003. The prison camp had earlier been the scene of horrific sexual crimes after Japanese soldiers screened the Dutch inmate population for sex slaves.
5   This precept was later codified in a code of conduct for intelligence officers that Lubis retained in all his subsequent intelligence roles. Interview with Irawan Sukarno, 11 March 2003.

6   This claim is contentious, as official Indonesian military texts recognize the 1948 graduates of the Military Academy in Jogjakarta as the country's first properly trained lieutenants.

7   Not by coincidence, Brani is pronounced *berani*, the Indonesian word for brave or courageous.

8   Interview with Suhario Padmodiwirjo, 30 April 2003.

9   Rubijono had been trained by the Allies during World War II; for a time he served in New Guinea when General Douglas MacArthur was in residence.

10   Padmodiwirjo interview.

11   Interview with Nasuhi, 27 May 2003.

12   For a brief period during 1949-1950, Lubis flirted with the idea of creating an intelligence organization within the defense ministry known simply as Defense Department Intelligence (*Intelijen Kementerian Pertahanan*, or IKP). Upon Simatupang's order, IKP was superceded by BISAP.

13   In a play on Indonesian words, Lubis lamented that "*BISAP habis diisap.*" Translation: "BISAP disappeared by sucking" – a reference to Simatupang sucking the life from it. Padmodiwirjo interview.

14   Interview with Kartono Kadri, 15 April 2003.

15   The CAT exfiltration from North Sulawesi, codenamed Eagle Flight, is recounted in a mission brief filed in the papers of C. Joseph Rosbert at the Air America/ CAT Archives (University of Texas –Dallas).

16   Kenneth Conboy and James Morrison, *Feet to the Fire* (Annapolis: Naval Institute Press, 1999), p. 80.

17   The full membership in the BKI, all of whom were at the inaugural ceremony, included air force Colonel Siswadi and Lt. Colonel Sudarmono, police Commissioner Oemar Chatab and Assistant Commissioner Samsudin, army Colonel Imam Soekarto and Lt. Colonel Djoehartono, navy Lt. Colonel Djasmani, Imam Soebardjo from the attorney general's office, and Mochtar Tayib from the Ministry of Foreign Affairs. Navy Colonel Pirngadi was named BKI chief, and Soeprapto from the *Biro Keamanan* was his deputy. The BKI permanent staff included Moeljadi Milono and Kartono Kadri from *Biro Keamanan*, and Police Assistant Commissioner Soebianto.

18   Kadri interview.

19   Paul F. Gardner, *Shared Hopes, Separate Fears* (Colorado: Westview Press, 1997), p. 155.

20   Kadri interview.

CHAPTER TWO

DURNA

The BPI was born into a nation undergoing severe growing pains. Indonesia's economy was worsening by the year, the result of Sukarno's support for quasi-socialist policies that included the abrupt nationalization of Dutch investments. National security, meanwhile, was still threatened by resilient rebel pockets on the islands of Sumatra and Sulawesi.[1]

Complicating matters was Sukarno's fixation on West New Guinea. The western half of a hot, humid island on the eastern extreme of the Indonesian archipelago, it contained a thousand distinct tribal cultures and languages – a fifth of the world's total – with most tribes in isolation from each other due to the exceedingly harsh topography. Though a hostile land, the Dutch had seen fit to retain control over it when they granted sovereignty to the rest of Indonesia in 1949. This infuriated Sukarno; retaking the territory had therefore become the president's favorite nationalist refrain since the start of the Republic.

Sukarno had not limited his campaign to words. As early as 1952, he had consented to sporadic attempts by the military to infiltrate teams – sometimes armed – of pro-Indonesian natives. These had been amateurish affairs until 1960, when the near-total defeat of the rebels on Sumatra and Sulawesi allowed Jakarta to devote more attention to wresting control of West Irian, Indonesia's preferred name for West New Guinea.

At least initially, the redoubled campaign to seize West Irian was envisioned as an enhanced program of covert guerrilla infiltrations overseen by the army. General Nasution, who had ultimately outmaneuvered cousin Zulkilfi Lubis and returned as army chief in 1955, gave a lead role to his head of intelligence, Colonel Magenda, who in turn handed primary control to one of his deputies, Major Rudjito. Assisted by three other officers, Rudjito's plan was dubbed Operation A.

Always ambitious, Subandrio lobbied to have his intelligence personnel participate in Operation A. His request was approved, though the BPI, with a skeletal staff and no agents inside West Irian, initially had little to offer. As one senior agency official recalled, this began to change in mid-1960:

> Our first contribution came after Sukarno gave us control over a huge cargo vessel that had been procured with Japanese war reparations. We named it the *Wapoga*, after a river in West Irian. The boat came with simple instructions from Sukarno: 'Play with it, but don't sink it.'[2]

The *Wapoga* was soon pressed into service. Steaming back and forth across the Indonesian archipelago, the BPI shuttled over one hundred Irianese men and their dependents to Jakarta. There the agency was given access to a vacant dormitory stocked with bunk beds. Dependents remained at the dorm; eligible males were turned over to Rudjito's Operation A, which had established a paramilitary training camp near Bogor.

Very quickly, Operation A fizzled. In November 1960, Rudjito launched his first infiltration attempt with a third of the Bogor-trained guerrillas pooled by the BPI. The mission was a resounding failure – all were rounded up by the Dutch in short order – as was a second attempt using another third in September 1961.

Frustrated, the officers of Operation A made one last try. With the BPI launching a recruitment drive to bring the Bogor contingent back up to strength, some 111 Irianese guerrillas were dispatched toward the front in January 1962. Accompanying them were three West German-made torpedo boats, loaned by the Indonesian navy to land the insurgents along the southern coast of West Irian. Also present were several BPI radio operators, all of whom had received Morse training on Saipan almost a decade earlier.

For Operation A, the third time was not to prove a charm. When the torpedo boats left their forward post on 15 January for the final run toward West Irian, a pair of Dutch warships was waiting over the horizon. As two of the Indonesian vessels peeled off, the Dutch placed the third in its sights and delivered a crippling blow. Going down with the ship was Commodore Yos

Sudarso, Indonesia's chief of naval operations; another 51 guerrillas and seamen were plucked from the water and sent to Dutch prison cells. The BPI radiomen were the first to relay the grim news to Jakarta on their Morse sets.

Predictably, the reaction in the capital was scathing. Army intelligence took severe heat for the fiasco, and Rudjito's Operation A from that point forward was relegated to the sidelines. In its place, the military fast-tracked a two-phased campaign to be overseen by a soft-spoken major general named Suharto. For the first phase, Suharto planned a far bolder series of infiltrations using elite airborne and seaborne units. They would stage from the forward launch sites previously established by Operation A; the BPI radiomen, made redundant by army communications specialists, were sent packing. As the second phase, Suharto laid plans for a massive conventional invasion, generously inflated with bluff and bravado.

With the BPI out of the infiltration business, the agency scrambled to stay relevant in the retaking of West Irian. One area where they made a contribution was in chaperoning key Irianese tribal leaders who had come over to the Indonesian side. Eight leaders were eventually assembled, six of whom were later taken on an international lobbying tour. Juggling the competing egos and stifling the traditional inter-clan rivalries was a serious challenge for the BPI escorts. "It was all we could do," said one, "to keep them from fighting with each other."[3]

The BPI was involved in one other covert West Irian operation. In a parallel track to Suharto's military campaign, senior Indonesian diplomats and military officials in the second quarter of 1962 contemplated a legal end-run to beat the Dutch at their own game. Back in February 1961, the Dutch had allowed West Irian locals to vote for a Papua Council (*Dewan Papua*), with the added promise that the territory would become an independent state by 1970.

Although the Indonesian government was incensed by the Dewan Papua, some senior officials saw opportunity. Reasoning that the decisions of the council would be legally binding, they thought of ways to entice a majority of council members to support integration with Indonesia. Making some crude calculations, they figured that 51 percent of the council's votes could be bought with $1.5 million.

Placed in charge of the vote-buying scheme was the Indonesian consul general in Singapore, Colonel Sugiharto. Assisting him was senior BPI officer Kartono Kadri, who was dispatched for a secret rendezvous in Hong Kong with a senior Dutch member from Dewan Papua. After a cordial ice-breaking session, the Indonesian representatives got down to serious negotiations. Recalled Kadri:

> First, we agreed to give West Irian the status of a special province. Second, Riau at the time used Singaporean currency, so we agreed Dutch currency could remain in use. Third, we agreed to let Catholic and Protestant missionaries stay in place. We did not agree to a Papuan flag flying alone, but we said that it could fly below the Indonesian flag.[4]

With the decisions going his way, the Dutch councilman was eager to have the Indonesians transfer the promised cash to an Australian bank account. Before doing so, however, Sugiharto and Kadri requested a sign of good faith that the Dewan Papua was preparing to stage a vote on integration. After several days of waiting, however, the councilman failed to reestablish contact. The bribery attempt was subsequently aborted and the funds never transferred.[5]

Even without the council's vote, Indonesia ultimately won. On 15 August 1962, Indonesian and Dutch delegates signed an agreement charging a temporary United Nations administration with running the territory through the following May, after which the Indonesians would take full control until a referendum on self-determination could be held before the end of the decade. Though the victory was gained largely because of diplomatic strong-arming against the Dutch (especially by the U.S.), Indonesia's generals, and Sukarno himself, preferred to heap credit on their threatened military campaign – not any foreign helping hand.

All of this did not sit well with Subandrio. As the army basked in a post-Irian glow, the ambitious foreign minister-*cum*-intelligence chief was rubbed raw. Disparagingly compared to *Durna* – the duplicitous advisor to the king in the Javanese *wayang* puppet theater – Subandrio made little secret he was positioning himself as Sukarno's heir apparent. As he did not yet have any power base of his own, this prompted him to begin courting the PKI for critical political support. And because the PKI was the army's primary political rival (they were the only two organizations with strong, nationwide grassroots outreach), Subandrio, by association, fell out with the generals.

The rift between the top brass and the foreign minister had a major impact on the BPI. Throughout the West Irian campaign, the intelligence agency enjoyed cordial relations with all parts of the armed forces. But once the generals soured toward Subandrio, the BPI was cut off from the army's vast territorial information network. Army representatives also boycotted the informal JIEG trysts.

Other armed services quickly stepped in to fill the void. In a highly symbolic move, Sukarno ordered the air force, which was the most politically progressive of all the services, to give Subandrio the honorary title of air marshal. The police, meanwhile, forged especially close ties with the BPI: not only did they provide the intelligence agency with access to their domestic information network (which was second only to that of the army), but a police brigadier general was named to the new position of BPI chief of staff.[6] That general, Sugeng Sutarto, was the former head of police intelligence; a diehard Sukarnoist, he was also a member of the president's influential Supreme Advisory Council.[7] Two other police generals, Mudjoko and Bugi Supeno, were elevated as ministers reporting to Subandrio in the cabinet; while their ministerial roles were ambiguous, they underscored the growing nexus between the police and the spy chief.

The BPI's realignment among the armed services became readily apparent during Indonesia's next foreign adventure. On 27 May 1961, while Indonesia was still fully preoccupied with West Irian, Malayan and British government leaders floated a proposal to form a wider Malaysian federation. The concept envisioned a union of Malaya, the adjoining city-state of Singapore, and the three British colonies – Sarawak, Sabah, and Brunei – in northern Borneo. The plan would enable Britain to grant independence to these remaining states, but was still obliged by treaty to shield them under the Commonwealth defensive umbrella.

Geography dictated that Indonesia take interest in the proposal. Britain's Borneo holdings, after all, encompassed a relatively narrow strip along the northern coast of that island; the other two-thirds were governed by Indonesia as part of what Jakarta called Kalimantan. Sabah and Sarawak were contiguous, with Sabah lying to the northeast and Sarawak to the southwest. Together, they shared an extremely rugged 1,750-kilometer border with Indonesia's Kalimantan, most of which was unexplored and never properly surveyed.

For more than a year, Indonesia appeared mildly supportive of the Malaysia concept. Subandrio himself underscored in October 1962 that Jakarta had no claims over Borneo. But two months later, after a charismatic leftist politician from Brunei named A.M. Azahari bin Sheikh Mahmud staged a failed putsch to expel the British, Indonesia underwent a complete diplomatic reversal. Perhaps in need of a new foreign distraction for Indonesia's economic woes, or perhaps smarting from the army's gloating after the West Irian victory, Subandrio, in the opening of 1963, grabbed a lead role in crafting Sukarno's policy of *Konfrontasi* ("Confrontation") toward the emergent Malaysia and its Commonwealth patrons.

From the start, Confrontation was far less specific than Indonesia's West Irian campaign. Whereas Major General Suharto had been charged with the military conquest of Dutch-controlled territory, Jakarta did not talk in terms of annexing Borneo. Still, Jakarta began mimicking the West Irian formula by looking to forge guerrilla units from among Borneo residents that had taken refuge in Kalimantan. Among the most promising were about eight hundred ethnic Chinese that had spilled across the border in the immediate aftermath of Azahari's botched powergrab in Brunei. Chinese compromised over 30 percent of Sarawak's 818,000-strong population, plus another 23 percent of Sabah's 507,000 locals. Many of them, especially in Sarawak, belonged to communist political organizations.

Eyeing this pool of potential recruits, Subandrio was in the forefront mapping out a pilot plan of assistance. Because the Chinese refugees were communists – and the apolitical Subandrio was opportunistically embracing the left to gain support of the PKI – the intelligence chief dispatched one BPI officer (a Saipan alumnus) to West Kalimantan with orders to select ten Chinese for paramilitary training under police auspices in Bogor, West Java.[8] Once instruction was completed in the second quarter of 1963, these ten joined sixty more Chinese partisans – including women – on the border. Dubbed the Special Force (*Pasukan Chusus*, or Passus), this BPI-supported unit became the nucleus of the Sarawak People's Guerrilla Force (*Pasukan Gerilya Rakyat Sarawak*, or PGRS), which went on to stage sporadic armed raids into the westernmost corner of Sarawak for the next three years.

On a separate track, other members of the BPI took a page from the West Irian playbook when they were given control over a dormitory in East Jakarta. This was soon filled by left-leaning Malayan and Singaporean émigrés who were beckoned to the Indonesian capital aboard commercial flights, then ushered through immigration by a police officer working closely with the intelligence service. Mixed with hundreds of civilian volunteers from across Indonesia, they were shuttled to paramilitary training run by police instructors at the National Police School in Sukabumi, West Java, then incorporated into a covert military program called (again, shades of West Irian) Operation A.

Officially launched in July 1963, Operation A theoretically ran the gamut of unconventional warfare options against the Commonwealth. Among its stated objectives were intelligence, counter-intelligence, psychological warfare, and sabotage. The marines, whose senior officers were unapologetic Sukarnoists, and the police and air force, both of which were institutionally left of center, poured hundreds of their most elite troops into this operation, which included several quixotic attempts to start guerrilla uprisings on peninsular Malaysia. During one of these, in August 1964, the first team of BPI émigrés trained in Sukabumi attempted to reach Malaysia by speedboat. The results fell short of expectations:

> We had them island-hop toward the Malaysian coast, but a British aircraft spotted them at sea. The boat was bombed, killing twenty of the people we trained.[9]

Following this loss, the BPI largely withdrew itself from the paramilitary business. It remained engaged in Confrontation on other fronts, however. In one quasi-diplomatic effort, the BPI tried to attack Malaysia from within by encouraging Singapore to secede from the union. This took place in 1964, when Indonesia's spies took their case directly to Lee Kuan Yew, the Singaporean chief minister who had administered the city-state's government prior to its merger with Malaysia. Using Indonesian intermediaries of ethnic Chinese origin, they met with Lee at his law office on several occasions and made the case that Singapore was suffering most from Confrontation because of lost economic opportunities. And in the belief that Lee was an aficionado of cock fights, BPI operatives scoured Bangkok for the best quality cocks and discreetly presented them to the chief minister as a sweetener. Although Singapore eventually split from Malaysia in August 1965, it is a good bet the cocks were not a decisive factor.[10]

One other BPI covert operation linked to Confrontation took place within the Indonesian capital. Soon after the December 1962 Brunei revolt, the Indonesians had encouraged rebel leader Azahari to form a North Kalimantan "cabinet" inside Indonesia to legitimize his paramilitary campaign. With one exception, the cabinet members were Borneo leftists backed by Subandrio and the PKI. The exception was the cabinet's defense minister, the self-styled "lieutenant general" Abang Kifli, a Borneo native who had immigrated to Indonesia in the fifties and earlier served as assistant to the Minister for Religious Affairs.[11]

Very quickly, Kifli became a man under fire. Not only was he of the incorrect ideological pedigree, but he had the nominal backing of Subandrio's military archrival, General Nasution.[12] Worse, after being escorted to the border to participate in Operation A, the skittish lieutenant general abandoned the cause to dabble in business back in Jakarta. Purged from the rebel cabinet on account of his desertion, he was arrested on BPI orders and confined to a prison cell for several months. No sooner than had he been released, Kifli fled to the Filipino embassy in downtown Jakarta and requested asylum.

For Subandrio, Kifli's asylum bid was a personal slap. Aside from Sukarno, Subandrio was the most visible Indonesian figure supporting Confrontation. Diplomatically, that campaign depended in part on the fiction of Azahari's cabinet-in-exile; now that its former defense minister was giving up the fight, Subandrio was infuriated. To bring Kifli under heel, he gave orders for the BPI to snatch him out of the Filipino chancery.

To that time, the BPI had never conducted an abduction, much less from inside an embassy.[13] The mission was handed to a team from police intelligence; because of the connections of General Sutarto – the BPI chief of staff – police intelligence personnel by that time were being routinely seconded for BPI operations. Their target was a two-story building on Jalan Diponegoro, a main thoroughfare through Menteng that hosted a mix of embassies and upscale residences. The Filipino embassy was occupied by either diplomats or local staff at nearly all hours – with one exception. On Sunday evenings, maids from embassy row would congregate at the end of the road to eat and gossip. As the embassy would theoretically be empty, the BPI intended to strike during this narrow window of opportunity. Appropriately, the operation was codenamed *Babu-Babu*, slang for "servant."

At the appointed hour, two police captains used a grappling hook to scale the upper floor of the embassy. Making their way down to the ground floor, they found Kifli resting in a makeshift bedroom. Not only was he bundled off, but a radio was also stolen in order to leave evidence of a robbery in the event Filipino diplomats filed a police report. The humbled Kifli went on to spend the rest of Confrontation in detention.[14]

Outside Indonesia's borders, the BPI was growing more aggressive. As Subandrio was both foreign minister and spy chief, the intelligence agency had carte blanche over information gathered by Indonesia's diplomats.[15] Still unsatisfied, the BPI pushed to have its own personnel stationed overseas. In 1963, three initial billets were granted. One was in Singapore, a second, filled by the Saipan graduate known as Doc, was in Rangoon, and the last, filled by a second Saipan alumni nicknamed Duffy, was in Bangkok.

By the following year, the BPI counted six more officers in foreign slots. Five were in Asia: Hong Kong, Kuala Lumpur, Phnom Penh, Tokyo, and Vientiane. One other, in Morocco, kept tabs on the Arab world. In hindsight, none scored any notable intelligence coups: primarily monitoring local conditions from open sources, they duplicated efforts already accomplished by the foreign ministry.

The BPI was operating on one other piece of foreign soil. Sharing half an island with Indonesia's West Timor, Portuguese Timor was a tiny colonial backwater that would appear to have little worth coveting. But at the same time Indonesia was taking on the Commonwealth during Confrontation, Subandrio in mid-1963 authorized his intelligence organization to initiate a covert project to bring all of Timor under Jakarta's control.[16] As a first step, a 22-person rebel Timorese cabinet mysteriously appeared in the Indonesian capital during August. A circular, bearing the stamp of the "Directorate General of the Central Presidium of the United Republic of Timor," claimed that it would soon be sending an envoy to the United Nations.[17]

In reality, the BPI-inspired rebel cabinet was notional. It contained no actual members, and, aside from the single circular in August, had no other statements issued under its name. Needless to say, no rebels from the United Republic of Timor made an appearance at the United Nations.

Slightly more substantive, the BPI in late 1963 deployed a single officer to West Timor to oversee a longterm propaganda effort to woo residents of the Portuguese colony. Because the frontier between the two halves of the island was fairly porous (visitors only received a stamp on the hand to gain entry), the BPI officer requisitioned a large supply of beer and *kecap* (Indonesian soy sauce) and made repeated forays to markets in the colonial capital of Dili. Along the way, he made low-key attempts at indoctrination. Before making any inroads, however, the officer was reassigned to open the BPI post in Cambodia; the Timor project was cancelled with Portugal none the wiser.

Compared to sideshows like Portuguese Timor, the diplomatic and political battles in Jakarta were far more treacherous. On 16 September 1963, PKI-backed student mobs – driven to a frenzy when Malaysia was officially inaugurated that month – stormed the British embassy in the Indonesian capital and left it a smoldering wreck. That same evening, the BPI's Kartono Kadri and Dr. Rubijono – Sukarno's personal physician and code officer – passed through the police cordon and picked their way through the water-drenched ruins. Gathering up hundreds of pages of soaked documents strewn among the hastily-abandoned offices, they carried them to a nearby police barracks for drying and processing.

The haul was enlightening. Among the recovered papers was an accurate analysis of the unhealthy competition between the Indonesian army and air force, as well as a highly critical analysis of former air force chief Suryadarma. But all these paled to a compilation of communiqués from the British ambassador, Sir Andrew Gilchrist. Written in decidedly undiplomatic prose for internal consumption, one of his dispatches intoned, "Sukarno at this time is like a cornered rat." The last entry, hurriedly jotted in Gilchrist's handwriting, said that stones thrown by the mob were coming through his window.

Collecting the seventy most revealing pages – including the "cornered rat" reference – the BPI provided bound copies to First Minister Juanda Kartawijaya and Deputy First Minister Leimena. Though Sukarno was not directly briefed (Juanda feared his outburst would be too severe), the president eventually learned of Gilchrist's unflattering assessment and made a veiled reference to "cornered rat" in a subsequent speech.

Gilchrist's musings – with some significant alterations – would later resurface with a vengeance. In early May 1965, after a year of Indonesia lurching further to the left, BPI Chief of Staff Sutarto released a bombshell. According to the police general, the army top brass had formed a secret cabal – a *Dewan Jenderal* – that was quietly mobilizing for a coup d'état against Sukarno. Though Sutarto claimed his information was corroborated by four sources, most were openly affiliated with the PKI. With no additional attempts to corroborate the report's validity, the police general passed word of his alleged discovery to the head of the PKI, who in turn announced it at a politburo meeting later that month.[18]

At virtually the same time Sutarto's rumor was making the rounds, on 15 May an envelope with a Jakarta postmark but no return address arrived at Subandrio's Menteng home. Inside was a British embassy telegram purportedly from Ambassador Gilchrist to the British Under Secretary of State from the Foreign Office:

TOP SECRET/PERSONAL
Sir Harold Caccia
March 24, 1965

I discussed with the American Ambassador the question set out in your letter No. 67786/85. The Ambassador agreed in principal [*sic*] with our position but asked for time to investigate certain [*illegible*] of the matter.

To my question on the possible influence of Bunker's visit to Jakarta the Ambassador stated that he saw no chance of improving the situation and that there was therefore no reason for changing our joint plans. On the contrary the visit of the U.S. President's personal envoy would give us more time to prepare the operation [*penciled in*: in the utmost detail].

The ambassador felt that further measures were necessary to bring our efforts into closer alignment. In this connection, he said that it would be useful to impress again on our local army friends that extreme [*penciled in*: discipline] and coordination of action were essential for the success of the enterprise.

I promised to take all necessary measures. I will report my own views personally in due course.

Gilchrist[19]

Immediately after receipt, Subandrio gave the paper – dubbed the "Gilchrist Document" – to Chief of Staff Sutarto, who in turn handed it to the police department's rudimentary forensic lab for verification. After a pro forma review, they declared that the paper was similar to that captured at the sacked British embassy but that the printing might be wrong. Downplaying doubts, Subandrio claimed he was convinced of its authenticity and gave it to Sukarno on 26 May.

The president's reaction was one of genuine alarm. For years, he had performed the delicate tightrope act of alternately leaning on the PKI and army for support. But by the opening of 1965, he had fully thrown in his lot behind the PKI and burned his bridges with the army brass. The Gilchrist Document not only suggested that army generals were conspiring against him, but it also confirmed Sukarno's long-held obsession that the U.S. and British governments were secretly plotting his ouster.[20]

The president wasted little time confronting his generals. At 1000 hours the next day, senior military leaders, including army chief Achmad Yani, were summoned on short notice. Presented with copies of the Gilchrist Document, the generals were pressed for comment on it and the *Dewan Jenderal*.

Yani denied both charges unequivocally. Very quickly, in fact, the army concluded that the Gilchrist Document was a fake – and a bad fake at that. Not only were there grammatical and stylistic errors – not likely be found in a letter between two senior diplomats – but the letterhead contained a critical spelling discrepancy: it read "British Embassy, Jakarta," whereas genuine stationery used the alternate spelling "British Embassy, Djakarta."

Even more damning was the document's unconvincing provenance. An unsigned cover letter in the same envelope sent to Subandrio's house claimed the Gilchrist Document was found at the Bogor villa of William Palmer. The representative for the American Motion Picture Association in Indonesia (AMPAI), the gregarious Palmer had long been a fixture on Jakarta's social circuit. For almost fifteen years, he had introduced many of Hollywood's newest films to private audiences; Sukarno himself was a frequent guest. But Palmer's high profile and popularity had made him a popular target of the Indonesian left. After several pro-communist newspapers in India and Ceylon printed spurious charges that Palmer was a CIA agent (and Radio Peking chimed in with denouncements of AMPAI), a PKI mob in mid-March trashed AMPAI's Jakarta office. On 1 April, the Indonesian press reported that PKI members had ransacked Palmer's Bogor villa.

That the Gilchrist Document came from Palmer's Bogor residence stretched credibility. It took either a fool or an innocent to think that a top secret British document would have been in the hands of the AMPAI representative. Just to make sure, army intelligence sent an officer to Bogor to confirm what had taken place at Palmer's villa. Surprisingly, the officer was told by Bogor police that the ransacking was vastly overstated: there was no evidence that anything had been taken from inside the villa.[21]

But choosing not to raise questions about its authenticity, Sukarno used it to his own advantage by way of leaks and private circulation. On 28 May, he dwelled on the issue of the document and the *Dewan Jenderal* at a meeting of army regional commanders. Embellishing further, he claimed to have concrete evidence of an "imperialist" plot to kill him, Subandrio, and army chief Yani ahead of the Afro-Asian Conference scheduled for July in Algeria.[22]

That same Algerian conference was shaping up to be the high point for the BPI. It was to take place ten years after the 1955 forum in Indonesia that established the Non-Aligned Movement; Sukarno had been a central fixture at the first meeting and was looking to make a major mark at the second. Stoking the president's considerable ego, the BPI, over the first half of 1965, had authored glowing assessments of keeping Malaysia out of the Algerian forum and of Indonesia emerging as a leading international player. With such high expectations, Subandrio had plans to publicly unveil the Gilchrist Document in Algiers.

The conference, however, was not to be. Just days before its scheduled opening, army officers in Algiers staged a coup d'état and forced its postponement. Angered over the loss of his soapbox, Sukarno lashed out at the rosy BPI intelligence assessments; there were even indications that Subandrio's stock with the president plummeted.[23]

The estrangement between Sukarno and Subandrio did not last. In events still shrouded in mystery, by August, a secret cell of top PKI ideologues were deep into a conspiracy with sympathetic military officers to eliminate senior army generals in late September and seize power. Though they did not participate in planning, evidence strongly suggests that both Sukarno and Subandrio were aware of the plot and were hardly opposed to the idea of having the legs figuratively cut out from under their army competition. But perhaps hedging his bets, or perhaps tasked with managing the post-coup transition in Sumatra, Subandrio on 29 September conveniently left the capital for Medan.

The following night, the powergrab commenced. Though the coup initially went according to plan – six out of seven targeted army generals were brutally murdered in the early morning hours – things quickly veered from the script. Losing momentum for a series of reasons – among the most important, lackluster support from Sukarno and surprising backbone displayed by Major General Suharto – the PKI and their military compatriots were on the defensive within a day.

Incensed, Suharto lost little time rallying the bulk of the army against its opposition. Over the remaining months of the year, anti-communist militias and vigilantes, sometimes armed and trained by army units, spearheaded a pogrom against the PKI and its sympathizers. Though estimates vary widely, tens of thousands, and perhaps hundreds of thousands, perished. For all intents and purposes, Indonesia's communist party ceased to exist by the beginning of 1966.

While the epitaph was being penned for the PKI, Sukarno and his closest advisors were stubbornly clinging to power. Among them, no figure earned more scorn than Subandrio. Pliable and opportunistic (despite being Washington's bête noire, for example, he had a son studying at the University of North Carolina), Subandrio was especially reviled by the army for his callous reaction to the murder of the six generals and his diehard defense of the PKI.

Condemned by association, the offices that Subandrio controlled were on the receiving end of the public's anger. On 8 March 1966, student groups attacked the foreign ministry. And on 12 March, one day after Sukarno was browbeaten into signing an ultimatum that delegated Major General Suharto all the necessary authority to guarantee security and stability, the army mobilized against the BPI. Even though the intelligence agency had been removed from Subandrio's direct control in December 1965, it remained tainted as his legacy. Several truckloads of troops pulled in front of the organization's headquarters on Jalan Madiun, firing bullets into the windows of its upper story. Although two dozen senior officers were nowhere to be found, twenty-one members of the BPI's support staff, occupying the lower floor, were led off into detention.[24]

The next day, the army moved to temporarily take control over the empty BPI headquarters. Named as caretaker was Brigadier General Sugiharto, the same officer involved in the aborted vote-buying scheme during the West Irian campaign. He had been promoted to army intelligence chief in November 1965; his predecessor, Siswondo Parman, was one of the six murdered generals.

Reviewing the BPI's files, Sugiharto found intelligence reports that were as politically biased as they were overly conspiratorial. Not unexpectedly, particularly harsh were the agency's findings on several pro-Western army officers. One of those singled out for sharp condemnation was Lieutenant Colonel Aswis Sumarmo, a member of the foreign section in army intelligence. As part of his foreign liaison portfolio, Aswis Sumarmo periodically met the

CIA's resident station chief in Jakarta, B. Hugh Tovar. Putting its own fanciful spin on this, the BPI charged that the lieutenant colonel secretly rendezvoused with Tovar, who captured conversations on a recorder hidden in his piano. Called in by Sugiharto to review the accusation, Aswis Sumarmo explained that intelligence chief Parman authorized the meetings, which he openly conducted in full military uniform. "Tovar did not even own a piano," he added.[25]

Such slanted analysis only stoked the army's hatred of the BPI leadership. Between 18 and 21 March, the top officers of the spy agency were tracked down and arrested. Three accused of PKI sympathies, including General Sutarto and Kartono Kadri, were given lengthy prison sentences. A defiant Subandrio, appearing in court during mid-year, was condemned to death.[26]

1   The BPI managed to infiltrate two agents into the rebel movement in North Sulawesi. The first served as the aide to rebel Colonel Warouw. The second, a Saipan graduate, was eventually promoted to battalion commander. Both managed to smuggle occasional intelligence reports back to Jakarta, where their families were being housed and fed by the BPI.

2   Kadri interview. Kadri was head of the BPI's Section Two, which was responsible for both foreign and domestic information collection and evaluation. Section One was charged with general administration and Section Three handled research and analysis. Later, during the Confrontation against Malaysia, the BPI created a Section Four that dealt exclusively with the North Kalimantan campaign. *G-30-S Dihadapan Mahmillub 3 di Djakarta (Perkara Dr. Subandrio)*, Volume II (Djakarta: PT Pembimbing Masa, 1966), p. 30.

3   Ibid.

4   Ibid.

5   This vote-buying operation was first detailed in a 29 March 1992 article in *Media Indonesia*. Putting an anti-communist spin on the failed bribery scheme, the article claimed that the operation was betrayed by members of the PKI. In reality, it failed because the Dutch council member, who was looking to profit behind the back of his own government, got cold feet.

6   According to the 1959 presidential decree that created the BPI, the agency was to be headed by a chief and deputy chief. Since its inception, however, the deputy chief position was never filled. The position of BPI chief of staff, filled by Sutarto, was not defined in the 1959 decree.

7   In 1945, Sutarto had been militia member in *Pesindo*, a socialist youth organization. The Supreme Advisory Council (*Dewan Pertimbangan Agung*) to which he belonged was a small body authorized under the 1945 Constitution that offered Sukarno alternate advice from the cabinet. *Gerakan 30 September, Pemberontakan Partai Komunis Indonesia* (Jakarta: Sekretariat Negara Republik Indonesia, 1994), p. 44.

8   Drs. Soemadi, *Peranan Kalimantan Barat Dalam Menghadapi* (Pontianak: Yayasan Tanjungpura, 1973), p. 56.

9   Kadri interview.

10   Ibid. Part of the BPI's effort to draw Singapore away from the Malaysian fold is recounted in *Kompas*, 22 July 1979.

11   Interview with Marwan Abdul Kadir, 13 May 2003; interview with Robert Martens, 14 May 2003. Marwan was Kifli's police escort officer for a year; Martens was a political officer at the U.S. embassy during 1963-66.

12   The rivalry between Subandrio and Nasution deepened in 1962, when reforms proposed by First Minister Juanda Kartawijaya would have had Subandrio's BPI report to Nasution (who, among other titles, was the deputy first minister). Not surprisingly, Subandrio opposed the realignment and the BPI continued to answer directly to the president. Robert Lowry, *The Armed Forces of Indonesia* (New South Wales: Allen & Unwin, 1996), p. 70.

13   The BPI had never conducted an abduction, but it was widely accused of hiring thugs to hound intellectuals in Jakarta who showed pro-Western sympathies. Martens interview.

14   Kadri interview; Kadir interview.

15   The ambitious Subandrio claimed a total of nine government titles by that time, including first deputy prime minister.

16   Subandrio authorized this operation even though he had publicly denied any territorial claims on the island of Timor. See Dr. Subandrio, *Indonesia on the March*, Volume II (Jakarta: Department of Foreign Affairs, 1963), p. 293.

17   *Foreign Broadcast Information Service*, East Asia edition, 13 August 1963, p. **rrr**3.

18   When Subandrio was under investigation in 1966, he was asked his opinion about the *Dewan Jenderal*. "I considered it only a 'whispering campaign,'" said the intelligence chief. "Also, it regarded a domestic matter, and the BPI was not concerned with domestic matters." Considering the overwhelming evidence of the BPI's highly politicized domestic role during 1965, Subandrio's denial rings especially hollow. Central Intelligence Agency, Research Study, *Indonesia 1965:*

The Coup that Backfired, December 1968, p. 200.

19 A photocopy of the Gilchrist Document is found in Let. Kol. C.K.H. Ali Said S.H. and Let. Kol. C.K.H. Durmawel Ahmed S.H., *Sangkur Adil* (Djakarta: Penerbit Ethika, 1967), p. 51.

20 Declassified U.S. documents reveal the CIA had, in fact, implemented a limited political action program beginning in Fiscal Year 1962 aimed at bolstering moderate Indonesian elements and reducing the influence of the PKI and the People's Republic of China (the primary external sponsor of the PKI). This program, which apparently was extended annually through 1965, primarily consisted of covert liaison with, and support to, anti-Communist groups; there were additional plans as of February 1965 to initiate black letter operations, media operations (possibly including black radio), and political action within existing Indonesian organizations and institutions. See Document 110, "Memorandum Prepared for the 303 Committee," dated 23 February 1965, in *Foreign Relations of the United States*, Vol. XXVI (Washington, D.C.: Government Printing Office, 2001). These CIA efforts were in support of an overall U.S. policy to promote a non-communist Indonesian republic still headed by Sukarno, and did not implicitly or explicitly seek a military-led alternative. There is no indication that the CIA effort was conducted in cooperation with British counterparts (as stated in the Gilchrist Document).

21 Sumarmo interview. Perhaps realizing the Palmer story was weak, Indonesian leftists later claimed that the Gilchrist Document came from the razed British embassy – even though the Bunker visit (not to mention the March 1965 date on the document) was more than a year and a half after the embassy was sacked.

22 Questions remain as to who forged the Gilchrist Document. In a declassified 1968 document, the CIA listed three likely suspects motivated by a desire to instigate firm action by Sukarno against the generals: Subandrio, the PKI, and the Chinese. But according to Ladislav Bittman, a Czech intelligence officer who defected to the United States in 1968, his agency, in cooperation with Soviet counterparts, forged the document and passed it through a leftist Indonesian ambassador in Europe who had cooperated in return for an apartment and a steady stream of female companions. Bittman further claimed that the rumors against William Palmer had been spread by Czech intelligence to journalists on their payroll in South Asia. *Indonesia 1965: The Coup that Backfired*, December 1968, p. 196; Ladislav Bittman, *The Deception Game* (Syracuse, N.Y.: Syracuse University Press, 1972), pp. 107-109 and 119-120.

23 *Indonesia 1965: The Coup that Backfired*, p. 278. In a rushed press conference in Cairo following the cancellation of the Algiers conference, Subandrio issued a public statement about the Gilchrist Document to Egypt's *Al Ahram* newspaper.

24 B. Wiwoho and Banjar Chaeruddin, *Memori Jenderal Yoga* (Jakarta: PT Bina Rena Pariwara, 1991), p. 195. Aside from its Jalan Madiun headquarters, the BPI owned safe houses across Jakarta from where it ran its informant networks.

25 Sumarmo interview.

26 Subandrio's death sentence was never carried out. In 1995, he was released from prison along with several other senior officials involved in the failed 1965 coup.

CHAPTER THREE

SATSUS INTEL

A lthough Sukarno still carried the title of president, Suharto increasingly consolidated his grip on power. Over the first half of 1966, the inscrutable, underrated major general methodically consolidated his political grip in Jakarta using a traditional Javanese blend of threat, bluff, negotiation, and cajolement. In the field, he was much less nuanced. Heading the Operational Command for the Restoration of Security and Order (*Komando Operasi Pemulihan Keamanan dan Kertiban*, or Kopkamtib), the military über-office which he created three days after the communist-led coup attempt, the general gave no quarter in mobilizing the armed forces – and especially the army – against PKI remnants.

As Kopkamtib chief, Suharto developed a tremendous appetite for intelligence. All regional commanders were designated Kopkamtib executives, and they tasked their local informant networks for tactical intelligence requirements. This was supplemented by an intelligence task force (*Satuan Tugas Intelijen*, or STI) intended as the blunt-force investigative arm within Kopkamtib. Still wanting more, Suharto on 22 August 1966 established a strategic intelligence agency directly responsive to himself as Kopkamtib chief.[1] Known as the State Intelligence Command (*Komando Intelijen Negara*, or KIN), this new body was to report on international and national security, including political, social, economic, and domestic and foreign military security matters. The BPI, which had been under army caretakers for the previous five months, was formally dissolved and its salvageable assets merged into KIN.

Despite its modest quarters in the Jakarta neighborhood of Tebet, KIN had the potential to be the country's most powerful intelligence organization to date. After all, Suharto himself was listed as its chief and he enjoyed virtual martial law-type powers as to what measures could be taken to guarantee order.

Beneath Suharto, many of the remaining top KIN slots went to Central Javanese acolytes. This was a matter of self-preservation: owing to his meteoric rise amid cutthroat chaos, as well as his own ethnic heritage steeped in the Javanese penchant for spinning conspiracies, the aloof and naturally suspicious Suharto was compelled to favor trusted army subordinates from his home province.

One such Central Java native was Brigadier General Yoga Sugomo. Bespectacled and slightly rotund, Yoga had spent World War II in a Tokyo military academy. Staying in Japan for a short period after the war, where he worked as an Allied translator, he returned to Indonesian soil after the war of independence had already commenced and found himself attached to the short-lived intelligence organization, the Fifth Section.

When the Fifth Section folded, Yoga remained in Central Java. It was there that he came to know Suharto, a regimental commander in Jogjakarta four years his senior. Except for a couple of periods – attendance at a military intelligence primer in England during 1951, and a three-year tour as the defense attaché in Yugoslavia beginning in 1962 – Yoga spent most of the fifties and early sixties as an intelligence officer answering to Suharto in units from the Central Java military command. For KIN, Suharto selected Colonel Yoga as its chief of staff.

Another top KIN officer from Central Java was Ali Moertopo. Three years Suharto's junior, he, too, had spent the fifties in Central Java alongside the major general. When Suharto was mobilizing for the West Irian campaign, Ali landed an intelligence role and, though he saw no military action, earned a reputation as an efficient troubleshooter. Remaining answerable to Suharto during Confrontation, he managed a Special Operations (*Operasi Khusus*, or Opsus) unit against the Commonwealth and then, showing flexibility, was instrumental in negotiating a swift end to that conflict just eleven days before KIN was founded. Within KIN, Lieutenant Colonel Ali was named head of its foreign intelligence desk.

The position of KIN's deputy chief was the most critical. This was because Suharto, like Subandrio in the BPI, was too busy wearing other hats and would likely cede de facto control of KIN to his deputy. Chosen for this slot was

Major General Soedirgo, a former Peta officer whose intelligence training began under Japanese tutelage during World War II. During the independence struggle, he had entered the Military Police and started working his way up its ranks. Twice schooled in the U.S., the dapper Soedirgo (he was regularly voted best-dressed officer) had risen to Military Police commander by the time of the 1965 coup attempt.[2] Suharto had briefly elevated him to army intelligence chief before naming him in October 1966 as KIN deputy.

The selection of Soedirgo was born out of necessity. He was not part of Suharto's Central Java inner circle, but his Military Police background was critical. The reason: there is often a close relationship between the police and domestic intelligence services; since Indonesia's civilian police were tainted by their ties to the BPI, the Military Police were the next best alterative. Much like Sutarto's role in the BPI, Soedirgo would be expected to exploit synergies between KIN and his former unit.

KIN was not the only intelligence unit gaining momentum during Suharto's early months in power. At the same time Lieutenant Colonel Ali Moertopo was named head of KIN's foreign intelligence desk, he maintained a second role as head of Opsus, the ad hoc troubleshooting unit that answered to Suharto since the West Irian campaign.

As Opsus chief, Moertopo had repeatedly proven to Suharto his ability to reliably execute sensitive, deniable tasks with minimal staff. Confrontation had been an especially busy period for his task force. Assisted by two special forces majors – Leonardus "Benny" Moerdani and Aloysius Sugiyanto – Moertopo had recruited a civilian shipping company owner and used his transport fleet to infiltrate army commandos sheep-dipped as merchant marines into Malaysia and Thailand. Other concerns were run by Opsus operatives posing as shipping and Garuda airline executives in Bangkok and Hong Kong. The idea was to strike at Malaysia from unexpected directions, though they scored no successes after more than a year of trying.

Ironically, the end of Confrontation was when Opsus made its greatest mark. Once Suharto had amassed sufficient confidence by early 1966, he pragmatically decided to end the costly campaign. The Opsus officer posted in Bangkok, Benny Moerdani, shifted to Kuala Lumpur and handled much of the initial truce negotiations. With its direct line to Suharto, Opsus cut through bureaucratic red tape and fast-tracked the formal end to the conflict that August.

Another discreet foreign assignment soon followed. In 1966, the United States, which was fast mending ties with Indonesia, earmarked emergency aid for Jakarta consisting of rice and unprocessed cotton. In order to process the cotton before delivery, Washington solicited bids from several Asian nations. Among them, the contract was won by the Republic of China on Taiwan.

At the time, Indonesia had virtually no contact with Taiwan. The Indonesian government had long held a "One China" policy, formally recognizing only the People's Republic. Prior to October 1965, in fact, Sukarno had enjoyed especially close relations with Beijing; the PKI's closest foreign ally was the Chinese. But following the failed coup, Jakarta's new rulers demonized mainland China as much as the PKI. Though ties were never formally cut, there was a tit-for-tat expulsion of diplomats in April 1967. The Chinese embassy, a massive, austere building hidden behind a high red wall in Jakarta's Chinese quarter of Glodok, permanently closed its doors.[3]

At the same time relations with the People's Republic were deteriorating, Opsus in late 1966 was opening channels with Taiwan. On the pretext of inspecting the mills that would process the U.S. cotton, Opsus officers began monthly visits to Taipei. There, they were hosted by the National Security Bureau (NSB), Taiwan's primary intelligence agency. In 1967, the NSB granted permission for Opsus to station a single officer in Taiwan under private commercial cover; the officer's mission was to promote Indonesia's economic interests (read: solicit aid) and to monitor developments in mainland China. In return, two NSB officers were hosted in an annex to the Opsus headquarters on Jalan Raden Saleh.[4]

During the same period, another Opsus operation engendered a sense of déjà vu. Colonel Zulkilfi Lubis, whose legacy as intelligence chief was checkered at best, had fled Jakarta and became a top rebel leader in Sumatra during the late fifties. In 1961, he accepted a government amnesty offer – only to be jailed by vindictive members of the Sukarno regime. Not until late 1965 did Lubis win his freedom and, with espionage still in his blood, he approached Moertopo for a job in Opsus.

Lubis, it turned out, was full of clever ideas. To discreetly network across the Middle East, he received Opsus seed money to open an Indonesian restaurant in Saudi Arabia that would act as an intelligence front. Few patronized the eatery, however, and the promised intelligence leads never materialized. Exhausting his funds, Lubis returned to Jakarta.[5]

In March 1967, semantics caught up with reality. After having already milked de facto presidential powers from Sukarno a year earlier, Suharto took a critical step toward codifying his political role that month when parliamentarians designated him acting president.

As acting president, Suharto stepped away from his symbolic post as KIN chief. Marking his departure, KIN underwent a redesignation. On 22 May, the State Intelligence Coordination Agency (*Badan Koordinasi Intelijen Negara*, or Bakin) was formally invested by presidential decree. Little changed besides the name: its strategic mandate stayed fixed, and virtually all the KIN section chiefs (with the exception of Ali Moertopo, who took his exit to focus on Opsus) retained their portfolios under Bakin. With Bakin answering to Suharto as acting president (but no longer its chief), Major General Soedirgo was elevated to the top slot. And showing greater clout, as well as some bureaucratic creep, Bakin received a larger headquarters on Jalan Senopati in South Jakarta.[6]

Like KIN, Bakin's upper echelon was dominated by active-duty army officers. But below the top tier, many of the remaining members were civilian bureaucrats and Bakin itself was designated as a civilian intelligence agency. This made it eligible for liaison relationships with foreign civilian counterparts (an unwritten rule among friendly intelligence organizations is that civilian bodies are predisposed toward dealing with each other rather than with military intelligence organizations). Until that time, however, Indonesia's intelligence organizations had been reclusive. During the BPI era, links had been forged with only a handful of counterparts from non-aligned nations like Egypt and Yugoslavia; during 1963, a pair of BPI students had trained in each of these nations.[7]

Bakin, by contrast, came out of its shell from the start. The agency was quick to create a Liaison Group, the purpose of which was – as the name implied – to coordinate contact with foreign counterparts. For the first few years of Bakin's existence, at least, there was only one counterpart that counted: the CIA.

For Bakin, ties with the CIA promised several advantages. Cash-strapped and possessing limited human resources, the Indonesians needed help with funding and training. And since anti-communism was now its new mantra, the Suharto regime was hypersensitive about foreign communist nations aiding and abetting Indonesian leftists that had escaped apprehension; the U.S. could shed light on such ties by providing trace searches on communist spies masquerading as diplomats.

For the CIA, operations in Indonesia were attractive on several counts. First, with the U.S. increasingly mired in Indochina, it was in Washington's interest to aid Jakarta in keeping communism out of insular Southeast Asia; cordial relations with Bakin could support this policy.

Second, Sukarno's leftist brand of non-alignment had led to a robust and diverse presence of communist diplomatic missions in Jakarta. With the exception of the People's Republic of China, these embassies had remained in place after the change of government. Sukarno's tilt to the left had also resulted in purchases of advanced weapon systems, including bombers, submarines, and missiles from communist states. For the CIA, all of this offered the possibility of unilateral or joint recruitment of penetration agents. It also offered the chance to scrutinize advanced communist weapons; this was especially important given the fact that some of these systems could not be found in Asia outside of China. Moreover, some of them, such as the SA-2 surface-to-air missile, were being used to shoot down American planes over Indochina.[8]

Overseeing the budding relationship with Bakin was CIA Station Chief Clarence "Ed" Barbier. A Japanese linguist with naval intelligence during World War II, he had served in that capacity alongside U.S. marines during the Pacific campaign. Transferring to the CIA soon after its inception, he had overseen liaison relations with South Vietnam's intelligence service in the late fifties, only to be wounded in the shoulder with a stray round during a 1960 coup attempt by disenchanted paratroopers.[9]

In July 1966, Barbier arrived in Jakarta in his first posting as a station chief. In a telling change, he was officially listed as "Special Assistant to the Ambassador." This diplomatic euphemism was often reserved for CIA station chiefs who were openly declared to a host nation. This implied a comfort level in diplomatic ties that had not previously been shared between Jakarta and Washington: the two previous Indonesia station chiefs, by contrast, were not declared to the Sukarno government and were instead listed as "First Secretary/

Political" – a title intended to camouflage the chief among bona fide diplomats.

Fishing for good sources of intelligence, Barbier's station found fertile ground. With the Indonesian government having thrown leftists on the defensive, there were literally hundreds of potential targets who were psychologically broken and economically desperate. In many cases, these persons were willing to curry favor with the new authorities; they were amenable to networking among, and reporting on, their former comrades.

One such target was Suhaimi Munaf. Born in 1925 in West Sumatra, Munaf married into a family whose patriarch was the top figure in the West Java-centered Indonesian Islamic Education Party (*Partai Tarbiyah Islamiyah Indonesia*, or Perti). Despite a small following, Perti held a disproportionately high profile during the Sukarno era. This was because the PKI (which, theoretically, should have been atheistic) had been looking to burnish its credentials among the Islamic masses and Perti was one of two minor Islamic parties that had prostituted themselves as willing cheerleaders.

On account of his father-in-law's position in Perti, Munaf was also given a prominent role in the party. With a sharp pen (he freelanced for leftist publications) and a pixie's grin, Munaf was coddled by the PKI and appointed as the token Perti representative on several Indonesian delegations to communist nations. In 1959, he ventured to Moscow. In 1964, he traveled to both Moscow and Havana. And in mid-1965, he spent a month in Beijing.[10]

Not surprisingly, authorities in the Suharto administration (which came to be known as the New Order, as opposed to Sukarno's Old Order) were quick to label Perti as a PKI proxy and eventually sought to punish its leadership. In February 1967, the law caught up with Munaf; arrested for political crimes, he would spend the next twenty months in a Jakarta prison cell.

Munaf, it turned out, had admirers from afar. For several years prior to 1965, members of the U.S. embassy had noticed him at diplomatic functions and were properly impressed with his easy access to foreign communist representatives. Making initial contact during a 1964 reception, they asked for his help – which he subsequently offered – in arranging a meeting with his prominent father-in-law.[11]

Fast forward to late August 1968, as Munaf was being readied for release from prison. The CIA station had dusted off what little it knew of him and judged Munaf to be a good potential penetration agent. It also knew he was vulnerable: he had no waiting job and his son had suffered a nervous breakdown during his incarceration. What's more, the New Order was being less than consistent in how it treated former leftists: although Munaf had served out the sentence handed down by the Jakarta authorities, Kopkamtib often re-arrested political criminals on a whim.

To make its pitch, the CIA station sought help from the Military Police. Similar to Suharto's motivation for appointing Soedirgo as Bakin chief, the CIA had taken pains to forge links with the Military Police for several important reasons. First, the Military Police had robust powers of arrest, especially for political misdeeds. Second, it was well versed in investigative skills. Third, unlike the tainted civilian police, the Military Police had not been emasculated after the 1965 coup attempt. Fourth, Indonesia's Military Police contained a large percentage of civilian members, which made it easier for the CIA to justify establishment of a liaison with a military unit.[12]

Fifth, and perhaps most important, several top Military Police officers had been schooled in the U.S. during the early sixties and were predisposed toward the West. This included the assistant for intelligence, Colonel Nicklany Soedardjo, a wiry workaholic and diehard Cold Warrior who had attended Fort Gordon in 1961.

After the CIA forwarded a discreet request through Nicklany, the Military Police on 2 September administered a psychological test to Munaf. They found him of high mental aptitude, though somewhat stubborn and not easily influenced. This suited the CIA, which again turned to Nicklany to personally make a recruitment pitch. Munaf was receptive, especially when the colonel hinted he was eligible to be sent by Kopkamtib to a new penal colony for political criminals being established in the Malukus. Assigned the codename Friendly/1, Munaf was to be unilaterally handled by the CIA, though select personnel within the Military Police (and Bakin) would be kept appraised of his revelations.

Friendly/1's mandate sounded simple. He was to re-establish contact with his former leftist colleagues, both foreign and domestic. And playing off sympathy over his incarceration, he was to solicit employment at a foreign communist embassy. The CIA preferred the embassies of either the Soviet Union or Democratic Republic of Vietnam (popularly known as North Vietnam), but the Cuban embassy was considered the best chance because Munaf previously enjoyed close ties to Ambassador Jacinto Vasquez.

Putting this mandate into practice, Friendly/1 encountered early difficulties. When he sought out two former acquaintances, he found them cordial but distant. Perhaps suspicious about New Order informants, both were unwilling to talk about politics.

Foreign embassies were equally challenging. Having been out of circulation for twenty months, many of Friendly/1's diplomatic contacts were stale. When he knocked on the door of the Cuban embassy, he was told by an unfamiliar face that the ambassador was out of the country; no further details were offered.

Though initially rebuffed, Friendly/1 was persistent. Returning to the Cuban embassy near the end of September, he found Vasquez had returned to the post. After a warm reunion, the Cuban ambassador revealed he had been touring Hanoi and Beijing; authorities in both these capitals confided in him their determination to continue the Vietnam struggle indefinitely (these findings were duly reported back to the CIA). On a less welcome note, Vasquez said there were no openings for employment at the Cuban embassy, and he himself was rotating back to Havana in two months.

Unfazed, Friendly/1 told his CIA handler that he intended to show up at the Soviet embassy for its October Revolution reception. Though he would not be sporting an invitation, he hoped to be recognized and allowed inside. The CIA recognized their newfound agent might have a short career. "He might be too brash because he needs cash," warned one memorandum shared with Bakin. "Some might ask how he got out of prison, and why he is asking so many questions."

Their fears proved unwarranted. When Friendly/1 arrived at the Soviet embassy – a very decadent, pastel mansion on Jalan Imam Bonjol – he easily worked his way into the reception and began re-establishing his foreign contacts. As yet raising no eyebrows of suspicion, he was poised to become an invaluable window into the foreign communist community in Jakarta.

Although the CIA had scored an early success with Friendly/1, Bakin chief Soedirgo did not last long enough in his post to share in the kudos. Ever since the 1965 abortive coup, Suharto had harbored suspicions toward a handful of army generals; high on his list was Bakin's top officer. Waiting until after being formally selected by the national assembly to a five-year term as president in March 1968, Suharto made his move.

In the case of Soedirgo, the charges against him were largely circumstantial. Though not a slavish Sukarno devotee, Soedirgo's role as the last Military Police commander during the Old Order meant he had much face time with the deposed president. Sukarno had also trusted Soedirgo enough to integrate Military Police members into the elite Cakrabirawa presidential guard regiment. And because the Military Police kept its finger on the pulse of security affairs around the Indonesian capital, it was assumed that Soedirgo must have had some advanced knowledge that a coup was in the offing.

For Suharto, all of this was damning. On 21 November 1968, he not only sacked Soedirgo as Bakin chief, but sent him packing to prison. Several other generals were jailed at the same time, primarily for having been sympathetic toward Sukarno, rather than because of any leftist persuasions.

With Soedirgo gone, Chief of Staff Yoga Sugomo temporarily filled the vacant top slot. But while he was instinctively trusted by the president and had a foundation in intelligence matters, Yoga was deemed to be of greater value in the armed forces. After just three months as Bakin head, he moved out and was simultaneously named chief of intelligence for the Ministry of Defense and Security, head of Kopkamtib's STI, and director of the new Strategic Intelligence Center under the Ministry of Defense and Security.[13]

Chosen as the new Bakin chief was Major General Sutopo Juwono. A former Peta officer, Sutopo had been associated with intelligence since the days of Brani. He continued as an understudy of Zulkilfi Lubis for nearly a decade, serving in all of the intelligence incarnations that came and went through the mid-fifties. He was also something of an academic, lecturing at the army staff school during the early sixties.

Not until late October 1965, just weeks after the abortive coup, did Sutopo's career start to show true promise. At that point, he was elevated to chief of staff for the Jakarta military region, a sensitive slot normally reserved for promising officers on the fast track. Two years later, he returned to the intelligence world with a pair of important hats: chief of army intelligence and intelligence assistant for Kopkamtib.

After turning in good performances in these roles, Sutopo on 10 March 1969 became Bakin's second chief. Though he did not have Soedirgo's deep personal links with the Military Police, that nexus remained strong because of an internal restructuring. Under Sutopo, there were now two operational deputies, both of whom were Military Police alumni.[14] Deputy I, Brigadier General Poerwosoenoe, was placed in charge of state security. Though this title was rather ambiguous, his mandate included counter-subversion, psychological warfare, and counter-propaganda operations.

Deputy II, in charge of intelligence collection and analysis, was Colonel Nicklany. Still retaining a second hat as intelligence assistant in the Military Police, he had been personally called to Bakin by Sutopo: the two had grown close while the hyper-caffeinated Nicklany was filling an additional role as Kopkamtib deputy intelligence assistant under Sutopo.

Nicklany, in fact, had long been a pivotal player in military intelligence. Back in early 1965, he had overseen the creation of a special intelligence unit within the Military Police. Given the wordy title of Military Police Intelligence Operative Detachment (*Detasemen Pelaksana Intelijen Polisi Militer*, or Den Pintel Pom), its unstated purpose was to keep track of the PKI. Very quickly, it was recognized as the most capable intelligence unit of its kind within the armed forces.

In early 1968, Nicklany, in his role as Kopkamtib deputy intelligence assistant, quietly put out word to key members of Den Pintel Pom that he was contemplating a new unit that would specialize in foreign counter-intelligence – catching spies operating on Indonesian soil. Three Den Pintel Pom members, including its commander, Major Nuril Rachman, spent April and May penning an operational plan for sixty men (ten active-duty personnel, fifty civilians) drawn from the Military Police. "It will cost a lot," concluded Nuril. "We will need a lot of equipment." "Don't worry," promised Nicklany, "you'll get it."[15]

Shortly thereafter, following an appearance by the CIA's Ed Barbier at Military Police headquarters, did the reason for Nicklany's confidence become apparent. Over the remainder of the year, covert American largesse provided for sixty salaries, surveillance vehicles, rental of a safe house on Jalan Jatinegara Timur in East Jakarta, and the latest Sony TC-800 tape recorders and QTC-11 telephone taping equipment.[16]

The result of all this was a unique formation. Formally inaugurated on 16 November 1968, it was initially known as the Special Intelligence Operatives Unit (*Satuan Khusus Pelaksana Intelijen*, or Satsus Pintel), soon shortened to Special Intelligence Unit (*Satuan Khusus Intelijen*, or Satsus Intel).[17] Reflecting its bifurcated pedigree, it answered to both the Military Police Assistant for Operations and, after 1969, to Deputy Nicklany in Bakin.

Unique about Satsus Intel, too, was the continued American help it received. Besides underwriting its budget, U.S. assistance extended to training. In September 1969, the CIA dispatched veteran instructor Richard Fortin to provide a two-week class in basic surveillance tradecraft. This included such skills as how to discreetly track vehicles, how to conduct a covert stake-out, and how to handle agents.[18]

Although they were the prime sponsors, the Americans were not the only foreigners helping at the outset of Satsus Intel. Also in late 1969, MI6, the British foreign intelligence service, dispatched a single officer to give a seminar in agent handling. And in November 1970, a British citizen named Anthony Tingle arrived to give four weeks of instruction in information collection. Passport aside, Tingle was actually a 50-year old Israeli brigadier working for that country's Mossad intelligence service.

Granting permission for an Israeli instructor had not been easy. Indonesia, with the world's largest Muslim population, did not have diplomatic ties to the Jewish state. But Nicklany was pragmatic: "We will get the Israelis because they are the best in the world," he opined to one Satsus Intel officer.[19]

Diplomatic sensitivities aside, Tingle was well received by his Indonesian students. Holding his classes at Satsus Intel's rural Cipayung training center south of Jakarta, he spent considerable time expounding on the nuances of false flag operations – the recruitment of agents under false pretenses.[20] This was a Mossad specialty, which often found need to entice Arabs into cooperative relationships by masquerading as Europeans, fellow Arabs, or anyone other than an Israeli. Tingle lectured with singular intensity and not a hint of humor. "He never smiled, never laughed, never wanted girls," said one student. "And I ended up learning more from him than any instructor before or since."[21]

Well before Tingle's arrival, Satsus Intel had already been declared mission-ready. By the close of 1968, the unit had opened personnel dossiers, known as 201 files, on virtually every Communist bloc diplomat and family member stationed in Indonesia. Also opened were installation files for key communist diplomatic addresses.

No foreign target was more closely scrutinized than the Soviet Union. During the Old Order, the PKI had sided with Beijing in the Sino-Soviet rift; Chinese influence, as a result, had flourished at the expense of the Soviets. But after the 1965 upheaval, the Chinese were sidelined and the Soviets were determined to fill at least part of the vacuum. As early as 1967, in fact, Opsus chief Ali Moertopo had received reports that Soviet diplomats in Surabaya were making initial contact with PKI members in East Java who had gone underground.[22]

Keeping track of Soviet activities in Indonesia was easier said than done. The overall size of the Soviet presence was formidable. There were usually no less than 140 families stationed in Indonesia, divided among an embassy, a cultural center, an office for economic cooperation, an information section, a sprawling residential compound, an Aeroflot office, and a Morflot office in Jakarta, as well as a vacation bungalow cluster south of the capital and consulates in such far-flung locales as Banjarmasin, Medan, and Surabaya.[23] All told, there were more than 90 accredited diplomats and over 170 others holding business or other visas; of these, no less than 60 Soviets at any given time were believed to be involved in espionage. And of these, members of the KGB (the Russian abbreviation for Committee for State Security, the Soviet civilian intelligence agency) outnumbered members of the GRU (the Russian abbreviation for Chief Intelligence Directorate, the Soviet military intelligence body) by a ratio of over two to one.

Complicating matters further, the Soviet spies often came well prepared for the job. Many spent years studying the Indonesian language, and often served multiple tours in the country. A case in point was Anatoliy Babkin. Born in 1931 in Moscow, Babkin first arrived in Jakarta in 1956 as a lowly political attaché. Five years later, he was back in the Indonesian capital, this time staying long enough to be promoted from third secretary to second secretary. In 1966, Babkin returned for the third time as a first secretary, and in July 1969, he began a fourth tour with the rank of counselor. A CIA trace report, given to Satsus Intel at the onset of his fourth arrival, correctly warned that Babkin was the *rezident* – the KGB's equivalent of station chief.

If that were not enough, Satsus Intel had to worry about far more than just the Soviets. Two other Warsaw Pact nations – Czechoslovakia and East Germany – had an extremely active intelligence presence in Jakarta, with the Soviets coordinating all of their activities.[24] Other communist nations, like

North Vietnam and the Democratic People's Republic of Korea (better known as North Korea), also had large embassies that undoubtedly concealed spies.

With inadequate personnel to cover all potential targets, Satsus Intel played the odds. In April 1969, it initiated a random schedule of covert stakeouts in front of the Soviet embassy.[25] Special attention was given to vehicles assigned to suspected spies, including *Rezident* Babkin (Babkin was easily remembered among Bakin officers, who joked that his name and their organization differed by only one letter.[26])

The North Koreans also received early attention. In mid-1969, Satsus Intel opened a file on Pyongyang's embassy on Jalan Teuku Umar. That November, when the unit received word that the embassy was locally printing thousands of copies of North Korean dictator Kim Il Sung's writings and giving them away – a highly sensitive issue given the New Order's disdain for communism – Satsus Intel tracked down the offending publishing house; a visit by government officers soon convinced it to desist.

As 1969 came to a close, Satsus Intel – and its co-parent Bakin – could claim its first tentative forays into the internecine skirmishes of the Cold War. This modicum of experience would prove invaluable as Indonesia's spies, and spycatchers, were drawn into Southeast Asia's hottest battlefield: Indochina.

1   This date is still celebrated as the anniversary of Indonesia's current intelligence organization, the State Intelligence Agency (*Badan Intelijen Negara*, or BIN).

2   Soedirgo first took the Military Police Advanced Officer Course at Fort Gordon, then the Command and General Staff Course at Fort Leavenworth.

3   In the absence of a diplomatic presence, China's interests in Jakarta were represented by Romania through the late eighties.

4   Interview with Aloysius Sugiyanto, 3 May 2003.

5   Interview with Soehardi Oetomo, 23 April 2003. In a bit of a stretch, when Saudi Arabia's King Faisal toured Jakarta in 1970, Lubis claimed that his earlier operations in the Saudi capital laid the foundation for the visit.

6   On 28 April 1967, the former BPI headquarters on Jalan Madiun was formally inaugurated as a KIN (later Bakin) training site.

7   The two students in Yugoslavia studied basic intelligence tradecraft; the pair that went to Egypt were trained in maintaining intelligence files, allegedly an Egyptian specialty. Kadri interview.

8   Beginning in 1967, CIA officers based out of the U.S. consulate in Surabaya launched
     Operation HABRINK, the covert acquisition of technical details (and in some cases,
     actual samples) of Soviet military hardware like the SA-2 missile, the Whiskey-
     class submarine, the Riga-class warship, and the Tu-16 bomber. Details of
     HABRINK were publicly revealed when one of the CIA officers involved, David
     Henry Barnett, was convicted in 1980 for selling details of the operation to the Soviet
     Union. Entries in Bakin Personnel File [hereafter BPF], "David Henry Barnett."

9   Correspondence with David Zogbaum, 29 November 1999. Zogbaum was serving
     under Barbier in Saigon at the time of the 1960 coup.

10   Interview with Suhaimi Munaf, 20 March 2003.

11   Ibid.

12   The CIA normally focused on counterpart relations with civilian intelligence
     organizations, leaving the Defense Intelligence Agency (via the defense attaché's
     office) to focus on links with foreign military intelligence units. Exceptions existed,
     however. During the early sixties, for example, the CIA forged close ties to South
     Vietnam's military intelligence agency because that country's civilian outfit was
     deemed corrupt and incompetent. For details, see Kenneth Conboy and Dale
     Andradé, *Spies & Commandos* (Lawrence, Kansas: University Press of Kansas, 2000).

13   Once Yoga departed, the Bakin chief of staff slot was abolished.

14   Besides the two operational deputies, Deputy III was in charge of administration.

15   Conversation recounted by Bram Mandagi, one of the three persons involved with
     writing the Satsus Intel operational plan. Interview with Bram Mandagi, 3 June 2003.

16   By the early seventies, Satsus Intel's surveillance fleet totaled 16 motorcycles, 3
     Mercedes sedans, 2 Toyota Corollas, 3 Volkswagens, 1 Toyota jeep, and 1 Datsun
     van (with its rear windows covered, the van was used as a covert photography
     platform).

17   By 1970, the terms Satsus Pintel and Satsus Intel were being used interchangeably
     in internal documents. By March 1973, Satsus Intel was being used exclusively.
     During that month, members of Satsus Intel were declared "honorary employees"
     of Bakin. While this did yet make them full-fledged members of the intelligence
     agency, it did make the spycatchers eligible for Bakin employee benefits.

18   Interview with Benny S., 14 February 2003; Mandagi interview.

19   Interview with Very Pelenkahu, 3 June 2003.

20   The Cipayung training center had been a vacation site confiscated from Dewi
     Sukarno, the Japanese bargirl Sukarno took as his fifth wife.

21   Although Satsus Intel coordinated Tingle's visit, the class he taught was primarily

comprised of Indonesian army officers destined to become military attachés. In February 1973, Mossad dispatched a second officer to Cipayung to give a course in counter-espionage and the use of agents in counter-intelligence. This second class was comprised wholly of Satsus Intel members. Pelenkahu interview.

22 Anton Ngenget, a former PKI member who resumed networking with former colleagues after the 1965 coup attempt, began contact with Ali Moertopo in 1967 and reported on the attempted inroads by Soviet diplomats in Surabaya. Entries in BPF, "Anton Ngenget."

23 The vacation bungalow was at Cipayung, a town near Bogor that ironically also hosted the Satsus Intel training center.

24 The other Warsaw Pact nations – Poland, Bulgaria, Romania, and Hungary – each fielded a single intelligence officer who was usually less aggressive. The Soviets made little secret of the fact that they were coordinating the activities of their satellite intelligence services. KGB *Rezident* Babkin would occasionally organize weekend holidays for Warsaw Pact intelligence chiefs at a seaside hotel on the southern coast of Java. While ostensibly on holiday, the chiefs would often wade out into the surf to carry on discussions – thereby frustrating any attempt by Satsus Intel to monitor their conversations.

25 To provide continuous surveillance of the Soviet embassy, Satsus Intel in April 1970 began secret construction of a permanent survey post on the opposite side of the street.

26 Interview with Jacob Sutardi, 16 April 2003.

CHAPTER FOUR

INDOCHINA

I n 1970, Bakin underwent its second reorganization in as many years. Swapping numbers, Nicklany became Deputy I, and Poerwosoenoe, Deputy II. Redefining roles along geographic lines, Deputy I was now charged with foreign intelligence operations; Deputy II handled domestic operations. Showing continued organizational growth, each of these deputies was authorized to oversee five directorates apiece, up from two the previous year.

Nicklany, in particular, was busy taking his mandate to heart. Renowned for his love of chess and insane work schedule (he spent Sundays in the office), Nicklany was itching to take members of Deputy I beyond Indonesia's borders. "With containment in mind," explained one senior Deputy I officer, "he wanted to deploy officers to nations on the frontlines of communism."[1]

Nicklany's choices of frontline states were somewhat surprising. In 1970, the first Bakin officer was posted to the Indonesian embassy in Vienna, Austria. The second, dispatched the same year, went to Kabul, Afghanistan. Neither had training as an intelligence officer in the classic sense – the first had served in the Ministry of Agriculture for more than a decade; the second was on loan from the air force – and their marching orders reflected this lack of experience. "They were only supposed to monitor press opinion," said the Deputy I officer; "not to recruit agents or conduct any kind of clandestine activity."[2]

At the same time, Nicklany's creation while in the Military Police – Satsus Intel – was quickly maturing as a counter-intelligence task force. From the outset, the unit had three primary targets: the Soviet Union, North Korea, and (reflecting Washington's preoccupation with the war in Indochina) the Vietnamese. Vietnam's presence in Jakarta was rather unique. Because of the Old Order's left-leaning foreign policy, both Indonesia and North Vietnam had upgraded their respective consulates to embassy status. What's more, Sukarno in 1964 had agreed to host an information office for the communist National Liberation Front (NLF) of South Vietnam, popularly known as the Viet Cong.

That NLF information office, which was afforded diplomatic status, held particular interest for the U.S. There were only five others in the world, and the Jakarta office was the only one in Asia.[3] Most were headed by senior revolutionaries who theoretically would be privy to the wartime strategies and negotiating positions of both the NLF and their North Vietnamese patrons.

There was another reason for American interest. In mid-April 1970, the CIA's penetration agent, Friendly/1, reported to his handler that an Indonesian national working at the NLF office was a recruitment waiting to happen. That Indonesian, a 39-year old male from West Java, had been a member of the PKI since his early twenties. In 1959, he had joined the PKI-controlled labor union, Sobsi, and for several years had been involved in translating Sobsi's newsletter into English.

Following the abortive 1965 coup, Sobsi was abolished by government decree. Desperate for employment, the translator knocked on the door of the NLF information center. He was not exactly a stranger to the Vietnamese: over the previous two years, he had volunteered his time to help the NLF publish an infrequent propaganda sheet called *The South Vietnam Bulletin*. Returning the favor, they offered their unemployed comrade the regular job of turning this bulletin into a weekly publication.

Though he was now gainfully employed, the NLF's translator was still dogged by problems. Not known for magnanimity, Kopkamtib was patiently working its way through the backlog of former PKI members to exact punishment; in October 1967, the translator was served notice to appear before Kopkamtib officials for questioning. Arrested on arrival, he spent the next two months in prison.

Though once again a free man, the translator was not fully absolved of past political sins. As Friendly/1 had discovered, there remained the constant possibility of re-arrest by Kopkamtib or other elements of the Indonesian security apparatus. To exploit this fear, the Military Police on 1 May 1970 ordered the translator to appear at its headquarters for an encore interrogation. Conducted by the Satsus Intel commander, Major Nuril, the questioning was followed by a weeklong background investigation, then a recruitment pitch. On 19 May, he agreed to a clandestine relationship and from that point forward was known by the crypt *Mawar* ("Rose").[4]

For the remainder of that year, Mawar held regular meetings with his Satsus Intel handler. In an unusual arrangement, Satsus Intel employed an indirect system of contact between its agents and case officers. Satsus Intel employed agent handlers – known by the Indonesian contraction for "secret activity" (*kegiatan rahasia*, or girah) – to act as middlemen who would receive a list of requirements from a Satsus Intel case officer, then go into the field and pass these requirements to the agent. In return, the agent's findings would be passed back to the girah, who would relay them to the case officer. This system was enacted to protect the identity of the case officers. "Our faces were known to the Soviet embassy since our days in the Military Police," said the Satsus Intel operations chief. "Jakarta can be a small city, and if they saw us making contact with agents, it would blow the entire operation."[5]

Mawar spent much of his first year providing biographic data on the NLF's diplomats in Jakarta. Until 1967, the information center had counted just two members: a senior revolutionary named Le Quang Chanh, and Chao Phong, a chubby, junior assistant who bore a striking resemblance to a cherubic Mao Tse-tung. The two had initially worked out of a cramped residence in posh Menteng. After 1968, they moved to a more spacious office-*cum*-residence on Jalan Sunan Ngampel in Kebayoran Baru; previously owned by the Bank of China, the building was donated to the NLF after China yanked its diplomatic presence from Jakarta.

Following the shift to Sunan Ngampel, the NLF office received a new chief. With Chanh promoted to a higher posting, his replacement was Huynh Van Nghia. Fluent in Russian, the relatively senior Nghia retained Chao Phong as his assistant.

In February 1971, the NLF again shuffled its Indonesia office. With Nghia remaining as chief representative, Chao Phong was replaced by Nguyen Huong Minh, a 40-year old Catholic who had been fighting for Vietnam's liberation since 1945. Rising to the rank of captain in the Viet Cong, Minh had not neglected his studies. Fluent in French and Japanese, he saw himself as more of an intellectual than a knee-jerk ideologue.

While Mawar's anecdotal information about the NLF representatives was welcome, deeper insights were limited. Mawar, after all, could not understand conversations conducted in Vietnamese. In addition, Mawar only worked normal business hours and was confined to his workspace in a corner of the ground floor; sensitive conversations no doubt took place afterhours and in rooms outside of Mawar's hearing range.

But given Mawar's unique access inside the NLF office, the CIA and Satsus Intel in early 1971 hatched plans to use him in a daring joint technical operation. Codenamed *Kuning* ("Yellow"), the project called for Mawar to install one, and perhaps two, listening devices in the Sunan Ngampel office.

By mid-February 1971, the general outline for Kuning was approved. Yet to be finalized, however, was the optimal location for the bugs. Based on Mawar's findings, the upper floor – where bedrooms were located – was not a good bet because the Vietnamese diplomats did little there besides sleep. On the ground floor, choices included a front guest room, an inner dining room, Mawar's work area, and an office used by Nghia. Of these, Mawar suggested that the most interesting conversations took place in the guest and dining rooms.

Having narrowed down potential locations, a decision had to be made as to where the bugs would be concealed. Mawar was initially tasked with compiling a list of decorative items, such as porcelain vases. After none were found to be suitable, the decision was made to instead use what was euphemistically called a woodblock: a battery-powered transmitter imbedded within a 27-centimeter-long block of wood. With a range of about 150 meters, it would be able to provide a signal for more than three months before needing a change of batteries. Sharp tacks protruding from one side would allow it to be innocuously affixed to the bottom of any piece of furniture.

On 21 July, Mawar kept a scheduled meeting with his handler at the Blok M bus terminal. There he received instructions to return in six days to receive the woodblock wrapped in a sheet of newspaper. He was to then take the bug to the NLF office and affix it to the bottom of the sofa in the guest room.

As instructed, Mawar on 27 May returned to the bus terminal. His girah handed him the paper-wrapped package, which he promptly stuffed inside a beaten, leather bag and walked the short stretch to his office.

Mawar's heart was pounding as he entered the NLF residence and took a seat at his tiny work station. On any given day, he would wait for the latest news to be sent from the North Vietnamese embassy (it came from Hanoi via Morse); he would then prepare the English version of the NLF newsletter and translate relevant sections into Indonesian. A noisy mimeograph machine at the rear of the office turned out the final product.

That afternoon, Mawar went through the motions of his job. Waiting until the two Vietnamese were out of the office, he opened his leather bag. Unwrapping the woodblock, he examined its exterior. Aside from a tiny hole on its side, there was nothing to betray its electronic contents.

Stealing into the front guest room, Mawar made a beeline for the sofa. Reaching underneath, he pressed the two tacks on the top of the woodblock into the couch's wood frame. Once it felt secure, he withdrew· to his work station; less than a minute had elapsed. By 1425 hours, he was back at Blok M briefing his handler.

The good news was not to last, however. Down the street from the NLF office, the CIA had rented a small office under the name of a notional clove company.[6] Inside, a Vietnamese-American linguist named Lee was monitoring the feed from the woodblock and translating relevant conversations. But after less than two months in operation, Mawar picked up a disturbing revelation: the NLF was planning to renovate the guest room and the old sofa was to be discarded. Thinking quickly, on 24 August, he retrieved the woodblock and turned it over to his handler.[7]

Waiting until after a new sofa was delivered, Mawar again took possession of the woodblock on 29 September and had it back in place that same day. Still, Murphy's Law was alive and well. Whether because no revealing conversations were taking place near the couch, or because the signal was muffled, nothing of significance was being relayed to the listening post. At year's end, Mawar once again retrieved the device and the CIA reconsidered its options.

In January 1972, Operation Kuning was set for a fresh start. This time, the woodblock was to be placed under a cabinet in the dining room. Despite the complicating presence of a third Vietnamese national – a chauffeur named Son had arrived in the interim – Mawar found opportunity on 27 January to install a woodblock without incident.[8]

The third time would not prove a charm. The following noon, Mawar peered into the dining room and froze. Lying on the floor under the cabinet was the woodblock; the two tacks had apparently not been sufficiently strong to hold it in place. Fortunately for the translator, Nghia and Son were visiting the North Vietnamese embassy at the time, and Minh was in his bedroom.

Returning the bug to his handler, Mawar received a modified version – this time with four tacks – on 10 February. The translator successfully installed the audio device that afternoon; not leaving anything to chance, he made a habit of ensuring the tacks continued to grip the bottom of the cabinet every morning thereafter.[9]

His perseverance paid off. Within two weeks at its new location, the woodblock was mining intelligence gold. On 23 February, Nghia was heard lamenting about the office's perilous financial state; the phone had been out of service for a week, and they were reduced to paying a repairman in cigarettes because they had no cash. Two days later, Nghia was telling a senior NLF visitor from Paris that they were forced to rely on the Cubans, North Koreans, and North Vietnamese for handouts.

The woodblock also revealed that not all was well between the NLF and North Vietnamese. On 25 March, Nghia counseled his two compatriots to be cautious around North Vietnam's overbearing representatives, and that their most sensitive documents should be kept hidden away in the attic. Five days later, when two diplomats from the North Vietnamese embassy visited the NLF office, Nghia complained they did not have enough money for food expenses; Hanoi's representatives were less than sympathetic, but tried to appease them by offering to pay for a holiday to Bandung.[10]

At other times, the audio voyeurism was comical. The NLF diplomats had recently purchased two dogs, and the reason soon became apparent. Three days before they were to host a 14 July reception for fellow communist representatives, the following exchange was recorded and transcribed:

Son: There are Eastern dogs and Western dogs. Eastern dogs taste better.
Nghia: Whenever we entertain the North Koreans, we eat dogs.
Son: We should kill one and keep the other.
Minh: What do you mean? Thirty people and one dog? There is not much left after you skin them.

More substantial, the bug picked up internal strife among the NLF personnel. As revealed in a late February intercept, Minh and Son had not spoken to each other for three weeks due to the latter not repaying borrowed money. Nghia was heard lecturing Son to make good on his tardy debt, but bad blood persisted.

Though the intellectual Minh was seething toward Son, he was very much a free spirit. During a 23 March intercept, Minh started whistling a tune to the NLF's pet bird. Continuing the tune, he began drumming his spoon on the table, then tapping his feet to complete the one-man band. (On the daily transcript sheet, the CIA interpreter jotted the commentary: "Is this guy happy or what?")

The CIA, it turned out, had one other inside source of information about the NLF cast. Back in 1966, the agency had established contact with a resourceful 29-year old Indonesian named Subandi. Born in East Java, Subandi had entered the Indonesian marine corps as an officer cadet and was one of eight junior officers selected in 1964 for training in Quantico, Virginia. Returning in February 1965, he became disillusioned by the leftist tilt among many top marine officers; penning a letter of resignation to his commander, he abandoned the corps and headed for his home province.

Returning to Jakarta after the October 1965 coup attempt, Subandi was out of a job but full of ideas. In August 1966, he contacted Lieutenant Colonel Pramuko, a fanatical Sukarno supporter (and fellow Quantico graduate) who was influential in the leftist newspaper *El Bahar*. Though he had no background as a journalist, Subandi professed leftist sympathies and, with Pramuko's help, landed a job at the paper.

Subandi also maintained contact with the defense attaché's office at the U.S. embassy. When it heard he was joining the staff of a left-wing paper, it saw opportunities and quickly introduced him to an officer at the CIA station. The decision proved fortuitous, for the personable Subandi, exploiting his press credentials, was soon on the invitation list for countless communist embassy receptions. Assigned the crypt Friendly/2, by 1968, he was passing on information to his case officer on a weekly basis. [11]

Perhaps none of Friendly/2's connections were better than those he forged with the NLF information office. Soon after joining *El Bahar* in 1966, he had befriended Chao Phong. Chao Phong, in turn, introduced Subandi to his successor, Nguyen Huong Minh, in early 1971.

Initially, relations between Friendly/2 and Minh were cordial but distant. With Chao Phong, who had resided in Jakarta for eight years, Subandi could easily communicate in Indonesian. Minh, however, spoke no Indonesian and only broken English. But Minh, it turned out, was eager to make friends outside his office. He liked alcohol and was especially eager to troll for female companionship; to avoid suspicions of his prudish comrades, he had even concocted an elaborate bogus tale that a war injury left him impotent. (Minh also warned Nghia that if he worked too hard, he was prone to a relapse from the faux ailment.)

Between Minh's love of the flesh, as well as his feud with chauffeur Son, the CIA judged him ripe for recruitment. Given the task was Friendly/2, who on 2 April 1972 convinced Minh to share a car ride to Bogor. As Friendly/2's leftist credentials were deemed beyond reproach, the trip raised no eyebrows within the NLF office.

En route to Bogor, the two bonded. Significantly, Minh made a point of noting he was a nationalist, not a communist. Sealing their friendship, the two stopped at a hotel and had the proprietor introduce some amiable female escorts.

Over the next month, Friendly/2 managed to meet Minh during several afternoons. Claiming that he had gotten lucky and fallen upon a financial windfall, Subandi said he wanted to share his newfound gains with an obliging Minh. Not until 2 June did their trysts turn serious. Perhaps sensing that Friendly/2 was vying for more than just social conversation, Minh again stressed he was a nationalist and not a communist. The two agreed to discuss that point the following week.

As promised, Minh slipped out of his office on 10 June and rendezvoused with Friendly/2. They then drove to a Tebet safe house and, with no others present, Subandi made his pitch. Without mentioning whom he represented, he promised a generous stipend for Minh's active cooperation. Minh thought for a moment, repeated his assertion that he was a nationalist, then offered his consent. From that point forward, Minh went by the crypt *Kasuari* – the Indonesian spelling for cassowary, a flightless bird indigenous to New Guinea that can disembowel a foe with its sickle-like claws.

On 21 June, Friendly/2 and Kasuari had their second meeting at the Tebet safe house. During that occasion, they agreed to the terms of a monthly retainer, as well as a bonus in U.S. dollars to be paid at the end of his Indonesian tour. The following month, during a third Tebet huddle, Kasuari was tasked with three areas of interest: What were the differences in war plans between the NLF and the North Vietnamese? What were the last instructions given to the North Vietnamese delegation prior to the Paris peace talks? Why was the NLF still getting its directives from Hanoi and not dealing directly with the South Vietnamese regime?

While Kasuari went back to collect answers to these queries, the CIA and Satsus Intel were developing other windows into the NLF office. Ever since March 1972, they had experimented with a new technique called a "hot mike," which involved the activation of a cradled telephone by sending a current through the line rather than planting bug in the telephone itself. Focusing on the telephone located inside Nghia's office, the hot mike technique allowed remote monitoring of conversations held in that room. And beginning in January 1973, Satsus Intel also initiated a more conventional telephone tap ("teltap") on the NLF phone line.

As a result of all these sources, there were few secrets left inside the NLF residence. As before, many of the intercepted conversations were hardly serious political diatribe. During a November 1973 meeting with two North Vietnamese diplomats, for example, Minh waxed eloquently about his taste in women. "Russians are too big," he opined. "Germans are prettier than Italians."

Other conversations were of special interest to the Indonesians. On 11 April 1973, and again on 23 October, those in the NLF office were heard complaining about a photographic display at the Indonesian armed forces museum. Featuring pictures of captured Viet Cong weaponry, the display rubbed the thin-skinned NLF representatives raw; they agreed to send a report to Hanoi and file a diplomatic complaint. Other discussions revolved around attempts to entice Indonesian journalists to run stories favorable to the NLF.

This multitude of secret channels also protected Kasuari. Back in December 1972, Mawar passed word that Nghia, the chief representative, had asked the NLF's new Indonesian chauffeur to report on Kasuari's movements. Alerted to this, Kasuari took added care around the chauffeur and was able to avoid further suspicion while passing frequent reports to Friendly/2.

These secret meetings continued until mid-1974. At that point, with Chao Phong having returned to Jakarta (this time as the top NLF representative), Kasuari was scheduled to leave Indonesia for a stint in North Vietnam. Looking to maintain its covert relationship, the CIA in early July had Friendly/2 arrange a rendezvous at a beach house along the Jakarta waterfront. On the designated day, two CIA officers – one poorly disguised with a fake moustache – were waiting inside. Kasuari, indicating his consent to further contact if and when he was again posted outside of North Vietnam, soon afterwards boarded a merchant ship bound for Hanoi.

After Kasuari's departure, the CIA's interest in the NLF office appeared to wane. With U.S. combat troops having already departed Indochina, a shaky ceasefire remained in effect in South Vietnam. The lease on the agency's listening post near Jalan Sunan Ngampel was allowed to expire at the close of November; just days short of that, Mawar removed the woodblock under the cabinet and turned it over to his handler.

But by the opening of 1975, with the Vietnam truce having effectively collapsed in December and Saigon suddenly looking more vulnerable than ever, the NLF office was once again a top item of interest. Not by coincidence, Kasuari, along with two other NLF colleagues, arrived in Jakarta on 22 January; together with Chao Phong, that office was now four strong.

Within days after Kasuari's arrival, Friendly/2 reestablished contact and arranged for a night meeting outside the massive Senayan sports stadium. Huddled in a car, Kasuari's comments were explosive. "The final offensive is on," he told Friendly/2. "The war will be over by March."[12]

Friendly/2 immediately passed this information to the CIA station, though U.S. intelligence officers were not exactly swayed by the alarmist hearsay. Still, the CIA and Satsus Intel had already decided to proceed with Kuning II, the re-installation of bugging devices at the NLF office. On 1 February, a new listening post, situated on the second floor of an office sporting the name of a fictional Australian engineering firm, was operational. After one false start – due to a faulty transmitter – Mawar by 27 March had placed a woodblock back under the dining room cabinet.

As it turned out, the bug picked up NLF reactions during the final weeks of the Vietnam War. Remarkably, the NLF's diplomats were far from euphoric. On 29 April, as North Vietnamese tanks were bearing down on the outskirts of Saigon, Kasuari spent the morning complaining of a tooth ache. He was joined at the dining table by Tran Nam Tien, one of the new NLF arrivals, who was interested in little more than preparing a cup of noodles. "These are nutritious," he claimed, "because they are made from flour and egg yolks."

Chao Phong, the office chief, was equally shallow. Seemingly oblivious to the pivotal events in his home country, he offered nothing more than a critique of Tien's meal. "A complete meal for just 45 rupiah, just add hot water," he mocked. "I'm sick of noodles."

One day later, the South Vietnamese regime was no more. As diplomats from across the communist world came to offer their congratulations to the NLF's Jakarta representatives, Satsus Intel rushed plans to expand its audio coverage of the Sunan Ngampel office. By 10 June, Mawar installed a second woodblock under the sofa in the front guest room. Two weeks later, the bugs picked up a conversation between Chao Phong and the Yugoslavian press attaché. "Socialism is the prevailing wind in Asia," beamed the attaché. "Maybe in the Philippines," countered Chao Phong, "but religion is slowing down the trend in Indonesia."

Apart from this brief exchange, the bugs revealed little else of value. And with the Vietnam War now over, it was deemed only a matter of time before the North Vietnamese did away with the NLF fig leaf and consolidated their control over a unified Vietnam. In anticipation of this, when the woodblock batteries expired in the third quarter, Mawar turned the two devices over to his handler and neither was replaced. During September, the teltap was discontinued. As predicted, by year's end the NLF office was set for closure.

Not missing a beat, Satsus Intel was already turning its attention toward the North Vietnamese embassy on Jalan Teuku Umar. Since September 1969, in fact, the unit had kept North Vietnamese diplomats under random surveillance. But in November 1975, with Operation Kuning II having been concluded, Satsus Intel and the CIA penned plans to shift one of the NLF woodblocks to the North Vietnamese diplomatic post.

Security precautions at the NLF office and the North Vietnam embassy, it turned out, were worlds apart. Whereas the NLF had eventually hired four Indonesian nationals (a cook, a maid, a chauffeur, and Mawar), the North Vietnamese granted access to no Indonesian employees other than Mawar (who continued occasional work as a translator at Teuku Umar after the NLF packed its bags). Although Mawar was able to identify several good locations for a woodblock, he was never alone long enough in the crowded embassy to install a bug. After four months of casing, the plan was quietly shelved.

Satsus Intel was not the only Indonesian intelligence unit taking an interest in Indochina. During the 1970 Bakin reorganization, Brigadier General Ali Moertopo was named Deputy III, a new post charged with Special Operations.[13] From his time as Opsus troubleshooter, Moertopo was well prepared to handle such clandestine operations on behalf of Bakin. But because he was among the most trusted of Suharto's inner circle (among other things, he was named the president's personal assistant for socio-political affairs), the general was allowed to retain his autonomous – and redundant – role as head of Opsus. And because he considered Opsus to be more prestigious than his deputy slot at Bakin, Moertopo gave his full attention to the former and kept his second position a hollow shell with a skeletal staff.

As before, Opsus remained busy developing fast, effective solutions to Suharto's eclectic mix of problems. Some of these issues were domestic: it was Opsus operatives who choreographed the 1969 pro-integration landslide vote in West Irian. And Opsus social engineers, equipped with copious amounts of cash, were behind the growth of the Golkar political machine that underpinned the New Order.[14]

Opsus, too, continued to handle discreet overseas ties when conventional diplomacy was problematic. Opsus, for example, had helped set the stage for the creation of the Association of Southeast Asian Nations (ASEAN). Additionally, Opsus had focused significant effort on Indochina, especially South Vietnam. There, the Indonesian government had closed its Saigon consulate ever since the Old Order upgraded its Hanoi presence to an embassy. Though the foreign ministry appeared determined not to reverse this decision, in early 1968, with Saigon still smoldering after the Tet Offensive, an Opsus officer made a brief fact-finding trip to South Vietnam.[15]

Two years later, Opsus was back in Indochina. This time, its focus was on the besieged nation of Cambodia. In March 1970, in a process eerily similar to what happened in Jakarta during 1965, Prince Norodom Sihanouk – a flamboyant, mercurial civilian leader who once been a close ally of Sukarno – was replaced in a bloodless putsch by his underrated military chief, General Lon Nol.

From the start, Lon Nol was under pressure. Along Cambodia's eastern border, North Vietnamese troops held sway; across much of the rest of the countryside, a brutal, homegrown guerrilla movement – the Khmer Rouge – was fast spreading. Professing his opposition to both these communist threats, the besieged Cambodian leader appealed to the West, as well as like-minded nations in Southeast Asia, for diplomatic and military aid.

Indonesia was quick to answer the call . On 6 April, a joint Indonesian mission comprised of military and Opsus officers arrived in the Cambodian capital of Phnom Penh for a two-week tour. Their goal was to determine if the Lon Nol regime would survive and, if so, what kind of Indonesian support was appropriate. Their final written report, issued on 21 April, concluded that Lon Nol's regime would survive at least for the short-term, though it was ambiguous as to what type of assistance Jakarta could or should render.

Privately, Ali Moertopo was far more forceful. As part of a covert assistance package, he gathered hundreds of AK-47 rifles – which had been the mainstay of the Indonesian armed forces during the waning years of the Old Order – and rushed them to the Cambodian army. This delivery was overseen by three Opsus officers, one of whom remained in Phnom Penh as part of a permanent posting.[16]

In March 1971, Opsus was back in South Vietnam. This time, Moertopo dispatched two officers to Saigon under cover as representatives of the Indonesian Chamber of Commerce. Neither had any intelligence training, and they were tasked only with passive monitoring of the security situation.[17]

For the next four years, the pair kept their fingers on the pulse of Saigon's diplomatic and business community. "We were there to see if the place was going to sink," explained one. In early April 1975, they returned to Jakarta and reported the end was imminent. Though Indonesia's generals scoffed at this dire prediction, Saigon was history by month's end.[18]

1   Interview with Sunarso Djajusman, 30 March 2003.

2   Ibid.

3   The other NLF information centers were located in Denmark, Finland, France, Norway, and Sweden.

4   Interview with Mawar, 19 March 2003.

5   Mandagi interview.

6   Cloves are a key ingredient of Indonesia's *kretek* cigarettes. See Mark Hanusz, *Kretek, The Culture and Heritage of Indonesia's Clove Cigarettes*, (Jakarta: Equinox Publishing, 2000).

7   As of 1972, the CIA had given its combined operations with Satsus Intel the cover designation Joint Task Force (JTF); this designation, found on internal memoranda exchanged between the two organizations, remained in usage through 1974.

8   During February 1972, thought was given to placing a listening device in Mawar's typewriter, which was being sent out of the NLF office for repairs. This option was dropped in favor of the woodblock.

9   Mawar interview. In June 1972, when the woodblock was removed for a change of batteries, it was outfitted with five tacks for added assurance.

10 Satsus Intel tailed the NLF on their April 1972 road trip during the appropriately
    titled "Operation Bandung."

11 Interview with Subandi, 18 March 2003.

12 Ibid.

13 Prior to 1970, Bakin's Deputy III was in charge of administration. After the 1970
    reorganization, Bakin administrative matters were handled by the new position
    of Deputy IV.

14 Despite its small size, the Opsus budget rivaled even that of Bakin. Its money
    came from domestic government sources (Suharto ensured that it received
    generous sums from state-owned enterprises), Chinese business leaders looking
    to curry favor with the New Order, and foreign donors (primarily the Republic
    of China on Taiwan). So plentiful was its funding that in at least one case, a sizable
    check from Taiwan was not cashed but instead kept as a souvenir. Interview with
    Pitut Soeharto, 9 May 2003.

15 Sugiyanto interview.

16 One of the three Opsus officers sent to Cambodia was Willy Pesik. A 52-year old
    native of North Sulawesi, Pesik had been a diplomat at the Indonesian consulate
    in Saigon during the mid-fifties. Joining the rebel movement in his native North
    Sulawesi late that decade, he went into exile in Malaysia following the rebel defeat.
    Pesik eventually returned to Indonesia in 1966 to join Moertopo's Opsus. He forged
    good relations with the CIA station and, given his Vietnam background, attempted
    to develop sources for the agency within the North Vietnamese embassy and NLF
    office in Jakarta. But in a telling display of inter-unit suspicions, Satsus Intel placed
    Pesik under surveillance during early 1970. So as not to get embroiled in local
    rivalries, the CIA curtailed contact with Pesik and used only Satsus Intel for
    operations against the NLF and North Vietnam. BPF, "Willy Pesik"; interview
    with Stuart Methvan, 1 June 2003.

17 Interview with Firdaus Wadji, 3 March 2003.

18 Ibid.

CHAPTER FIVE

SIDESHOWS

From early on, Satsus Intel did not limit its activities solely to catching spies. Its first major diversion outside the world of espionage came on 16 July 1970.[1] That afternoon, nine-year old Timothy "Timmy" Pesik was returning home from school near Jakarta's Chinese quarter. Near the school, a black sedan pulled up to the curb. Witnesses later claimed two young men exited the vehicle and told the boy his mother had been involved in an automobile accident. In tears, Timmy got in the back seat and the car sped off.[2]

An hour later, a handwritten note was found at the gate of Timmy's house. The writer demanded 20 million rupiah for his safe release, to be paid in three days at a location to be stipulated in future correspondence.

Word of the kidnapping spread like wildfire across the Indonesian capital. Not only was it the first time a prominent child was abducted – Timmy's father, ethnic Chinese businessman Tan Gwan Tjae, owned a profitable pharmaceutical company – but the ransom demand was jaw-dropping. Given the exchange rate of the time, as well as the more modest 1970 standard of living in Indonesia, 20 million rupiah was, by any account, an astronomical amount.

The Indonesian police, moreover, were out of their league. By coincidence, the Jakarta metropolitan police chief was a close acquaintance of Satsus Intel commander Nuril, and he had heard rumors that Nuril's unit had some unique surveillance capabilities. After a quick appeal for help, Nuril consented. At 2215 hours, he passed word to his men: Satsus Intel was to take the lead in what was darkly codenamed Operation *Tumpas Bersih* ("Clean Extermination").

For Satsus Intel, the kidnapping promised to be an ideal testing ground for all of its skills. By the following morning, it had initiated a teltap on the Tjae residence. It had also established a discreet 24-hour stakeout near the house in the event the kidnappers attempted to drop off another ransom note; to blend into the surroundings, one member of their surveillance team was disguised as a beggar and kept vigil from a garbage heap down the street.

In the end, the telephone proved the kidnappers' undoing. Perhaps unfamiliar with the ability to trace a call, the perpetrators contacted the family to renegotiate the ransom (they were now prepared to accept the still princely sum of 6.5 million rupiah). Satsus Intel was able to identify the incoming telephone number, match it to an address, and put that location under surveillance. On the evening of 27 July, police stormed the locale, found a shaken but otherwise healthy Timmy, and apprehended five kidnappers. Characteristically, Satsus Intel shunned the limelight and took no credit.

Satsus Intel soon shouldered additional mandates. At the opening of 1971, a presidential decree charged Bakin with investigating currency counterfeiting. In Bakin doublespeak, such cases were codenamed *gigi palsu* – "false teeth."[3]

Following the decree, Bakin's first exposure to "false teeth" came in January 1971 after receiving a classified CIA memorandum about an American national named Bernard "Larry" Tractman. Born in Philadelphia, Tractman, 49, had operated an aviation transportation firm during the late sixties in the Philippines and Indonesia. Records also indicated that he had approached the U.S. embassy in Jakarta during May 1969 to seek help in selling demilitarized tank landing ships to an Indonesian firm.[4]

Not all of Tractman's business activities were legitimate, however. According to information gathered over the second half of 1970, the U.S. government suspected he was the head of an international counterfeiting syndicate. These suspicions grew more concrete in November 1970, when he was fingered as having passed bogus deutschemarks to Indonesians transiting Singapore.

The next month, December 1970, Tractman grew bolder. Meeting up with a shady Chinese-Indonesian businessman named Muchsien Rustandi, he offered Rustandi the chance of making a quick fortune if he helped transfer US$ 6 million from Hong Kong to Bangkok. The catch: Tractman said the bills were demonetized dollars he had smuggled from the Philippines to Hong

Kong in a diplomatic pouch before scheduled destruction.

Agreeing to be Tractman's bagman, Rustandi crisscrossed Southeast Asia on eight occasions during the first half of 1971. Much of his time was spent carrying suitcases of cash – not demonetized bills this time, but fake dollars, Philippine pesos, and Indonesian rupiah printed by Tractman and his associates in Hong Kong.

The counterfeiting syndicate, it turned out, also had political dimensions. Rustandi was told the dollars and rupiah had been ordered by prominent Indonesian generals – Tractman had earlier befriended them during his business jaunts – who needed the fake cash to defray the cost of the April 1971 legislative elections.

The story was much the same for the Philippine pesos. Tractman, a longtime resident of Manila, had grown close to Sergio Osmena, a disgruntled former senator who was bitterly opposed to President Ferdinand Marcos. Osmena reportedly wanted the money to support political allies in the upcoming November 1971 senatorial election. He also wanted weaponry, hinting that there would be an armed uprising if the polls were rigged by Marcos; an obliging Rustandi ultimately made several trips to Europe in search of night-vision devices, automatic rifles, and grenade launchers.

For its part, Bakin was primarily concerned with the rupiah counterfeits. Once alerted by the January 1971 CIA memo, the case was passed to Satsus Intel, which in turn attempted to pinpoint the whereabouts of Rustandi. But given his frequent travel and numerous aliases, the Indonesian courier proved slippery.

Not until September 1971 did they receive a break in the case. This came from the Singaporean police who, similarly alerted to the region-wide counterfeiting operation, arrested Rustandi after finding him in possession of fake dollar and rupiah notes.

Rustandi's detention proved short. Perhaps fearing details of their activities would come out in trial, Tractman and his Filipino conspirators posted bail in October, allowing their Indonesian accomplice to flee the city-state. Using yet another alias, he crossed the Strait of Malacca to Sumatra and assumed a low profile in the city of Medan. There Satsus Intel eventually picked up his trail, initiating covert surveillance of the suspect – appropriately named Operation Medan – in February 1972.

At that point, the scheming of the counterfeiters took a new twist. Sounding more like Walter Mitty than a hardnosed assassin, Tractman began talking up plans to kill Marcos on behalf of Osmena and his clique. Eight plots were reportedly hatched between February and September 1972, though none was ever actually launched. Rustandi participated in some of these, taking additional trips on behalf of the syndicate to Thailand and Malaysia.

By that time, the Indonesian authorities were growing tired of their wayward countryman. Late in 1972, after having pinpointed Rustandi's location with the help of Thai counterparts, Major Nuril flew to Bangkok and hustled him back to Jakarta on the next available flight. While not charged with any crime (perhaps because the Indonesian government was less than eager to expose the reported link between its generals and fake rupiah), Rustandi was sufficiently intimidated to again assume a low profile.

The Filipinos were less inclined to forgive and forget. In January 1973, General Sebastian Ver, chief of the National Intelligence Coordination Agency, ventured to Jakarta on the pretext of attending a regional intelligence forum hosted by Bakin. Ver had more on his agenda than the Bakin tryst: a Marcos appointee, he was more interested in crushing the plots against his president. To those ends, he hoped to contact Rustandi and gain his cooperation.

Rustandi, it turned out, was willing to talk to just about anyone. Rendezvousing with Ver, he answered the general's questions about his relationship with Tractman and others in the ring. Immediately thereafter, he approached Bakin and briefed them on Ver's convoluted take on events. While Indonesians are usually game for a good conspiracy, they had nothing on the Filipinos: Ver, said Rustandi, suspected a CIA hand behind Osmena's opposition to Marcos, and even claimed the Indonesian government was secretly training a guerrilla army on Java to bolster Muslim separatists in the southern Philippines.[5]

This last charge, without basis, was of obvious concern to Indonesia. On 30 March, Bakin chief Sutopo met Filipino Ambassador Modesto Farolan to discuss the Tractman counterfeiting ring and its link to anti-Marcos schemes. While finding the Filipinos still prone to conspiracies – Farolan pointed an accusing finger at the unlikely alliance of Libya and the CIA – Sutopo did his best to convince the ambassador that Indonesia wanted nothing more than cordial ties.

Satsus Intel, meantime, remained on the case for another year. Though Rustandi appeared outwardly contrite, teltaps in June and July revealed he was still in telephone contact with Tractman and was plotting to pass $100,000 in stolen securities. This information was passed to U.S. authorities, who began making arrests in July. For their part, Filipino officials detained five persons between December 1973 and April 1974, charging them in the attempted assassination of Marcos. A byproduct of all this was an end to the *gigi palsu* being printed in Hong Kong.

Another mandate handed to Bakin in 1971 was counter-narcotics operations, especially those with an international dimension. Its first exposure to the drug wars came the following year, when Deputy Nicklany received word of smuggling – probably including narcotics – by a 30-year old ethnic Chinese importer named Roby Cahyadi. Boasting close connections with a litany of generals, Cahyadi regularly browbeat customs officials along the Jakarta docks to turn a blind eye to his activities. Nicklany, not easily intimidated, gave Satsus Intel the task of collecting incriminating data.

Codenamed Operation *Kencana* ("Gold"), the spycatchers discovered how Cahyadi earned his. According to import regulations, Indonesian students studying overseas were allowed to import a single car without paying stifling duties. Cahyadi had exploited this loophole, paying students a nominal fee to import luxury automobiles from Hong Kong under their names. When the number of smuggled vehicles outstripped the number of students, an emboldened Cahyadi, benefiting from a growing roster of military officers on his payroll, began fabricating documents for nonexistent students.

In late 1972, Bakin turned its evidence over to the police. Although they were unable to collect evidence of drug smuggling, teltap transcripts from Satsus Intel left no question that Cahyadi was importing cars under false pretenses. He was given a stiff prison sentence in January 1973, and more than a couple of senior army officers had their careers torpedoed for complicity in the scheme.[6]

One other non-espionage mandate handed to Bakin was the so-called "China problem." Partially out of anger over China's sponsorship of the PKI, and partially out of envy over their growing economic clout, Indonesia's ethnic Chinese minority under the New Order were increasingly on the receiving end of social and cultural discrimination. There was also a thorny problem over citizenship: the People's Republic of China had long claimed that overseas Chinese were its countrymen; Indonesia, by contrast, did not want to recognize such dual citizenship. In 1967, Suharto had created a special staff to monitor anti-Chinese discrimination and sort out the citizenship issue. Two years later,

administration of this staff was handed to Bakin. In June 1973, Bakin expanded
the staff into the Agency for Coordinating the China Problem (*Badan Koordinasi
Masalah Cina*, or BKMC).

While the BKMC was a passive reporting body, Satsus Intel took a more
discreet look at the foreign aspect of the China problem. In order to keep tabs
on possible links between Indonesia's ethnic Chinese citizenry and overseas
communists, the spycatchers by 1972 had established a 25-man censor unit to
scan virtually all of the mail coming and going to communist nations, especially
the People's Republic of China. Using steam tables and ivory tongs, letters
were surreptitiously removed, photographed and, when applicable, translated
from Chinese into Indonesian.

Expanding on this, Satsus Intel penned plans in April 1973 to create a
dedicated 75-man China task force with its own surveillance teams, electronics
experts, and transcribers. Codenamed Phoenix, its cover was to be a travel
agency, a real estate company, or income tax consultancy. Funds were not
approved, however, and Phoenix was stillborn.[7]

In October 1973, Bakin experienced yet another internal restructuring. With
Lieutenant General Sutopo still at the helm, the agency subdivided its previous
divisions into a record six deputies, each with six directorates. Under this new
table of organization, Deputy I returned to handling domestic intelligence,
Deputy II oversaw state security, Deputy III was still responsible for special
operations, Deputy IV was mandated with foreign intelligence, Deputy V
handled clandestine intelligence operations (including counter-intelligence),
and Deputy VI was responsible for administration.

In hindsight, there were several problems with Bakin's continued growth.
For example, many of the deputies now had overlapping mandates: Deputy I,
for example, was virtually synonymous with Deputy II. Similarly, Deputy V
had elements in common with at least two other deputies. As redundant offices
competed for limited budgets and human resources, this did little to encourage
efficiency or improve the agency's overall intelligence product.

Moreover, Deputy III remained part of Bakin in name only. In a
compromise move, Ali Moertopo, who by then had earned his second star,
had grudgingly ceded most of the overseas portion of his Opsus empire. By

early 1973, all of his officers stationed in overseas posts – Cambodia, Hong Kong, Singapore, Taiwan, and South Vietnam – had their positions transferred to Bakin administration.

Still, Moertopo resisted submitting the more politically-sensitive domestic elements of Opsus to Bakin oversight. To the contrary, he had shifted his fast-expanding Opsus to a series of converted residences along Jalan Tanah Abang III near downtown Jakarta. From there, the general used his pregnant coffers – some of his war chest flowed from state-owned enterprises and Indonesia's emergent ethnic Chinese tycoons, some came courtesy of Taiwan – to browbeat and manipulate political and social support for the New Order. "Moertopo had no permanent friends or enemies, just relations of convenience," said one longtime Opsus aide. "He did not seek to be king, just kingmaker."[8]

Moertopo's intransigence over Opsus was set against a backdrop of growing tension among Indonesia's senior military officers. In one camp was Moertopo himself. Opposing him were several high-ranking Peta veterans led by Sumitro, a rotund, gregarious general who had taken over the powerful slot of Kopkamtib deputy commander in 1969.

As an organization, Bakin was largely sympathetic to Sumitro. This included intelligence chief Sutopo Juwono, a fellow Peta alumnus who bristled at Moertopo's refusal to merge his Opsus assets. Deputy Nicklany, though not a Peta veteran, shared Sumitro's contempt for the insubordinate Moertopo. So great was Nicklany's disapproval that in January 1972 he authorized Satsus Intel to briefly place a teltap on Moertopo's office to troll for suspicious or incriminating behavior.[9]

By the opening of 1974, the infighting was fast coming to a head. In what was apparently an attempt to embarrass the opposing camp – and possibly gain in Suharto's eyes – both Moertopo and Sumitro were trying to court support from Jakarta's vocal university population.[10] In this, Sumitro came out on top. During the third week of January, during a state visit by the Japanese prime minister, thousands of these students began staging violent riots in the capital ostensibly against Tokyo's economic imperialism. Not by coincidence, many of their placards demanded that the president's personal assistants (read: Moertopo) be dismissed. They also burned Moertopo's effigy along with that of the Japanese prime minister.

Bakin had not been fully caught off guard by the rallies. On 14 January, one day before the first demonstrations, Satsus Intel had already initiated

Operation *Bunglon* ("Opportunist"), planned as a monthlong intelligence-gathering operation against Jakarta's most politically active students. Bunglon had several components. On 15 and 16 January, field operators mingled among the demonstrators to gain information on student leaders. Because many of the demonstrators hailed from the University of Indonesia, a teltap was placed on that institute's rector. And on 15 January, Satsus Intel penned a report on the movements of Moertopo, including details of a trip he took to Jogjakarta the previous week.[11]

Also tied to the rioting, Satsus Intel conducted a background check on a U.S. embassy diplomat. That diplomat, Second Secretary Robert Pringle, had been the embassy's designated officer for student liaison; because he had socially met most of the university activists leading the riots, that link rang warning bells in Bakin. Though the check did not extend beyond completing a thin dossier on Pringle, it was a sensitive move, given that CIA largesse made Satsus Intel possible.[12]

After two days, the riots – which were soon dubbed the Malari Affair – subsided.[13] But Suharto was looking for heads to roll for the lapse in security; playing no favorites, he left none of the implicated generals unscathed. Bakin chief Sutopo, who had never quite warmed to the president and vice versa, was sacked almost immediately. Sumitro lost his Kopkamtib post in March.

Even Ali Moertopo saw his star wane. Heeding one of the criticisms of the students, Suharto abolished the offices of his personal assistants. In an equally significant move, Moertopo was forced to close down his autonomous Opsus and formally merge the entire operation to his existing post as Bakin Deputy III. More than just semantics, Deputy III was now tasked with *Penggalangan* – literally, "Conditioning." Ironically, this term had been popularized by the PKI in reference to its attempts at lobbying (and subverting) social institutions. Among its many covert projects, Opsus had continued this tradition of discreetly molding public opinion. Said one Deputy III officer:

> We focused on the five M's: Muslims, the military, mass media, *mahasiswa* ["students"], and money [business leaders]. We tried to shape their views, to bring them over to our side in order to further national development.[14]

Within Deputy III, directorates were formed for each of these five target groups. One final Deputy III directorate, reflecting its lineage with Opsus, retained that name and handled particularly sensitive covert operations.[15]

There were some winners in the Malari Affair. Feeling the need to bring in fresh blood, Suharto beckoned the former Bakin Chief of Staff, Major General Yoga Sugomo, from his position as the Indonesian deputy representative at the United Nations.[16] Not only was Yoga untainted by the student riots by virtue of being in New York at the time, but he had a strong Bakin background as well as Suharto's implicit trust. On 28 January, he became Bakin's third chief.

Yoga made his mark almost immediately. Whereas Sutopo Juwono was never accused of being a Suharto sycophant, and steadfastly refused to sugarcoat intelligence reports according to the president's tastes, Yoga was more politically astute. This was apparent on 20 April, when he gave Suharto a 50-page classified Bakin analysis of the Malari Affair. While the report included muted references to the competition between Moertopo and Sumitro, the analysts conveniently concluded that student dissatisfaction could be traced back to a multitude of external influences, including everything from the Asia Foundation to Libya.

Early under Yoga's watch, an area of growing concern was the Portuguese colony of Timor. Three months after he took command of Bakin, a small group of disgruntled army officers overthrew Portugal's authoritarian government in a bloodless coup nicknamed the Carnation Revolution. They were motivated in large part by their bitter counter-insurgency experiences in Africa, where Lisbon had been combating leftist independence movements in its colonies of Angola, Guinea-Bissau, and Mozambique for a decade. Not surprisingly, the coup leaders gave priority to negotiating a commonwealth that would allow Portugal a de facto exit from Africa.

This sudden policy reversal had major implications for Portuguese Timor. Long a neglected colonial backwater, native Timorese had traditionally been politically apathetic. But within a month of the Carnation Revolution and the subsequent mad dash to arrange for a commonwealth, Timorese sentiment began to shift when Portuguese officials lifted restrictions on forming indigenous political parties. The three that took shape reflected the options open to locals: enter into Portugal's proposed commonwealth, demand full independence, or merge with Indonesia.

For Indonesia's intelligence services, Timor had long been a black hole. During the BPI era, there had been the brief, inconsequential flirtation with sowing integrationist seeds. Since that time, Bakin's interest in the colony had been sparked on just one occasion. That took place in 1970, when the CIA passed word that Soviet journalist Vitaly Yevgenyevich Lui – alias Victor Louis – was heading to Southeast Asia. Louis, an infamous source of Soviet disinformation who often did the KGB's bidding, sparked a frenzy of speculation among Western intelligence agencies every time he made a made a journalistic foray outside of Moscow.

This time around, Louis was tracked as far as Bangkok – and then disappeared. As there was reason to believe he might be heading to Indonesia – possibly to write about the penal colony on Buru Island – Satsus Intel was put on alert. Since its founding, that unit had stationed a liaison team at Jakarta's international airport, where they matched arrivals against a black list of international terrorists and other undesirables.[17]

True to his reputation, Louis managed to evade the immigration cordon. Using an alias, he transited Indonesia and mysteriously appeared in Portuguese Timor. This set both Indonesian and U.S. intelligence officials on edge: the journalist's jaunt to Portugal's colony, it was feared, might signal a greater Soviet interest in that territory.

In hindsight, that never happened. But four years later, with Lisbon reassessing its links to its colony, Portuguese Timor suddenly became a Bakin priority. This was driven home in June 1974, when the leaders of the Timorese party advocating integration with Indonesia (known by the Portuguese acronym *Apodeti*) crossed the border into West Timor and sought an audience with Indonesia's top intelligence officials.

Taken to Jakarta, the group was received by Deputy III Ali Moertopo. Having now fully merged Opsus into Bakin, he was charged with formulating Indonesia's clandestine response to Timor's decolonization process. After seeing off the delegation, he turned to one of his long-serving officers, Colonel Aloysius Sugiyanto. Since the Opsus merger, Sugiyanto had been named Deputy III's Director of Cultural Affairs. A Catholic – like a third of Timor's residents – the colonel was instructed to visit Timor's oceanside capital of Dili on a fact-finding mission.

In July, Sugiyanto received a visa stamp from the Portuguese consulate in downtown Jakarta, then flew to Dili via a commercial flight from Darwin,

Australia. He made the trip under the guise of a marketing officer for a fictitious trading house in Surabaya. Using this same business pretext, Sugiyanto frequented the Portuguese colony on a near-monthly basis. The real purpose of his travels was to gather general intelligence on the emerging Timorese political parties and their chief personalities. Though Indonesia had obvious common ground with Apodeti, he made a point of visiting all three. Said Sugiyanto:

> I would be met at the airport at Dili by representatives of Apodeti. After talking with them, I would go back to the hotel and see the [leaders supporting a Portuguese commonwealth] for a coffee. Later that night, I would have dinner with [those supporting independence]. It was like that on each trip.[18]

While Sugiyanto was busy visiting Dili, Moertopo had established a wider strategic intelligence operation relating to Timor during the third quarter of 1974. Known as Komodo – after the gargantuan monitor lizards that populate the Indonesian island of the same name – the operation was based in the West Timor capital of Kupang, with a forward post at the border town of Atambua. Modest in size, Komodo consisted of a dozen Deputy III civilians and army personnel on secondment to Bakin. Catholics and Protestants were disproportionately represented on the team in order to give them religious common ground with many of Timor's residents.[19]

From intelligence gathered by Komodo, warning bells began sounding in Jakarta by year's end. Some of this was due to the leftist shift displayed by those Timorese advocating independence.[20] Concerning Jakarta as well were developments in Africa. In September 1974, a second wave of younger, more progressive army officers had taken control in Lisbon. Ditching the earlier proposal for a commonwealth with its colonies, Portugal now wanted a faster, complete divorce. Following from this mindset, in January 1975, Lisbon reached agreement to grant independence to Angola before year's end. With Portugal all but certain to encourage a similar outcome in Timor, those Timorese supporting a commonwealth now became the second party to advocate full independence.

Eyeing these events, Suharto's key security advisors were torn. Although fearful that Portuguese Timor might ultimately be handed over to anti-Indonesian parties – and especially communists – they were reluctant to intervene with an overt military force. Moertopo, for one, advocated a continued clandestine attempt at swaying the Timorese population and lobbying support from Portuguese officials. Already, part of the Komodo effort was aimed at underwriting the Apodeti integrationists and channeling limited financial incentives to the party that previously advocated a commonwealth. In January, Komodo expanded its operations to include pro-Indonesian radio broadcasts from Kupang in various Timorese dialects. Suharto himself was prone to agree with this indirect approach, in large part because he remained sensitive to Indonesia's international standing – especially in the U.S. and Australia – and did not want to be tarred with his predecessor's penchant for foreign adventurism.

Many of his generals, however, were more hawkish. As the senior intelligence officer in the Ministry of Defense and Security, General Benny Moerdani – the former Opsus operative – had authorized a competing covert operation – codenamed *Flamboyan* – to provide the military with tactical combat intelligence in the event of Indonesian military intervention.

By February 1975, an eight-man Flamboyan staff led by Colonel Dading Kalbuadi had set up camp alongside Komodo's forward outpost at Atambua. There, they found that Komodo had established a modest cross-border agent network, and had been running a physical fitness training course for several hundred recruits dispatched by Apodeti leaders.

As this was happening, the situation in Portuguese Timor was growing more confused. Jakarta was particularly alarmed by a January pact between the two parties supporting independence: both were now focusing their opposition against the pro-Indonesia Apodeti.

Confusing signals, meantime, were coming from Portugal. In private conversations with Moertopo during a round of shuttle diplomacy, some leaders in Lisbon had sympathized with Jakarta, and had even seemed to acquiesce to eventual Indonesian control over their colony. Other Portuguese leaders, however, spoke of Timor's eventual independence after proper preparation.

All of this was taking place as communism was on the ascendance in mainland Southeast Asia. Pro-Western governments in Cambodia, Laos, and South Vietnam were all in their final dying weeks. Reflecting Jakarta's sensitivity to this shift, the Bakin-produced propaganda broadcasts from Kupang grew more shrill, including apocryphal reports of Chinese communist advisors arriving in Dili. Further stoking Jakarta's paranoia was the arrival of three openly-leftist Portuguese officers – two majors and a captain – to assist Timor's military governor.

Prompted by all these developments, Bakin's Operation Komodo was ratcheted up several notches in March. Part of this focused on channeling covert political support to Apodeti. At the same time, Sugiyanto ventured to Dili and looked to drive a wedge between the two parties supporting independence. This he did by playing favorites, targeting a few of the political leaders for Indonesian largesse.

Forging ahead on a separate, but parallel, track, Colonel Dading laid plans to assume control over the Apodeti training program at Atambua. By late April, an army special forces training team arrived on the border and began a simple paramilitary regimen for 400 Apodeti recruits. Some of the special forces personnel also conducted reconnaissance patrols along the border, and even crossed incognito into Portuguese Timor on fact-finding forays.

As this was taking place, the political landscape in Timor was lurching in unpredictable directions. While Moertopo continued to fete a string of Timorese political leaders visiting Jakarta, inter-party bickering, and even intra-party bickering, was on the upswing. This reached the breaking point on 9 August, when one faction seized control of Dili, stole rifles from a police armory, and turned them against the other two. As chaos spread, the Portuguese military governor ordered his paltry detachment of airborne reinforcements to withdraw to the piers and not take sides.

These events put Jakarta – and Lisbon – at a temporary loss. To assess the situation, and pass on key directives from Lisbon, Portuguese Major Antonio Joao Soares arrived in Jakarta on 14 August for a one-day layover before heading to Kupang on his way to Dili. Taking note of his diplomatic passport upon arrival at Jakarta's international airport, Bakin rushed plans for Satsus Intel to place him under surveillance. As his disembarkation card indicated he was staying the night at the Borobudur Hotel, Satsus Intel operatives headed in that direction.

By the time Satsus Intel arrived at the Borobudur, Soares was resting in his room. The Indonesian authorities did not yet know the intent of his visit, but surmised that he might be carrying sensitive documents. To get a look, they hatched a scheme to introduce a cramp-inducing drug into his bottled water. Once he developed stomach problems, went their thinking, he would leave the room to seek medical attention, allowing Satsus Intel operatives to secretly enter his room. But although the spiked water was given to a hotel bellboy for delivery, the major never stirred.

The following morning, 15 August, a courtesy letter from the Portuguese consulate was delivered to the Foreign Ministry. In it, Indonesian authorities were formally notified that Soares, described as a military attaché, was destined for Kupang via Bali. From Kupang, the major planned to board an aircraft for Dili that was being dispatched by Timor's military governor.

By the time Satsus Intel was notified of the contents of the letter, Soares had already slipped the hotel stakeout and was at the airport waiting for a Garuda flight to Bali. More determined than ever to see the contents of the major's briefcase, Benny Moerdani tasked Colonel Dading with gaining access. Benny listed three options: take the briefcase by force, stage a fake robbery, or use a "magician's approach."

On the evening of 15 August, Dading departed Jakarta on the trail of Soares. Accompanying him was a four-man team: one major from his Flamboyan operation, as well as three members of Satsus Intel. The latter included a photography specialist, a member of the censor section proficient in opening flaps and seals, and field operative Hans Hamzah. One of the few ethnic Chinese in Satsus Intel, Hamzah had a gift for languages – he spoke six – and was an expert in lockpicking.[21]

Arriving in Bali at 2135 hours, Dading's team met up with liaison officers at the airport and was told that the target had gone to the Ramayana Hotel on Kuta beach. They also reported he was booked to leave early the next morning on the Merpati Airlines flight for Kupang. Unfortunately, three Australian journalists in the same hotel were also on that flight. As they had yet to get a photograph of Soares, the team could still not pick their mark with certainty.

Brainstorming before getting some sleep, Dading reviewed their options. The Satsus Intel members said they wanted no part of anything other than Moerdani's third suggestion, the magician's approach. With Dading nodding his consent, the team woke early and was at the airport by 0600 hours, two hours before the flight to Kupang was scheduled to depart. Hamzah was standing behind the Merpati desk, having gained airline approval to pose as the branch manager. From that vantage point, he was able to glance at the passports of each Caucasian arriving for check-in.

At 0625 hours, Soares presented himself with two heavy bags. Improvising, Hamzah falsely claimed the major's ticket needed to be endorsed by immigration officials before he could be allowed to board the flight to Kupang. Soares grew livid, insisting he was on an important diplomatic mission and had to get to Kupang by noon to catch the governor's chartered plane. But Hamzah stood his ground, telling Soares he would personally escort the Portuguese officer to the closest immigration branch to rush the necessary stamp. Grateful for assistance, the major agreed to depart immediately.

Driving 16 kilometers, by 0740 hours, the pair was sitting in the guest room at Bali's immigration branch office. Soares nervously eyed his watch; Hamzah, in his faux role as Merpati manager, calmed the major by claiming he could delay the flight for over an hour.

Meanwhile, word of the ruse had earlier reached the immigration chief, who readily agreed to play along. After making Soares wait twenty minutes, he granted the major an audience. As Soares prepared to meet the chief, Hamzah suggested that he leave his bags in the guest room where a pair of armed guards could keep watch over them. The major thought for a moment, then agreed. Smiling widely, Hamzah led Soares into the chief's office and closed the door.

Satsus Intel quickly went into action. Taking momentary leave of Soares, Hamzah pulled out his picks and opened the bags in seconds. Inside one was a pair of thick bundles; opened by the censor expert, they contained maps, notes, and classified orders. All were carefully photographed by the third Satsus Intel member, with Colonel Dading standing witness to the proceedings.

All the while, the immigration chief was doing a fine acting job. After placing calls to his headquarters in Jakarta, he eventually produced some visa documents and had Soares laboriously fill them out. Not until 0920 hours, after getting word that the photography was concluded and the bags were back in the guest room, did he return the major's passport with a two-day transit visa.

Rushing back to the airport, Soares was irate to find his Merpati flight had already departed. To ease the inconvenience, Hamzah helped him book a seat on the next Kupang flight, two days hence. Still in character, he took the major out to dinner and drinks that evening.

The following noon, 17 August, Dading and the team flew back to Jakarta. Their operation, codenamed *Kuta* as an afterthought, earned kudos for all involved. Documents found in the two bundles confirmed that Portugal was looking to cut and run. One critical letter ordered the military governor to evacuate all Portuguese troops to Ilhe de Atauro – the Isle of Goats – 16 kilometers north of Timor.

With advance word of Portugal's decision to forfeit its colony – its departure for Atauro took place a week after Operation Kuta – Jakarta was fast running out of patience. On 23 August, the Indonesian consulate in the Timorese capital was evacuated by sea. By month's end, Indonesian special forces personnel assigned to Flamboyan were authorized to begin cross-border raids. While Komodo operatives continued with an indirect approach, hawks among the top brass were telegraphing what increasingly appeared an inevitable military solution. When an overt invasion eventually took place in December, Bakin's role in Timor was relegated to something less than a footnote.

1   In March 1970, Satsus Intel was mobilized in a case of mistaken identity. That month, newspapers around the world began to circulate stories that Ronald Biggs, the fugitive mastermind behind the infamous 1963 Great Train Robbery in England, had fled to Australia, Rhodesia, or Indonesia. These rumors gained momentum on 24 March, when Bakin was notified that a man with that last name had arrived in Indonesia from Australia. After Satsus Intel chased leads for three weeks, it was discovered that the Indonesian arrival was not Ronald Biggs but Donald Biggs, a 56-year old clergyman from Tennessee.

2   Bakin Case File, "Timy [sic] Pesik."

3   Bakin was involved in one counterfeiting case prior to the 1971 presidential decree. This took place in November 1970, when Satsus Intel was notified that a Singaporean woman, Chiong Chiang Kun, was implicated in passing fake Indonesian, Thai, and U.S. bills. Under the apropos codename Operation Lady, the unit conducted stakeouts and teltaps against Chiong and her local contacts for two months.

4   BPF, "Larry Tractman."

5   BPF, "Rustandi."

6   BPF, "Roby Cahyadi."

7   Bakin Case File, "Phoenix."

8   Pitut Soeharto interview.

9   BPF, "Ali Moertopo."

10 Bakin chief Sutopo Juwono was also forging his own ties with student activists; among them was Taufiq Kiemas, later the husband of President Megawati

Sukarnoputri. Panda Nababan, ed., *Tanpa Rakyat Pemimpin Tak Berarti Apa-Apa* (Jakarta: Pustaka Sinar Harapan, 2002), p. 61.

11 Bakin Case File, "Malari."

12 Not surprisingly, the CIA was not informed of the Pringle assessment. The CIA, in fact, kept its distance from the January riots and the military personalities involved. One exception: on 1 February, the CIA station passed a special memorandum to Bakin about an 18 January Japanese-language newspaper article that detailed a 16 January meeting of the Australian Union of Students, during which time, the union pledged to support Indonesia's protesters. Bakin Case File, "Malari."

13 Malari was a contraction for *Malapetaka 15 Januari*, or "Disaster of 15 January."

14 Irawan Sukarno interview.

15 The Opsus Directorate within Deputy III was primarily concerned with recruiting and handling Muslim extremists.

16 In 1971, Yoga had forfeited his three military intelligence positions over a serious security breach. While transiting Singapore en route to West Germany for a briefing of Indonesian military attachés on 15 October 1970, he lost a briefcase containing classified documents. Although he insisted one of his subordinates was to blame, Yoga was held responsible and sent off to New York under a cloud. *Memori Jenderal Yoga*, p.220.

17 Mandagi interview.

18 Interview with Aloysius Sugiyanto, 25 May 2001.

19 Part of the Komodo effort revolved around clandestine radio broadcasts from Kupang using local Radio Republik Indonesia facilities. Most of the broadcasts were gray, meaning that the station did not make any claims about its sponsorship but – given its openly pro-Indonesian, and often anti-Australian, editorial position – there was little doubt that it was being run by Jakarta. A smaller portion of the radio broadcasts were black, meaning that they purported to be communications between Timorese units within Portuguese Timor. The black broadcasts largely consisted of fake tactical instructions intended to sow confusion among the ranks of the anti-Indonesian Timorese angling for independence. Interview with Alex D., 8 September 2003.

20 While anecdotal, Sugiyanto noted that the independence advocates (known by the Portuguese acronym *Fretilin*) had a stack of Mao Tse-tung's red books stacked in their Dili office. Sugiyanto interview.

21 BPF, "Antonio Joao Soares."

CHAPTER SIX

GATOT

T hey did not take us seriously at first," said veteran spycatcher Bram
Mandagi. "They weren't trying too hard to avoid surveillance."[1] *They*
were the two dozen KGB and GRU officers stationed in Jakarta,
Medan, and Surabaya during the early seventies. Given the collective call sign
Gatot (a common Javanese surname) by Satsus Intel, some of the Soviets
reflected their professional disrespect through uncharacteristically poor
tradecraft. Example: Boris Liapine, a KGB operative masquerading as the
deputy cultural attaché, stood apart as a heavy drinker among countrymen
who generally had a high tolerance for alcohol. Satsus Intel operatives often
followed him until the early morning hours in Menteng's swankiest nightspots,
where he regularly drank himself into a stupor. This culminated at 0300 hours
on 21 April 1970, when an inebriated Liapine was nearly beaten senseless at
the 69 Club – he had provocatively doused his cigarette in the rice porridge of
a Solo dignitary – and was spared only after the discreet intervention of his
Satsus Intel tails.[2]

Another example was Vladislav Romanov, a suave Russian linguist who
appeared on the Soviet diplomatic list as a political attaché. With a penchant
for late night entertainment and Chinese girls, Romanov made little secret
that he was courting the daughter-in-law of the owner of Jit Lok Jun, a Chinese
restaurant in Menteng. Satsus Intel approached the girl soon after the affair
started, and she proved amenable to relaying pillow talk.[3]

But even while some of the Soviet intelligence officers had lapses in
professionalism, they remained exceedingly formidable opponents. Renowned

as the most dangerous of the lot was the KGB's Oleg Brykin, a chubby second secretary who had spent nearly a decade studying English (including a year at Harvard). Besides his linguistic talents and social skills (he regularly entertained at his house), Brykin had recruited the Algerian cultural attaché, who in turn attended most Western diplomatic functions and acted as his handler's spotter for potential agents. His particular focus seemed to be the British embassy; from teltaps and surveillance, Satsus Intel strongly suspected by early 1970 that Brykin had recruited both the British counselor and a secretary.[4]

Besides the cunning of spies like Brykin, countering the Soviets was complicated by other factors. Part of this had to do with bureaucratic ineptitude on the part of the Indonesian government. Back in late 1968, when Satsus Intel was first formed, the unit had requested files on all Indonesians who studied in the Soviet bloc. But the Ministry of Education claimed the files could not be found, then suggested that they had been destroyed at the Ministry of Foreign Affairs building when it was sacked in early 1966. Not until 1971 were they discovered by accident at the Directorate of Higher Education, providing Satsus Intel with a welcome, albeit belated, source of potential agent recruits.[5]

Another complicating factor could be traced to Great Britain, where the British government in September 1971 conducted a mass expulsion of Soviet diplomats suspected of intelligence activities. Two of them – Georgiy Penko and Yuri Lovkovskiy – were immediately redirected to Indonesia. The new Soviet ambassador, Pavel Kouznetsov, had also been expelled from London for espionage back in 1952. But when Satsus Intel requested files on the Soviets declared *personae non gratae*, MI6 initially offered little more than general biographical data; not until a year later, after repeated requests, did the British intelligence service provide more substantive information – such as habits and preferred operational methods – that could assist in surveillance.[6]

Offsetting all this, the Indonesians in mid-1972 received an intelligence windfall in the form of a 33-year old GRU captain named Nikolay Grigoryevich Petrov. Born in a collective northeast of Moscow as the youngest of four children, Petrov had been raised in a one-room peasant house overseen by a devoutly religious mother. Educated as an electrician, he had joined the army in late 1959, first serving in a tank training regiment then, three years later, enrolling in Indonesian courses at a military language school.

Petrov excelled as a linguist. In 1967, after five years of intensive

Indonesian, he was assigned as an interpreter for Project 055. Based in Surabaya, that project oversaw residual Soviet aid to the Indonesian navy (in a pragmatic move, the Soviets were still trickling military assistance to the Indonesian military despite the Westward tilt of the New Order). Two years later, he transferred to the aid desk at the Soviet embassy in Jakarta. There his linguistic talents – he spoke colloquial Javanese as well as Indonesian – came to the attention of the military attaché, who soon had Petrov working as the interpreter for his office.

Finishing the two-year overseas assignment, Petrov in July 1969 returned to his wife and three-year old son in Moscow. On account of his excellent performance at the military attaché's office, he was recommended for transfer to the GRU. Following an eight-month intelligence course, during which time Petrov was commissioned as a lieutenant, he was assigned to the Indonesia desk at GRU headquarters.

By the opening of 1971, Petrov, with his family in tow, was back in Jakarta as part of the ten-man GRU contingent in Indonesia. It was led by Colonel Nikolay Khakhalin, the GRU *rezident*, whose cover slot was senior press attaché.[7] The deputy *rezident*, Lieutenant Colonel Yevgeniy Chubshev, was the naval attaché. Others in the contingent were hidden in the cultural section and the Aeroflot and Morflot (Soviet shipping line) offices. Petrov, despite his army affiliation, was placed in a vacant slot on the naval attaché's staff. (A CIA trace report, provided to Satsus Intel on Petrov's arrival, correctly alerted the Indonesians of his suspected GRU affiliation.)

As the most junior of the ten officers, Petrov, for his first six months, worked as a translator and driver for the other GRU members. This gave him a wide sampling of the activities of his seniors, including exposure to their most successful penetrations of the Indonesian military. He learned, for example, that the GRU had recruited a particularly productive air force lieutenant in the technical branch. There was also at least one well-placed agent at the Surabaya naval base.

Among the most effective recruiters among the GRU contingent was Vladimir Abromov. As the chief Morflot representative, 48-year old Abromov had raised eyebrows after being expelled from Ghana for espionage back in 1966. But despite being under scrutiny ever since his arrival in Jakarta in August 1968, he had still scored an early success by placing a key bureaucrat working for the Indonesian army on the GRU payroll.

In 1970, Abromov scored again when he recruited Yamin, a 31-year old civilian who coordinated training programs at Indonesian navy headquarters. Yamin's cooperation proved a family affair: his wife assisted with photographing classified documents at their house in Kebayoran Baru. For his services, Yamin was paid a generous stipend of 50,000 rupiah (about $129) per month.

In June 1971, Petrov was paired with Abromov and began learning the ropes of agent handling from the seasoned Morflot veteran. The GRU, he found out, preferred meeting its agents at night around the Senayan sports complex. Some officers would park their automobiles at the stadium and leave them empty with the windows slightly open; their agents would then stroll by and toss a package – usually a film canister – onto the car seats. Abromov preferred a variant on this theme: cruising along the street in front of the sports complex, he would signal a curbside agent by blinking the headlights and placing a sheet of white paper on the dashboard. If the agent had a newspaper in his right hand, he wanted to toss a package in the open window; if the newspaper was under his arm, he wanted to get in the car and talk. In the case of Yamin, thought was even given to using his wife as a courier and picking her up on the curb, camouflaging her action among the prostitutes in the area.

In December 1971, after a six-month probation period under Abromov, Petrov was deemed ready to assume control over his first agent. Hiding on the floor of a car, he was driven to Abromov's house and bundled inside. Yamin and his wife soon arrived by foot, and the former was ushered into an upstairs bedroom. With Abromov using multiple counter-surveillance techniques – music was playing, water was running, conversations were whispered into ears, and the most important items were written on paper – Yamin was told that he would answer to Petrov from that point forward.[8]

Promoted to captain in March 1972, Petrov spent the first two quarters of that year honing his operational techniques. For example, he selected two roadside trees where Yamin was to affix an innocuous thumbtack in the event the agent wanted to rendezvous before a scheduled meeting. Petrov would drive by these trees each morning; if he saw Yamin's tack, that meant an emergency session was desired that same night. Petrov and Abromov also trolled the city by night – with windows down and music blaring to defeat recording devices – in search of ideal dead drops (discreet locations where small packages could be left for agents and vice versa).

In addition, Petrov worked on an emergency evacuation scheme for Yamin. According to his plan, the two would meet at the Jakarta zoo's monkey pavilion with the GRU captain carrying a newspaper under his arm. Yamin would ask where the paper was purchased; Petrov's answer would be where the Indonesian would go to await help from an extraction team.

On 6 June 1972, after eighteen months in Indonesia, Petrov's wife and son returned to Moscow for summer home leave. Petrov could not immediately join them, however, as he had scheduled a meeting with Yamin near month's end.

Alone, Petrov reveled in his newfound freedom. Just days after his wife's departure, he linked up with a prostitute. Then on 12 June, he spent the afternoon at a Menteng restaurant playing the slot machine and liberally helping himself to free beer. Within an hour, he had squandered all his cash.

Petrov did not take his losses well. Determined to win back his money – and, optimistically, earn extra to buy souvenirs for all friends in Moscow – the captain drove back to the embassy. One of his assignments during his first six months in country had been to handle the military attaché's cash fund; as a result, he knew the combination to the office safe. With the attaché coincidentally away on vacation, Petrov made a beeline for the safe, pocketed 350,000 rupiah (about $900), and sped back to the slot machine.

Predictably, Petrov's luck did not improve. By 1800 hours, he had lost all of the borrowed cash – a loss tempered only by the cloud of heavy drinking. In an alcohol-induced stupor, the captain conjured a vague new plan. As the restaurant was around the block from the U.S. embassy, Petrov figured he could present himself at the doorstep and sell information for cash.

At 1900 hours, Petrov put his plan into action. Pulling his Datsun into the deserted parking lot, he staggered up to the marine guard booth. He then blurted out the name of the defense attaché, which he recalled from diplomatic invitation lists. The marine, not knowing what to make of the visitor, began making frantic calls to the military attachés and members of the CIA station. But none were in the immediate neighborhood and, after waiting half an hour, an apprehensive Petrov turned around and returned to his car.

At that point, Petrov's comedy of errors ratcheted up several notches. Gunning the engine as he peeled out of the parking lot, he lost control of the Datsun, hit the curb, and managed to flip the vehicle on its side. A crowd soon began to gather, pushing Petrov's anxiety to the breaking point. After they helped him right the car, he put it in reverse and headed back to the U.S. embassy.

Returning to the marine guard booth, Petrov looked a mess. His car, severely dented along one side, had it even worse. By that time, the defense attaché, the CIA station chief, and several of the station officers had arrived on the scene. Taking Petrov inside the embassy, they administered rudimentary first aid and, at his request, gave him a stiff drink of scotch.

The added alcohol was probably not a good idea. In a fog, Petrov started barking orders in Russian. He then turned belligerent and, after throwing punches at the closest officer, had to be subdued. Demanding to leave, he got back in his Datsun, struck a parked car upon exiting the compound, and had another accident on the way home.

By the time Petrov reached the Soviet housing compound, his comrades were aghast. His Datsun was a wreck and the captain, sporting fresh dressings on his injuries, had obviously received recent first aid from persons unknown. But as Petrov was too inebriated to give sensible answers, he was taken to the house of the assistant air force attaché to sober up.

Not surprisingly, Petrov began to panic as the alcohol worked its way out of his system. Fearing he would be sent to prison or, worse, expelled from the party, he grew desperate. When he asked the wife of the attaché for a poison pill, she laughed it off. Rope burns later found around his neck attested to a suicide attempt in the bathroom.

By the next morning, 13 June, Petrov was feeling little better. Given some tea to ease his hangover, he became nauseous and retreated to the bathroom. Though still a committed communist, Petrov felt that his activities of the previous night left him no choice. Slipping out the back stairway, he took a pedicab to the house of the U.S. naval attaché several blocks away. Once there, he asked for, and quickly received, political asylum.

Back at the Soviet attaché's house, Petrov's disappearance was discovered within an hour. Word spread quickly among the military personnel, who initially speculated he was on another drinking binge. When an army attaché rang the assistant air force attaché early that afternoon, a Satsus Intel teltap recorded him sarcastically comment, "Sometimes, a drunk hides in the corner."

By later in the afternoon, however, the Soviet intelligence community began to fear the worst. What followed was forty-eight hours of panic, with the KGB *Rezident*, Anatoliy Babkin, manning a makeshift command post in the embassy as he dispatched all available KGB and GRU officers into the field to watch train stations, bus stops, and the airport. Throwing proper tradecraft by the wayside, they phoned Babkin with frequent updates. "It completely exposed them," said Bram Mandagi. "We were able to confirm all our suspicions as to who were really intelligence officers."[9]

There still remained the problem of spiriting Petrov out of the country. There had been one previous defection from Indonesia – an East German intelligence officer in 1970 – but he had been able to board a flight to West Germany before the consulate even noted his absence. Petrov's case was far more dangerous. From the teltaps, Bakin and the CIA knew that the Soviets were pulling out all stops in their search for the missing captain – and would probably resort to kidnapping or assassination if they determined his location. As a stopgap, the CIA had resorted to hiding him in plain sight – at the exposed, well-lit house of the deputy station chief.

After forty-eight hours, the CIA made its move. Dressing the captain as a U.S. marine, they drove him to Halim airbase and, after filling out a fake medical emergency report, loaded him aboard the weekly U.S. Navy flight to the Philippines. The Soviets did not detect the ruse and were still not fully certain about Petrov's fate for several weeks.

Shuttled to Washington, D.C., Petrov was resettled in Virginia under a new name. Given the call sign Houdini, he proved to be one of the most productive GRU defectors to that time. For the next two years, debriefings of Houdini yielded dozens of detailed intelligence reports; many of them, forwarded to Satsus Intel, dealt with the GRU officers in Jakarta and their successful recruits.

Petrov's tragic comedy had a dark ending. In the late seventies, after growing homesick for his wife and teenage son, Houdini rejected the advice of his CIA handlers and elected to return to the tender mercies of the Soviet state. He was never heard from again.

If the Soviet intelligence contingent in Indonesia considered Houdini's defection a setback, they did not show it. Continuing with an aggressive recruitment campaign, part of their effort was focused against the government's legislative branch. As revealed by Petrov, GRU Deputy *Rezident* Chubshev had already recruited a productive agent – his identity never conclusively determined – in the national assembly. And in 1976, the KGB's Valery Orlov was tailed as he tried – unsuccessfully – to recruit one of the expert staff working for the same body.

In August 1974, it was the Indonesian post office that became a Soviet target of opportunity. This started when 30-year old postal worker Franky Wena, looking to practice his English at a seafood restaurant near Jakarta's port, struck up a conversation with a dining KGB officer. Flattered by the officer's rapt attention, Wena embellished his résumé by claiming to be a Bakin counter-narcotics expert. This further stoked the spy's interest, who wasted no time offering large dollar incentives for each classified document Wena could procure.

Before their covert relationship progressed further, Wena got cold feet and confessed to his superiors. This confession was relayed to Bakin, which in turn passed word to the CIA station. Always interested in obtaining details about KGB handling techniques, the CIA forwarded a list of questions on 10 September for use in Wena's impending interrogation.

Incredibly, Wena reconsidered and decided to make one more attempt at scamming the Soviets. This time, he had an unlikely accomplice: a Bakin officer from Bali who, privy to Wena's initial confession, wanted a bite at the KGB's monetary inducement for classified documents. On the evening of 27 September, Wena ventured to the embassy and asked for his KGB contact. Carrying three classified memoranda provided by the conspiring Balinese officer, he angled for the promised cash reward. But perhaps suspicious of Wena's reckless approach, the KGB rebuffed him on that and half a dozen other unannounced visits. The postman's continued indiscretions were revealed through Satsus Intel teltaps and a subsequent interrogation; he eventually was sentenced to two years in prison.

On occasion, the KGB took aim at the CIA's Indonesian agents. Friendly/2, the former marine who had spearheaded the recruitment of Kasuari, had frequent social contact with KGB officers at communist diplomatic receptions during the late sixties. By 1970, these ties had developed to the point where the Soviets were tasking him with specific questions and offering monetary incentives. His responses, carefully drafted by the CIA, contained nothing more than open source material.

Friendly/2's delicate dance with Soviet intelligence lasted until August 1973. During that month, the KGB asked him to obtain a long list of personal data – including a citizenship card, driver's license, and birth certificate – for any middle-aged ethnic Chinese-Indonesian who had recently died. Scrutinizing the request, the CIA surmised that the KGB was looking to craft a fake biographical backstop – a "legend" – for an Indonesian exile they had recruited. Deeming this too dangerous to fulfill, the CIA ordered Friendly/2 to cease all further contact.[10]

Friendly/1, the former Perti leader, received similar attention. In late 1971, he was introduced to KGB officer Evgeni Cherniak at a diplomatic reception. The two began occasionally meeting early the following year, with Friendly/1 often providing tantalizing information vetted by the CIA.

On 8 July 1974, with Cherniak scheduled to conclude his tour later that month, the two met at a Filipino restaurant in Menteng. As time was of the essence, the KGB officer made a bold pitch. Provide reports on Chinese activities in Jakarta and U.S. intelligence officers posted to Indonesia, said Cherniak, and he would arrange for the Soviet embassy to provide goods that he could sell for a commission.

With Friendly/1 promising to sleep on the offer, he reported back to the CIA. On 26 July, with Satsus Intel watching from a distance, the agent again dined with the KGB officer. Alternately inducing and intimidating, Cherniak again pressed for help against the U.S. and China. "If you cause problems," he warned, "I have many friends who will respond to you and your family."

Cherniak requested one last meeting, this time at his house. On 30 July, with boxed household effects cluttering the floor, Friendly/1 arrived for their final tryst. A cheerful Cherniak offered a toast at the conclusion, though he never provided guidance on a follow-up point of contact. Perhaps suspecting his CIA links, Friendly/1 was never again pitched by the Soviets.

No Indonesian institution received more attention from Soviet intelligence than the armed forces. Satsus Intel, as a result, spent much of its time anticipating, and occasionally frustrating, covert contact between communist spies and Indonesian security personnel. In 1971, for example, they observed a KGB recruitment attempt against an adjutant to General Nasution. In July 1972, the spycatchers watched an army lieutenant receive a GRU approach. During mid-1974, in an operation codenamed *Jaring* ("Web"), Satsus Intel operators scrutinized a suspicious Indonesian code officer but were unable to get proof positive of espionage.[11] And during July 1975, in Operation Double Dagger, Satsus Intel documented repeated contact between a KGB officer and an army lieutenant assigned to military intelligence.

One of the longest running cases involved police Lieutenant Colonel Sukarno. During a routine tail of KGB officer Genediy Balkirev on the evening of 29 December 1976, Satsus Intel observed him park his car near the Menteng Cinema, cross the street to a second vehicle with Soviet diplomatic plates, and travel to Sukarno's house. After nearly an hour, Sukarno was seen returning Balkirev to the theater.[12]

Tipped off by this suspicious behavior, Balkirev and Sukarno became the subjects of stakeouts and teltaps. At the same time, Bakin approached the police leadership and discovered that Sukarno, who had previously served in a counter-narcotics unit and the foreign liaison section, had been making recent inquiries about army troop strengths.

For over two months, the Satsus Intel surveillance turned up nothing. Then on 19 March 1977, Balkirev arrived for another meeting at Sukarno's residence; as there had been no prior teltap indication, the two had apparently devised an alternate form of communication. A third meeting at the house was observed ten days later.

The next month, Bakin contemplated turning Sukarno into a double agent. Asked for comment, the CIA cautioned against the move. Instead, they suggested three alternatives: expelling Balkirev, revealing the espionage activity through an "inspired press leak," or raiding Sukarno's house during a meeting and propositioning the KGB officer.

In the end, the Indonesian authorities chose none of the above. Although Satsus Intel witnessed a fourth meeting in August, and continued its teltap of the Sukarno residence through February 1981, the police – probably not willing to wear the embarrassment of a conviction – tipped off Sukarno as to their suspicions then elected to bury the case without so much as a reprimand.

Arguably the most convoluted counter-intelligence case involving a member of the armed forces was codenamed *Ubur-Ubur* ("Jellyfish"). Counter-intelligence cases are often said to take place in a wilderness of mirrors, but in this instance, the wilderness was especially dense and the mirrors particularly plentiful. The focus was a 41-year old colonel named Susanto, who had arrived in Bangkok during 1968 to begin a three-year tour as naval attaché. He went there with a special added assignment: according to a 1 November memo signed by the head of naval intelligence, Susanto was to "watch the situation in Bangkok" by making contact with Soviet diplomats. This contact was initiated by his predecessor; Susanto was merely continuing the project.[13]

Taking his assignment to heart, Susanto met frequently with several of the local Russians. Most of them were known KGB officers, including First Secretary Gennadiy Vaoulin. Word of his inroads eventually got back to Jakarta, where it came to the attention of Indonesia's hardluck spymaster, Zulkifli Lubis.[14]

By that time, Lubis, answering to Ali Moertopo in Opsus, had returned from his bankrupt restaurant in Saudi Arabia and was looking for a new mandate. Establishing a front company in Blok M, he sold Moertopo on the idea that he would track worldwide developments in the communist world. While this was a broad subject, Lubis spent much of his time fixated on just one person: Brigadier General Soehario Padmodiwirjo.

Soehario and Lubis went back a long way. In 1946, Soehario had joined a fledgling intelligence unit that fell under the loose command of Lubis' Brani. For the next seven years, the former continued to serve on the various intelligence bureaus conceived and led by the latter. After that, however, the two parted ways. Lubis, clashing with the top brass, fled Jakarta and eventually turned up alongside U.S.-sponsored rebels in Sumatra. Soehario, remaining loyal to the Republic, ventured to the U.S. in 1957 and was the first Indonesian army officer to undergo airborne training at Fort Benning.

By 1961, their fortunes were worlds apart. Lubis, who had peaked as the deputy army chief before joining the rebels, was sent to prison after surrendering to the authorities. Soehario, by contrast, had been strengthened on account of his outspoken support of Sukarno and unabashed sympathy for the PKI. Back in 1959, for example, he had been selected as escort officer for visiting North Vietnamese leader Ho Chi Minh. And in 1962, while serving as a regional commander in Kalimantan, he took leave of his post in order to make a trip to Moscow to attend a peace conference.

During the turmoil of late 1965, their stars reversed. Lubis, the vindicated anti-communist, was released from prison and rebounded to his seat in Opsus. Soehario, sensing the shifting political winds, abandoned his Kalimantan command and sought asylum in Moscow, where obliging Soviet officials named him a visiting fellow at the Frunze Military Academy. While there, he took a side trip to Hanoi (he had a standing invitation from Ho Chi Minh since the 1959 visit), and, according to a CIA memo provided to Bakin, was linked to an exiled PKI cadre in Beijing that was assisting the Viet Cong. [15]

To be sure, Soehario was not the only general in the armed forces with leftist sympathies. But he was the only one to escape harsh New Order justice by refusing to return to his homeland. Obsessed with contacting the fugitive officer, and somehow convincing him to leave his Moscow sanctuary, Lubis figured he would try to forward a letter to Frunze. This was sent to Colonel Susanto in Bangkok during September 1969, who was instructed to pass it to one of his KGB contacts at the Soviet embassy. The letter was subsequently handed to First Secretary Vaoulin. [16]

By that time, Susanto's links with the Soviet embassy had snowballed. The CIA, which kept close watch on the Soviets with the help of facilitative Thai intelligence personnel, became aware of these links in November 1969 when an unidentified male driving an Indonesian embassy car – later identified as Susanto – was observed meeting Viktor Mizin, a KGB officer who ran agent operations in Thailand. By the following year, Susanto was being tailed while meeting two other Bangkok-based KGB officers, including *Rezident* Valentine Malakhov.

With warning bells ringing at the CIA, word of Susanto's growing Soviet ties was quietly passed to Bakin's General Sutopo. In December 1969, Sutopo dispatched a telegram to both the Indonesian ambassador and ranking defense attaché in Bangkok outlining Susanto's odd behavior. Four months later, on 29 May 1970, the ambassador wrote back defending his naval attaché and pointing out that he was fulfilling an assignment given by naval headquarters.

The ambassador's defense did not dispel suspicions, apparently. In June 1971, Susanto concluded his Thai tour and returned to Jakarta as the private assistant to the navy chief. While the colonel looked primed for even higher office, behind the scenes, the CIA was fretting over his earlier association with Soviet intelligence in Bangkok. Deputy Nicklany had shared those concerns, and on 17 December took the case to heart by conjuring plans for a complex disinformation operation. Rather than hauling in Susanto for questioning, he decided to embrace the colonel under the pretext of a Bakin special project to document his contacts with Russian spies. All the while, Nicklany would be plying the naval officer with false information and watching to see if he passed it to local Soviet intelligence officers.

On 8 January 1972, Nicklany's special project received final approval. Apparently unaware of the deep suspicion he had generated, Susanto reported to his new Bakin desk and spent February turning out numerous reports on his years in Thailand and the Soviets with whom he had connections.

The CIA remained unconvinced the links were innocent. In an 8 March memo to Nicklany, the station chief noted that the KGB often recruited overseas, then used clandestine means of contact when the agent returned to his or her home country. While stopping short of accusing Susanto of any wrongdoing, Nicklany was encouraged to use Satsus Intel to tap Susanto's office and his home phone.

The CIA's gut feeling seemed to bear fruit, at least initially. On 16 March, Satsus Intel launched Operation Ubur-Ubur against Susanto. Eight days later, operatives were following from a distance as the colonel, his wife, and two children drove their Holden to Blok M. Dropping off his family, Susanto slowly circled the block, apparently in a search for a parking space. From the opposite direction, a Fiat with Soviet embassy plates drove past; Satsus Intel later identified the driver as KGB officer Valery Yermolenko.[17]

Ten minutes later, Susanto's wife and kids returned to the car. Susanto drove less than 100 meters before letting them out a second time to purchase cake. The colonel, as before, remained behind the wheel.

Two minutes later, Yermolenko's car came back into view. Pulling abreast of the Holden, the Fiat flashed its headlights. After a full minute, Yermolenko pulled away and disappeared.

For Nicklany and the CIA, the encounter of the two vehicles at Blok M was too much to be a coincidence. Stepping up their investigation of the colonel, they discovered that he had spent time in Poland during 1958 while awaiting delivery of a destroyer. It was also discovered that two other Indonesian diplomats in Bangkok – a political counselor and third secretary – had extensive contact with the KGB during the same years as Sutanto.

Compounding suspicions were some of the questions asked by Susanto around Bakin headquarters. On 16 March, he reportedly asked colleagues if they had any information on Soviet-made rockets that had been sold by the

Indonesian armed forces to the U.S. He also asked if the U.S. had started producing AK-47 ammunition for South Vietnam.

But just like the investigation into Police Lieutenant Colonel Sukarno, Ubur-Ubur eventually fizzled. Although Satsus Intel teltaps and stakeouts continued for a year, Susanto was not documented making any further contact with Soviet officials. Furthermore, he could legitimately claim that all of his overseas contact with the Soviets had been upon written orders from his superiors. With no incriminating evidence emerging from the wilderness of mirrors, the case was quietly closed with more questions than answers.

1   Mandagi interview.
2   Ibid.; BPF, "Boris Liapine."
3   BPF, "Vladislav Romanov."
4   When the British counselor was subsequently posted to West Germany, Brykin was assigned to the same country shortly thereafter. This was considered more than coincidental, as KGB handlers often followed their top recruits from one country to the next.
5   The Soviets were also looking for potential agents among the hundreds of Indonesian students who had studied behind the Iron Curtain. Made Odantara, an ethnic Balinese who attended the Technical Institute of Chemistry in Moscow, was successfully recruited and, for five years, passed information on Japan's plastics technology during a subsequent scholarship in Tokyo. Odantara was arrested in a Tokyo restaurant during May 1969, after he was spotted receiving money from a Soviet intelligence officer.
6   Relations between Bakin and MI6 reached a low in late 1971, in part because of London's lack of cooperation regarding the expelled Soviet officers, and in part because Satsus Intel caught the MI6 station chief recruiting his own agent network in Jakarta. Etiquette among friendly intelligence services dictated that guest stations would not recruit unilateral agents in the host nation (or at least not be caught doing so). On account of both these issues, Bakin's Sutopo and Nicklany reported their displeasure to a visiting British delegation. Bakin also turned over to the delegation the surveillance files for the British embassy members who were thought to have been recruited by the KGB's Brykin. The MI6 station chief was subsequently recalled; his replacement was reportedly far more cooperative. Still, there were occasions through the remainder of the decade when the British would

drive Satsus Intel beyond frustration due to their suspicious behavior. In July 1978, for example, Indonesia's spycatchers watched a female motorcyclist hand a package through an open window of a car bearing British diplomatic plates that had stopped at a red light; both vehicles then sped off in opposite directions. This activity had all the hallmarks of a clandestine car toss. Mandagi interview; Bakin Case File, "Life [sic] Drop."

7   Soviet press attachés working from their information center for many years were less than successful in courting the Indonesian media. This began to change in early 1976, when the Soviets quietly offered major cash incentives for Indonesian editors to publish unflattering articles about the CIA and China. Bakin learned of this from a Satsus Intel agent codenamed Dahlia, who worked on the editorial staff of the army-sponsored newspaper. Information from Dahlia allowed Bakin to expose the plan that April and spike the articles before publication. BPF, "Dahlia."

8   Though an otherwise excellent intelligence officer, Abromov had a weakness for holding meetings at his house. When GRU headquarters found out he had invited Yamin to his residence, Abromov received an official reprimand. Bakin Case File, "Houdini."

9   Mandagi interview.

10 Subandi interview.

11 The code officer came under suspicion after conducting what appeared to be a brush pass with a Soviet intelligence officer in October 1973.

12 In March 1976, Satsus Intel was officially renamed the Bakin Operational Unit (*Satuan Pelaksana Bakin*, or Satlak Bakin). This change signaled the full integration of the unit under Bakin administration; from that point forward, all residual links to the Military Police were cut. To avoid confusion, the term Satsus Intel will remain in use in this book.

13 BPF, "Taufik Susanto."

14 Soviet intelligence was relatively active in Bangkok; during the fifties and sixties, five Soviet officials (one TASS reporter, four diplomats) were expelled from Thailand for espionage.

15 Padmodiwirjo interview; BPF, "Brig. Jend. Soeharjo."

16 The letter penned by Lubis was never received by Soehario. In 1973, however, the fugitive general received a surprise telephone call from Lubis, who had traveled all the way to Moscow on the pretext of pricing rice imports. Lubis appealed for Soehario to return to Jakarta, but the latter refused on account of his children

needing to complete their schooling. Not until July 1977 did Soehario board an Aeroflot flight to Indonesia; detained on arrival, he was subject to a prolonged interrogation. Soehario interview.

17 Yermolenko's KGB affiliation was strongly suspected since his arrival in Indonesia during 1967, but was not confirmed until the testimony of Houdini.

CHAPTER SEVEN

THE HERMIT KINGDOM

K orea has historically been known as the Hermit Kingdom, but those from contemporary North Korea have proven the moniker especially apt. Hailing from the most homogenous society in the world, its diplomats in Jakarta during the late sixties and early seventies displayed a sense of ethnic chauvinism and xenophobia exacerbated by the paranoia of Pyongyang's police state. The result of all this was a mindset steeped in dark suspicion toward virtually all Indonesians, fellow diplomats, and even each other.

The North Korean diplomats often took this to comical extremes. Fearing defections, for example, they could only leave the embassy in pairs, never alone. They would only patronize restaurants with loud music and poor lighting, apparently over fear of video and audio surveillance. They favored walking, rather than driving cars – and would dramatically pause every hundred meters on the sidewalk and turn around to see if they were being tailed. They also phased out all local staff working in the embassy compound, with the exception of two night watchmen who were fired every other month and replaced in order to prevent possible recruitment by the Indonesian authorities.[1]

Such idiosyncrasies aside, the North Koreans were arguably the most formidable opponent faced by Satsus Intel. Like the Soviets, many of their diplomats spent exceptionally long or multiple tours in Indonesia; as a result, they often were fluent in Indonesian and, as Asians, blended into the local society. And while only a couple of their diplomats were bona fide intelligence officers, it was often hard to tell the difference. "The North Koreans worked as a total team," said Bram Mandagi. "More than the other communist nations, we had to focus on their entire embassy."[2]

In the task of keeping tabs on the North Koreans, Satsus Intel had help. Within a year after its formation, the unit established a liaison relationship with South Korean intelligence. As Seoul had a vested interest in gathering data about Pyongyang's overseas operatives, it began to regularly trade biographical information with the Indonesians.[3]

Some of Satsus Intel's information about the North Koreans came from teltaps. Most communist diplomats were cautious about what they said over the phone; while the North Koreans were normally exceptionally discreet, exceptions existed. The most notable was a 40-year old political officer named Ho Chang Gon. Arriving in Jakarta in September 1969, Ho was a veritable home entertainment system for the teltap personnel transcribing his phone conversations. This first became apparent in October 1970, when he began calling restaurants several nights per week. With a heavy accent and limited English vocabulary, the repressed Ho would attempt to flirt with waitresses, invariably get frustrated and shout obscenities, and then hang up.[4]

Ho's crank calls continued for another two years. Growing progressively bolder, he started phoning bars and nightclubs near midnight, chatting up call girls in his broken English, and negotiating a price for an evening session. Listening in, Satsus Intel on two occasions mobilized surveillance teams outside the North Korean embassy and Ho's intended hotel rendezvous. But both times, Ho never left the embassy and Satsus Intel called off further nocturnal stakeouts.[5]

Ho's phone skills, or lack thereof, were inadvertently humorous on numerous other occasions. In August 1971, he answered the phone when George Moore, an Australian peace activist who was prominent in the anti-Vietnam War movement, called the North Korean embassy during a visit to Jakarta. Regardless of the question being asked by an exasperated Moore, Ho invariably responded with his favorite stock phrase, "Yes, I fully understand."

Another classic exchange took place in April 1972. Early that month, Ho called the secretary of Kopkamtib commander Sumitro to convey plans for an Indonesian military delegation to visit North Korea. During the same conversation, Ho asked for the telephone number of Bakin chief Sutopo Yuwono; the secretary promised to contact Bakin and have its representatives phone Ho.

One week later, a Bakin representative called – or tried to call – the North Korean diplomat. The resultant miscommunication went as follows:

Bakin (*in Indonesian*):	Is this number 49606?
Ho (*in English*):	No, this is number 49606.
Bakin (*in Indonesian*):	This is from Bakin.
Ho (in English):	What do you mean *Bapak* Kin? This is the Korean embassy!
Bakin (*in Indonesian*):	Maybe I have the wrong number. (*hangs up*)

Supplementing the information about the North Koreans gleaned from teltaps were reports from indigenous agents. Friendly/1, the CIA source shared with Bakin, had especially strong ties to the North Korean embassy. Aware of his strong leftist credentials during the Sukarno era, the Koreans had him back on their invitation list soon after his release from prison. Believing him worthy of recruitment, he had been courted by one of that embassy's most aggressive intelligence officers, Han Dong Chol. Han was especially persistent in pressing the agent for information about South Korean activities in Indonesia; on occasion, Friendly/1 provided open source answers composed by the CIA.

Friendly/2, the other CIA source shared with Bakin, was also close to the North Koreans. Buying into his cover job as a sympathetic journalist, they feted the agent in their own peculiar way. On 25 December 1971, for example, two of Pyongyang's diplomats made an unexpected visit to his house to give him a bottle of ginseng tonic and a New Year's card. In return, the North Koreans made unusual requests of the CIA's agent. In January 1973, for instance, they implored Friendly/2 to pen a congratulatory telegram to dictator Kim Il Sung for his most recent, redundant appointment as leader of the People's Supreme Committee.

At the same time, Satsus Intel was building its own agent network. Virtually all of its agents were codenamed after flowers; most, too, had leftist connections prior to 1965. By 1970, two recruits were forwarding regular reports: *Kamboja* ("Frangipani"), who worked as a secretary at the Polish embassy, and *Horstile*, a former female member of the PKI who was on the invitation list for most communist receptions.[6] By 1974, two others were actively reporting: *Anyelir* ("Carnation"), who had close ties to the Soviet embassy, and *Tulip*, a former Indonesian language instructor who spent three years in Leningrad.

One of Satsus Intel's best agents offered an excellent window into the North Korean embassy. Thomas Soetarjo had once been a promising youth leader in the left-leaning Indonesian Nationalist Party during the Old Order.

Showing a flair for the written word, his party organized a four-year scholarship for him to study journalism in Yugoslavia. Returning in 1964, he went on to play a prominent role in youth friendship committees promoting ties with countries like China, North Korea, and North Vietnam.[7]

Normally, such blatant leftist sympathies would have invited swift New Order retribution. But because Soetarjo had never been an official member of the PKI, he escaped the initial waves of arrests after October 1965. Still, he elected to press his luck by writing for quasi-leftist publications through the late sixties. This was a dangerous undertaking: invariably coming under government pressure, these publications would temporarily close, only to reappear under a new name.

Throughout this period, Soetarjo kept in frequent touch with the North Korean embassy. In a rare departure from their normal paranoia, the Koreans appeared to implicitly trust him. Not only had he been a loyal friend since the Old Order days, but he had a good pedigree by marriage: his wife was once a vocal leftist activist and her father, a former Sobsi union leader, was then interned at the PKI penal colony on Buru Island.[8]

The thought of recruiting Soetarjo was first raised by CIA agent Friendly/2. His contact with Soetarjo dated back to 1968, when the two were invited to a film presentation for sympathetic journalists at the North Vietnamese embassy. They continued to meet at communist receptions – especially at the North Korean embassy – where Friendly/2 was struck by a small but telling detail: Soetarjo was the only Indonesian who was granted access to the restroom in the rear of the North Korean compound.[9]

In December 1975, Friendly/2 met with his case officer. Outlining Soetarjo's background, he rated the journalist a "local leftist worthy of recruitment." His handler agreed that Friendly/2 should explore the possibility; two months later, the Indonesian agent made an unannounced visit to Soetarjo's house to further assess the potential recruit. There, he briefly chatted with the journalist's wife (a strong-willed woman who controlled the family's purse strings) and mother-in-law (a domineering matriarch and unrepentant leftist) before sitting down with the target himself. An international soccer match had just concluded, and Soetarjo – surprisingly – expressed pleasure that the North Koreans had bested the Indonesian team.

On 18 March 1976, Friendly/2 outlined his latest thoughts about Soetarjo. As there was no statute of limitations for Kopkamtib recriminations, he feared his past. The CIA agent also observed that Soetarjo had a wandering amorous eye, possibly brought on by living in a household with overbearing women. Both of these factors made him vulnerable to recruitment. "Have an officer take him to a restaurant and say that he knows his past," concluded Friendly/2. "Make him want to prove his loyalty."[10]

The CIA forwarded these opinions to Satsus Intel for consideration. The agency also noted two areas of concern. First, because Soetarjo was a committed ideologue, there was always the chance he might pretend to cooperate but, in fact, become a double agent for a communist intelligence service.

Second, there was the ever-present threat of a spoiling arrest by Kopkamtib. Due to security compartmentalization, as well as the often unhealthy rivalry among Indonesia's military and civilian intelligence agencies, Kopkamtib's heavy-handed powers of detention had frustrated more than a couple of intelligence operations. In May 1973, for example, Friendly/1 had been summoned for a repeat interrogation; only the quiet intervention of the CIA station had secured his prompt release. Mawar, the agent within the NLF office, had also undergone a brief incarceration. And in April 1974, a cooperative former PKI journalist going by the pen name *Melati* ("Jasmine") was roughed up in a Kopkamtib roundup; despite a swift release and profound apologies, he demanded to be released from the Satsus Intel payroll.[11]

Despite these concerns, Satsus Intel felt Soetarjo was too good to pass up. It also recognized that it might only have one chance to make a pitch. In something of an understatement, a 10 September memo to the CIA station noted that it would "need to recruit him in a careful way."

As it fretted for the next two months on the exact approach it would use, the ideal solution suddenly presented itself. The Satsus Intel deputy commander, Major Jacob Sutardi, had earlier served as an assistant to the defense attaché in Yugoslavia between 1958 and 1961. At any given time, there was an average fifty Indonesian students studying in that country, and they would often gather at the embassy for holiday celebrations. Included in that number was Soetarjo, who overlapped with Sutardi's tour for a year.

This coincidence was nearly overlooked. When Sutardi was reviewing surveillance photographs taken at a North Vietnamese diplomatic reception, however, he immediately recognized Soetarjo from his Belgrade days. This set in motion a staged encounter during the first week of December 1976. Boarding a pedicab, the major had the cyclist make a slow pass down the journalist's narrow backstreet. Spying Soetarjo near the entrance to his house, Sutardi expressed shock over their coincidental meeting and invited him for lunch in Menteng. Betraying no suspicion, the journalist readily agreed.[12]

On 21 December, Soetarjo arrived at the Paramount restaurant. Once seated in a quiet corner, Sutardi, looking to maximize shock effect, wasted no time telling the journalist he was being closely watched by the Military Police. Following the script earlier suggested by Friendly/2, Soetarjo was challenged to prove he was a patriot. "He will bend," stated a Satsus Intel report penned after the meeting.[13]

This prediction proved correct. On 8 January 1977, Soetarjo agreed to a secret oath. As a Catholic, he swore on a Bible his loyalty to the state and declared his intention to demonstrate he was not a communist. Within Satsus Intel, his call sign from that point forward was *Teratai* ("Lotus").

From teltaps, stakeouts, and reports filed by agents like Teratai, Satsus Intel was often able to keep one step ahead of North Korean designs. Pyongyang's most maddening indiscretion – from Jakarta's point of view – was its frequent contact with members of the Old Order. As early as 1969, the CIA had forwarded reports from Friendly/1 regarding continued North Korean links to prominent Sukarno-era figures. Over the decade that followed, this came to include former ministers, military officers, and publishers.[14]

Ironically, the North Koreans also contacted the remnants of a past Indonesian intelligence operation. During Confrontation, Subandrio's BPI had facilitated the creation of a North Kalimantan cabinet to confront the Commonwealth. Sukarno had even granted it diplomatic status, akin to what was extended to the NLF information office.

With the rise of the New Order and its fast negotiated end to Confrontation, the North Kalimantan cabinet became an embarrassing relic. But unwilling to completely turn their back on their former creation, the Suharto authorities allowed the top two North Kalimantan leaders – A.M. Azahari and Jais Abbas – to quietly continue the fiction of their movement from a pair of bungalows in Bogor.

In early 1975, for reasons not quite apparent, the two aging revolutionaries decided to end their decade-long hiatus. On 22 January, Jais Abbas was observed by Satsus Intel as he attended a lunch with North Korean intelligence officer Han Dong Chol. Azahari and Abbas had previously visited Pyongyang during the Old Order, and agent reports indicated Chol had professed continued support for their movement's leftist sympathies. Emboldened by the encounter, the two met several Arab ambassadors over the weeks that followed. The Iraqi ambassador gave them a particularly warm reception, and reportedly even offered guerrilla training in Iraq for North Kalimantan recruits. Only after the delivery of a stiff warning from government authorities did the pair retreat back to their Bogor residences and desist from further canvassing.[15]

On occasion, the North Koreans offered more than talk. For several years during the early seventies, for example, Pyongyang's diplomats were suspected of passing considerable sums of money to sympathetic Indonesian editors in return for favorable articles.

The North Koreans were also forging ties with some of Indonesia's ethnic Chinese business leaders. This included emergent tycoon Liem Sioe Liong, who was the subject of several shrill Bakin reports in June 1975. According to these reports, teltaps since 1972 had chronicled business inquiries by Liem to the North Korean embassy, culminating in a November 1973 conversation in which he requested a visa to visit Pyongyang. Two years later, Satsus Intel tracked major North Korean donations to a scholarship-granting foundation believed to be associated with Liem. And despite the fact that Liem eventually become one of the most important financial supporters of the New Order – and was particularly close to Suharto – Satsus Intel operatives surreptitiously opened his incoming and outgoing overseas correspondence for five years.[16]

For its part, CIA interest in surveillance of North Koreans in Jakarta was twofold. First, there was the ever-present fear that Pyongyang might abet terrorist activity in Indonesia. This was driven home in October 1975, when Satsus Intel watched North Korean diplomats collecting information on the physical security at the British, Dutch, French, German, and U.S. embassies. Diplomatic installations in Jakarta were attractive targets, read a 31 October CIA memo provided to Bakin, because there had not yet been a terrorist incident here and defensive plans had not been proven through experience. Although the CIA feared the North Koreans might pass on the embassy information to a terrorist organization, possibly the Japanese Red Army, no attacks materialized.

A second reason for the CIA's interest was the chance for a North Korean recruitment. Given the fact that their diplomats only left the embassy in pairs, the opportunity to cultivate a recruit was rare. There was an exception, however. In the early seventies, a North Korean political secretary returned to Jakarta for a second tour. Probably on account of his considerable time spent overseas, this secretary broke the North Korean archetype. Fluent in Indonesian, he was relaxed and confident at diplomatic receptions. He was forever in need of money, and, as the embassy's procurement officer, had mastered the art of overbilling and kickbacks.

All of this came to be known to Friendly/2, who learned of the secretary's financial sleight of hand when acting as a broker for new air conditioners at the embassy. A friendship soon developed, with the secretary discovering a novel method of discreetly meeting the CIA agent without an escort. During their private trysts, he was amenable to candid conversation for cash incentives.

In 1976, with the secretary nearing the end of his second tour, the CIA looked to make the relationship last beyond Jakarta. Friendly/2, who had developed good rapport with the departing political secretary, was the obvious candidate to make the pitch. In a plan codenamed "Briefcase", Friendly/2 would claim they would together be providing occasional help for a consulting firm in Lichtenstein.

As planned, Friendly/2 rendezvoused with the secretary and delivered his Briefcase patter. "Take a risk," he implored at the end.[17]

The secretary visibly stiffened. His lifetime of indoctrination kicking in, the North Korean curtly declined the offer and urged the CIA's agent to leave. One week later, he had departed Indonesia for the socialist paradise that was the Hermit Kingdom.

If North Korea had one competitor for the title of most sequestered, most idiosyncratic take on socialism, it was Democratic Kampuchea. Once known as the Kingdom of Cambodia under the mercurial, philandering Prince Norodom Sihanouk, the country had walked a left-leaning diplomatic tightrope through March 1970, after which Sihanouk was ousted in an army-led coup. The army chief, General Lon Nol, subsequently claimed the presidency and oversaw a pro-Western republic for five years.

It was to prove a bloody half decade for the people of Cambodia. Along its eastern frontier, North Vietnamese troops, dug into well-defended sanctuaries from which they could conduct their war against South Vietnam, held de facto control. In the remainder of the countryside, meanwhile, a puritanical communist guerrilla movement – the Khmer Rouge – made fast gains on account of moral support offered by a vengeful Sihanouk, occasional military assistance from the North Vietnamese, and gross incompetence on the part of the republican government.

During April 1975, Lon Nol's corrupt republic imploded. Marching triumphantly through the capital of Phnom Penh were highly-disciplined yet deceptively-ragtag Khmer Rouge guerrillas, who immediately put into practice their radical version of Marxism. All cities were forcibly emptied, transformed almost overnight into eerie ghost towns. Money was abolished; commerce came to a standstill. Virtually all of those associated with the previous regime or deemed tainted by education – teachers, for example – were summarily executed. All others, regardless of background, were forced to slave on communes in order to theoretically place the renamed Democratic Kampuchea on the fast track to self-sufficiency, socialist equality, and rapid development. Millions would ultimately perish, mostly from starvation.

The outside world, meantime, knew little of the horrific auto-genocide being perpetrated inside Democratic Kampuchea. Most diplomatic ties were cut; only a handful of embassies were permitted inside the gutted Phnom Penh, and foreign diplomats were relegated to something akin to house arrest. What few journalists that were allowed inside the country – invariably, known sympathizers – were closely chaperoned. Air traffic was limited to infrequent flights from the People's Republic of China, Kampuchea's primary foreign backer.

Indonesia was among the majority whose contact with Democratic Kampuchea was rare. Not that Jakarta minded: there was little love lost between the two nations. For one thing, anti-communism remained Indonesia's mantra; Jakarta was suspicious of all things communist, Kampuchea's mysterious blend or otherwise. What's more, Kampuchea was China's closest ally in Southeast Asia, and this ran foul of the latent anti-Chinese sentiment that permeated the New Order. Kampuchea was also one of the first and most vocal supporters of the leftist Fretilin separatist movement that was battling the Indonesian military in East Timor.

But in an attempt to maintain the appearance of cordial ties among Southeast Asian neighbors, in early September 1978, three years into Democratic Kampuchea's brutal social experiment, came word that top Khmer Rouge leader Ieng Sary planned a visit to Jakarta the following month. As both deputy prime minister and foreign minister, Sary had helped shape Khmer Rouge ideology and was one of the few that traveled outside that troubled, cloistered nation. His upcoming trip, part of a regional tour, was to lobby for support in Kampuchea's worsening border conflict with Vietnam.

Word of Ieng Sary's impending four-day visit soon circulated around Jakarta. Given Sary's unique perspective on the inner workings of the Khmer Rouge, the CIA on 15 September proposed a joint technical operation – codenamed *Bunga* ("Flower") – against the Cambodian foreign minister and his six-man delegation. The U.S. would underwrite the operation, and loan additional equipment to Satsus Intel.[18]

Six days later, Bakin chief Yoga was given the Bunga proposal for approval. Offering a fast green light, plans were finalized within seventy-two hours. Eighteen members of Satsus Intel would be involved, primarily to monitor wireless microphones placed in most of the hotel rooms used by the delegation, as well as taps on their telephones.

On 18 October, two days before Sary's arrival, Satsus Intel personnel visited Hotel Indonesia. Located at the most prominent traffic circle on Jakarta's main thoroughfare, that venue was at the time one of the few international-class hotels in the Indonesian capital. The hotel's security manager was highly cooperative, providing the team with access to a room next to the central telephone exchange on the ground floor; from there, shifts of teltap operators would ensure that the microphones were working properly over the entire four days. Once all tapes were compiled, translation of the transcripts would be conducted elsewhere.

Two days later, Ieng Sary arrived at Halim airport. All seven Kampuchean passports were quickly photographed by a Satsus Intel team operating in an immigration backroom. The delegation was then whisked to their hotel, with Sary – given the call sign *Lebah* ("Bee") – provided with a double suite on the fourth floor.

In the end, Bunga was a bust. What few words that the Cambodian diplomats uttered to each other – mostly in Khmer, occasionally in English – revealed nothing of import. And not a single telephone call was placed to any Jakarta locales, let alone to Kampuchea – for the very good reason that all Cambodian phone lines were cut to the outside world. With the xenophobic Phnom Penh regime an enigma to that time, Ieng Sary's visit did nothing to peel back the bloody veil covering the maniacal Khmer Rouge rule.[19]

1   A 9 November 1972 Satsus Intel memorandum noted that the North Korean embassy fired all of the local Indonesian employees shortly after the government banned the distribution of Kim Il Sung's works; the memo surmised the Koreans acted in retaliation.

2   Mandagi interview.

3   Ibid.

4   BPF, "Ho Chang Gon."

5   Interview with Max M., 19 April 2003.

6   Horstile is an Indonesian corruption of "horse tail," a reference to the agent's ponytail hairstyle.

7   Interview with Thomas Soetarjo, 7 March 2003.

8   Soetarjo interview.

9   BPF, "Teratai."

10 Ibid.

11 Melati was a costly loss for Satsus Intel. As deputy head of the Indonesia-China Friendship League during the Old Order, he had traveled extensively in China and was trusted among the communist embassies in Jakarta. He had particularly good contacts among the East Germans and North Koreans.

12 Sutardi interview. The operation to recruit Soetarjo was codenamed *Pendel* (Javanese for "Nail").

13 BPF, "Teratai."

14 In November 1972, Satsus Intel noted frequent contact between North Korean diplomats and the Old Order Minister of Sports, R. Maladi. Ironically, Maladi's own son had been recruited into Bakin in 1969.

15 BPF, "A.M. Azahari."

16 BPF, "Liem Sioe Liong."

17 Subandi interview.

18 Bakin Case File, "Bunga."

19 The Khmer Rouge government lasted just two more months before being toppled by a Vietnamese military invasion.

CHAPTER EIGHT

INTERNATIONAL TERRORISM

A cross the Middle East during the late sixties, socialism was making gains. In the case of Libya, it was uniquely blended with Islam and pan-Arab nationalism by that country's revolutionary leader, Moammar al-Gadhafi. But in most other Arab states, the embrace of leftist politics reflected more of a shrewd Cold War calculation than ideological conviction.

Iraq was a good example of such pragmatism. In July 1968, the nationalist Baathist party conspired with a handful of army officers to stage a bloodless coup. But even before the generals could warm their new seats, the Baathists outmaneuvered the top brass by month's end and seized full control. To safeguard their grip, the Baathists then reconciled with the Iraqi Communist Party, which they had earlier helped drive underground for almost a decade. This predictably won kudos from Moscow, which offered Baghdad a friendship treaty by 1972 and opened the floodgates of military aid.

The story was much the same in Syria. In 1966, a bloody coup broke out as factions of that country's Baathist party sniped at each other. Emerging strong was a relatively moderate wing under Major General Hafez al-Assad, who suppressed many of his communist political opponents later that decade. But after consolidating power in a November 1970 putsch, Assad dramatically improved relations with Moscow the following year, entered into a national front with the communists, and saw a spike in Soviet military largesse. Moreover, he pushed for more cordial ties with left-leaning Egypt and Libya, leading to a short-lived federation with both these nations in April 1971.

Further south, Cold War posturing was evident on the Arabian peninsula. In 1963, a leftist nationalist group had initiated a guerilla campaign against British colonial administrators controlling the port of Aden. The British abandoned the port four years later, giving rise to the People's Republic of South Yemen, consisting of Aden and the adjacent former protectorate of South Arabia. Two years after that, the country openly declared itself a Marxist state, changed its name to the People's Democratic Republic of Yemen, and was courted by both the Soviet Union and China.

For Indonesian intelligence, all of these nations joined Satsus Intel's top three concerns – the Soviet Union, North Korea, and North Vietnam – as potential sources of communist subversion.[1] Initially, the coverage by Indonesia's spycatchers was random. Beginning in September 1969, for example, infrequent casings were conducted at the Iraqi, Syrian, and Egyptian embassies.[2]

But by 1973, the surveillance of Arab targets had grown more refined. That February, Satsus Intel initiated Operation *Onta* ("Camel"), a ten-day stakeout and teltap against members of the Iraqi embassy and Yemeni consulate. Two further surveillance blitzes – Onta II and Onta III – were conducted against the same diplomats by the third quarter. Also in September, Satsus Intel drew up plans to permanently station a team at Jakarta's Kemayoran international airport; this team soon began archiving color photographs of Arab passports from over a dozen nations and comparing the names of arrivals to a terrorist watch list compiled by cooperative foreign intelligence services.

None of these countries stoked more Indonesian suspicion than Yemen. Part of this was due to an accident of history. Yemenis had been master seafaring traders, and dominated the boat crews from the Middle East that had landed on Indonesian shores generations earlier. As of 1973, an estimated half million Arabs holding Indonesian citizenship were of Yemeni descent; another 30,000 Yemenis were living in Indonesia but had yet to become naturalized citizens. Most lived in Central and East Java; of them, Bakin, in 1973, identified 109 residents of Yemeni origin who it believed were communist sympathizers.

The Yemeni consulate did little to dissuade the Indonesians of their fears. To the contrary, Satsus Intel, by April 1973, had catalogued a litany of suspicious activity by Yemen's diplomats. Besides frequent meetings with Soviet, North Vietnamese, and North Korean embassy personnel, consular members also hosted a large number of Arab-Indonesians at odd hours. And as of September 1972, the consulate was believed to have sponsored creation of a so-called Committee of Nine; as the name suggested, this was a nine-man council in Bogor comprised of Arab-Indonesians who sympathized with the Yemeni government.[3]

Reacting to this activity, Satsus Intel took several steps. For one thing, it continued periodic teltap coverage of the Yemeni consulate phones for almost a decade. For another thing, in June 1973, it began a "letter scanner" program against the consulate. Using steam tables and ivory blades, it surreptitiously opened mail to and from the consulate, copying all letters personally addressed to staff members, as well as correspondence that urged involvement in the internal matters of Yemen, urged the creation of an Indonesian political party in the name of Islamic solidarity, and, most importantly, encouraged contact with the Committee of Nine.

In hindsight, the Yemeni-sponsored Committee of Nine proved nothing more than a talk shop.[4] Far more serious was the threat posed by another Arab export: international terrorism. This scourge had its origins in the contentious Palestinian issue. By the late sixties, after the decisive Arab defeat in the Six-Day War, a large number of Palestinian independence groups had come into being. Countries like Libya, Syria, the Soviet Union, and China sponsored some; the larger factions often received simultaneous support from multiple foreign backers. In 1967, the Palestinian Liberation Organization (PLO) had been formed as an umbrella to coordinate their parallel campaigns. The PLO's largest faction, *Fatah* (Arabic for "The Victory"), had been founded a decade earlier by the fiery Yasser Arafat (Arafat also doubled as overall PLO chairman). But it was the second largest faction, the Popular Front for the Liberation of Palestine (PFLP), led by George Habash, which became synonymous with terrorism. A Marxist-Leninist group, the PFLP saw the liberation of Palestine as an integral part of the world communist revolution. To accomplish this, it received support from both the Soviet Union and China, and had forged contact with left-wing guerrilla movements around the world.

The PFLP was also the first Palestinian group to pioneer the use of international aircraft hijackings to popularize its cause. The first hijacking came in July 1968, when an Israeli El Al passenger jet en route from Rome to Tel Aviv was forced to divert to Algeria. Several similar incidents followed before climaxing in the dramatic seizure of four planes in September 1970, three of which were taken to an airfield in Jordan and (after being emptied) blown to pieces.

The Jordanian explosions had major repercussions for the Palestinian cause. For three years, King Hussein of Jordan had tolerated the presence of the PLO headquarters in his capital. But after the simultaneous hijackings, the king decided that the Palestinian radicals had gone too far. A day later, he declared martial law; another day after that, he ordered his army to evict the PLO. After ten days of brutal fighting that inflicted an estimated 3,000 fatalities, the remnants of the PLO fled to Lebanon.

Although defeated, Yasser Arafat was unrepentant and arrogant. By the third quarter of 1971, he was present at a series of meetings in Syria during which the PLO debated a future course of action. The PFLP's Habash, among others, wanted to escalate the cycle of violence outside of Israeli-occupied territories. Arafat straddled the fence, not willing to commit acts of international terrorism under the PLO name – though willing to turn a blind eye if such acts were done under a new name, which is exactly what happened.

In November 1971, four armed Palestinians gunned down the Jordanian prime minister in downtown Cairo, Egypt, in broad daylight. As one paused to drink some of the spilled blood, he shouted that they belonged to heretofore unknown Black September. Named after the month in which its members were expelled from Jordan, Black September was actually a conglomeration of the PLO's most violent members; the PFLP, in particular, generously provided expertise and volunteers. It had no single leader; rather, it drew some of the most radical PLO lieutenants, often times competing with each other to win Arafat's favor.

Very quickly, Black September demonstrated the extent of its international reach. In December 1971, some of its terrorists attempted to assassinate the Jordanian ambassador in London. Two months later, others sabotaged a West German electrical installation and a Dutch gas plant. And in July 1972, it blew up an oil refinery in northeastern Italy.

In September 1972, Black September terrorists conducted their most infamous act to date. Stealing into the Olympic Village in Munich, West Germany, they seized a team of Israeli athletes. At the end of the ensuing three-day drama, eleven Israelis and five of the eight Palestinian gunmen were dead.

After the Munich massacre, there were fears that Black September's attention might turn to Indonesia. In December 1972, the U.S. embassy in Jakarta received a letter purportedly from the "head of Black September" threatening American citizens if the U.S. did not immediately halt its bombing of North Vietnam. (The bombing did not cease, but no Americans in Indonesia were harmed.)[5]

Far more bizarre was an April 1973 letter posted to the U.S. consulate in Medan. Written in Indonesian and allegedly sent by the "Organization of Islamic Solidarity with Arab Palestine," it claimed credit for assassinating the U.S. vice consul and the manager of Mobil Oil, which had been engaged in oil exploration in Aceh. The letter further demanded that those involved in the Aceh murder be released; it expected a press response in a week. While there were some comments in the letter that hinted to a link with Black September, the CIA and Bakin were left scratching their heads because the assassinations for which it claimed credit had not taken place.[6]

By that time, in fact, events in Sudan had sealed Black September's demise. In March 1973, an eight-man Black September hit squad broke into a diplomatic reception at the Saudi embassy in Khartoum. After receiving radio directives from the PLO headquarters in Beirut, the squad executed one Belgian and two U.S. diplomats. These assassinations infuriated the Saudis and Sudanese – both of whom had supported the PLO – forcing Arafat to quietly suspend further Black September operations.

Still, not all Arab terrorists chose to listen. Beginning in July 1973, Bakin maintained a three-volume *Fedayeen* (Arabic for "Fighters of the Faith") handbook that listed 2,500 known terrorists. This was constantly updated with tips provided by cooperative foreign intelligence organizations. In October 1973, for example, the CIA warned Bakin that Algeria's senior diplomat in Jakarta had terrorist links during an earlier posting in Switzerland; among other things, he had provided known terrorists with Algerian passports. Similarly, in October 1975, the CIA alerted Bakin to a recent Libyan provision of passports to Arab extremists.[7]

More substantial CIA assistance was evident during the December 1975 visit to Jakarta by President Gerald Ford. Codenamed Zebra, the operation was a surge effort to watch all suspect foreigners ahead of Ford's arrival.[8] It was a major undertaking, with the CIA loaning Arabic, Chinese, Japanese, Korean, Russian and Vietnamese translators, as well as two video tape recorders for the airport and eight additional teltaps.

Initially, there was some reason for concern. Two PLO members had arrived in Jakarta from Malaysia on 27 November. Two days later, a Japanese national bearing the same name as a known ultra-leftist arrived from Manila. And on 1 December, Anatoliy Babkin, the former KGB *rezident* in Jakarta, landed aboard a flight from Singapore. But with Satsus Intel keeping all of these persons under close surveillance, Ford came and went without complications.[9]

CIA assistance also came in the form of training. The U.S. had been giving intelligence tradecraft instruction to Satsus Intel since the late sixties, but in August 1976, the agency shifted focus and offered a counter-terrorist course – on bomb disposal techniques – to twelve Indonesian students. Combating terrorism soon became the overriding emphasis of CIA training that year, with classes titled "VIP Protection" and "Terrorist Devices Threat and Response" offered over the next three months.

CIA primers on counter-terrorism remained a central theme over the next four years.[10] By 1980, five separate terrorism-related courses were taught by U.S. instructors, who rated the Indonesians (drawn from both Bakin and the military) as the most capable foreign students they had tutored over the previous half-decade.[11] The only minor gaff took place when the Indonesians, honing their VIP protection skills, were coached in the use of Israel's compact Uzi submachine gun. This was somewhat controversial: although Mossad had been quietly providing periodic assistance to Bakin since 1969, it was deemed too politically sensitive to stock weaponry bearing Israeli manufacturing stamps. Ever resourceful, the CIA put Bakin in touch with a Philadelphia arms dealer who procured the desired Uzis – but conveniently bearing the alternate stamp of a Potomac, Virginia firm.[12]

Among international terrorist groups of the seventies, the Japanese Red Army easily ranked as one of the most extreme. It traced its roots back to 1968, when university campuses across Japan erupted in protests over the planned extension of the U.S.-Japan security treaty. When that treaty was ultimately signed

Subandrio confers with President Sukarno, 1964 (Courtesy Ipphos)

Subandrio arrives to testify at his own trial, 6 July 1966. (Courtesy Ipphos)

Muhammad Saad Iqbal Madni, a Pakistani national deported from Indonesia in January 2002.

Surveillance photograph of Abu Daud

Umar Faruq immediately prior to his deportation, June 2002.

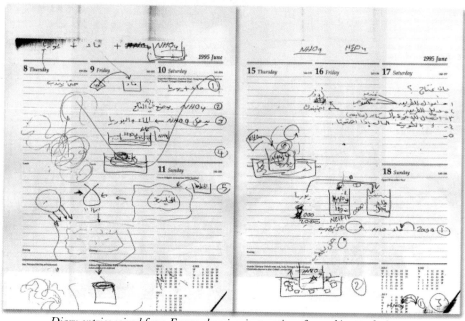

Diary entries seized from Faruq showing instructions for making explosives.

in 1970, most students dutifully returned to class. Against this conformity, however, an element of Japan's Communist League maintained a confrontational approach. Known as the Red Army Faction, its members grabbed headlines in 1970 when they hijacked a passenger jet to North Korea. They also began staging robberies of banks and post offices across Japan to finance their activities.

The following February, after internal fighting began to tear apart the Red Army Faction, one of its female members, Shigenobu Fusako, ventured to Beirut and contacted the PFLP. Like the rest of the PLO, the PFLP was still licking its wounds after being evicted from Jordan; the move to Lebanon was a blessing in disguise, however, as they were able to quickly establish terrorist training camps near Beirut. These were opened to both Arabs and like-minded radicals from around the world.

Returning to Japan, Fusako cobbled together a small core of ultra-leftist students who had roots in the defunct Red Army Faction. It was this group that ventured back to Beirut in November 1971 and, with PFLP assistance, founded the Japanese Red Army (JRA). It proved an odd, but lasting, marriage, with Arab militants and idealistic Japanese dropouts, many from good family backgrounds, repeatedly joining forces over the ensuing years. In May 1972, a mixed team of Japanese and Palestinians stormed the international airport in Lod, Israel, killing two dozen civilians and wounding over two hundred. In July 1973, another mixed team hijacked a plane to Libya and blew it up. After that was the seizure of the French embassy in The Hague and an abortive raid by Japanese and Palestinians on a Singaporean oil refinery in January 1975. Seven months later, five JRA gunmen burst into the U.S. consulate in Kuala Lumpur, took 53 hostages, forced the release of five jailed comrades in Japan, and successfully demanded a flight to Libya.

Just as with Black September, there were hints that the JRA might turn its attention to Indonesia. In October 1975, a foreign counterpart agency informed Bakin that Japanese radicals were possibly targeting Jakarta's President Hotel or the adjacent Wisma Nusantara office building, both of which had prominent Japanese ownership.

More precise information surfaced in January 1976. That month, foreign intelligence services tracked six JRA members who had rendezvoused at the North Korean embassy in India, then headed to Nepal, and from there to Bangkok. Detained and interrogated, the six provided details of the JRA's international support network. Included among those supporters, learned Bakin, were eight Indonesian nationals.

On 6 February, Satsus Intel was tasked with conducting discreet background checks on the JRA's Indonesian sympathizers. Of the eight, five were in Jakarta, two were in Jogjakarta, and one was in Semarang, Central Java. Focusing first on the Jakarta-based targets, warning bells immediately began sounding on one: neighbors of Bambang Noerdjoko revealed his father was a former PKI member incarcerated on Buru Island; his younger brother was also affiliated with the PKI and had fled to Hungary. And two years earlier, an unidentified Japanese guest, apparently bearing a letter from the exiled brother, had visited Bambang's Jakarta residence.[13]

Scouring its database, the CIA believed it knew the identity of the mysterious Japanese visitor. Takahashi Taketomo, 41, had been an assistant professor at Tokyo's Rikyo University before heading to the Middle East and joining the JRA as its intelligence chief and head of European operations. Highly resourceful, he was known to have befriended PKI exiles in Holland; with their help, in 1974, he had used a forged Dutch passport with an Indonesian name.[14]

That Taketomo had probably visited Indonesia seemed to confirm JRA's interest in the country. While the JRA was not all that large – as of March 1976, the CIA listed just 22 members still on the loose around the world – there were indications they were attempting a recruitment drive. Moreover, there was an unconfirmed report the group was looking to participate in a joint Libyan/PFLP attack in Jakarta during the second quarter.[15]

In the end, that attack never materialized. Still, the JRA was viewed as an extremely serious threat for another year. Some of Bakin's concern was a result of the nexus between Japanese radicals and PKI fugitives (such as that between Taketomo and Bambang's brother in Hungary). According to a January 1977 Bakin memo, the JRA was also known to have contacted four PKI members living in Belgium as of August 1974; that same year, a Japanese female had befriended two PKI members living in Canada.[16]

These concerns aside, the JRA was not aging very gracefully. Never large in number, many of its hardcore members by late 1977 were either killed or captured. Taketomo, their intelligence chief with the Indonesia connection, had been detained by Swedish police in July. Of its lesser committed members, most renounced their radical ways and slowly had their names removed from

CHAPTER EIGHT - INTERNATIONAL TERRORISM   131

the international terrorist watch list. In March 1980, immigration officials in Jakarta noted that one of the last remaining on the list – Yamada Yusiaki – had entered the capital en route to Bali. But when Satsus Intel dispatched operatives to investigate, they found an innocent, elderly golfer who shared the same name.[17]

The JRA, however, saved its worst for last. In April 1986, a 39-year old, bespectacled Japanese national carrying a passport under the name Hirofumi Ishida entered the Indonesian capital from Singapore. On 10 May, the same man, this time using a Japanese passport under the name Shunseke Kikuchi, checked into the President Hotel. It was later learned that both passports had been stolen from India two years earlier.

What came next was an attack as bizarre as it was dangerous. At 1100 hours on 14 May, two improvised mortar rounds arced toward the U.S. embassy compound. Fired from the park across the street, each consisted of three tin cans taped together and packed with a pound of TNT flakes. Neither of the rounds exploded.

Thirty minutes later, two more improvised mortars were fired from the eighth floor of the President Hotel toward the Japanese embassy across the street. One landed on the roof of the embassy's parking garage; the second veered toward the lawn of the Soviet embassy next door. Again, neither round exploded.

Another thirty minutes after that, a car bomb exploded in the parking lot behind the Canadian embassy. Seven cars were damaged and three persons wounded. JRA communiqués from the Middle East later claimed credit for all three incidents.

Neither Bakin or any of its foreign counterparts had any forewarning of the attacks. Although Satsus Intel scrambled to investigate, it soon determined that the person who checked into the President Hotel had already fled to Singapore, and from there to Moscow. Further investigation by U.S., Japanese, and Indonesian authorities discovered that the culprit was Tsutomu Shirosake, one of the JRA's most wanted. While elusive, Shirosake was eventually apprehended in Nepal during 1996 and extradited to the U.S. In November 1997, he was convicted of the attempted murder of U.S. diplomats and currently sits in a maximum security prison.

The jury is still out on another of Indonesia's brushes with international terrorism during the seventies. It began on 22 April 1977, when the CIA passed word to Bakin that "a source of unknown credibility" overheard plans of a pending attack on a Golkar election rally set for the following day near Jakarta's Senayan sports stadium. The name of the source was never given to Bakin, nor was it known if the rumor even originated in Indonesia. Acting on the tip, Satsus Intel operatives mingled with rally participants but observed nothing out of the ordinary.[18]

Perhaps related to this, perhaps not, three days later, a 26-year old Swiss national named Hugo Tinguely landed at Jakarta's international airport. Applying for a tourist visa on arrival, he told immigration officials this was his second trip to Indonesia; he stated his first visit, the previous October, was for "karate and girls." Raising no objections, the officials gave him a thirty-day stamp.[19]

But immediately after leaving the airport, foreign counterparts gave Bakin a different picture of Tinguely. He had just come from a month in Japan, they learned, where he was tailed by Japanese police during several meetings with JRA sympathizers. During his departure from Osaka, customs officials had spent nearly two hours pulling apart his luggage – blatant harassment meant to sour him toward a repeat visit.

Compounding matters was Tinguely's student affiliation. According to his visa application, he was studying in West Germany. Over the previous year, radical German leftists from the Baader-Meinhof Gang had grabbed headlines for a series of daring terrorist attacks. Their most prominent act had been the joint PFLP hijacking of an Air France flight to Entebbe, Uganda; Israeli commandos later stormed the terminal and freed the hostages.

Learning of Tinguely's German schooling and JRA connections, Bakin recalled the vague CIA warning about the Golkar rally earlier in the week and intuitively assumed there was a dark and direct correlation.[20] Rushing to place him under close surveillance, Satsus Intel at 2100 hours was ordered to track down the suspicious Swiss student. Codenamed *Puyun* ("Quail"), the operation was led by Hans Hamzah, the resourceful ethnic Chinese officer who had earlier conned Portuguese Major Soares in Bali.

At that late hour, Hamzah grabbed three available Satsus Intel operatives and immediately launched a search. From Tinguely's visa and customs forms, they knew he was carrying two pieces of luggage and indicated he would be staying at Hotel Palace in Central Jakarta. A quick visit, however, indicated no Swiss national had checked into Hotel Palace that night. Assuming that a student would likely reside at a budget establishment, they next headed to the guest houses along Jalan Jaksa that were popular with the hippie crowd. Still coming up short, at 2300 hours they ventured to the nearby two-star Hotel Bali Indonesia. Scanning the hotel register, they noted a Swiss national named "Ting" had checked in a couple of hours earlier.

Figuring there was a match, Hans beckoned the duty manager. The two, coincidentally, were old friends, and the manager readily agreed to provide the spare key to the suspect's room. When no one answered the door, they went inside and confirmed there were two pieces of luggage – the same number listed on Tinguely's customs form.

At that point, Hans put his linguistic talents into play. Sitting at the front bar, he waited until a lanky, blonde European male entered the lobby at 2320 hours and paused for a drink. A master of improvisation, Hans introduced himself as a Singaporean teacher and offered to buy a beer. Not only did Tinguely agree, but from almost the opening moments of their conversation, he shifted the topic to Japanese politics and the JRA.

Several beers later, the two called it a night. As a parting comment (and as an excuse to have a subsequent meeting), Hans said he knew of a guest house that was cheaper than their current hotel. Tinguely agreed to meet in the lobby the next morning to take a look.

As promised, Hans was waiting at 0800 hours. Taking Tinguely to a hostel on Jalan Raden Saleh, the Swiss national approved of the room and better rates. Thirty minutes later, his bags were shifted. Conjuring a quick excuse for continued contact, Hans offered to take him to Taman Mini Indonesia – a sprawling, somewhat gaudy cultural center on the southern outskirts of the city – the next morning. Again, Tinguely agreed.

Thus far, Satsus Intel had done a good job of keeping the Swiss suspect under watch. Not only was Hans building personal rapport, but a teltap was placed on his hostel room and a surveillance team stayed on Tinguely's tail from a distance.

But Satsus Intel was not alone. Ever since his appointment as intelligence chief for the Ministry of Defense and Security, Major General Benny Moerdani had assumed control over the intelligence task force fielded by Kopkamtib. By 1977, that task force was commanded by a brigadier general (outranking the Satsus Intel commander, a colonel) and had been afforded a generous budget to build surveillance teams and procure its own teltap gear.

Hearing of the Tinguely case, Moerdani demanded that his men participate in the operation. The resultant joint operation was coordinated in name only. Beginning on the evening of 27 April, surveillance teams from both Satsus Intel and the military were authorized to tail the Swiss. Their parallel coverage, not surprisingly, became excessive – and obvious. During their trip to Taman Mini Indonesia, Tinguely complained to Hans he was being followed by photographers. "Indonesia is full of spies," he noted at their subsequent lunch, correctly pointing to two of Moerdani's cameramen sitting at a nearby table.[21]

Though paranoid about the heavy-handed surveillance, Tinguely betrayed no suspicion toward Hans. He also made no secret of his rebellious ideological orientation. During their 28 April lunch, he lectured the faux Singaporean teacher about the JRA and the Indonesian religious extremist movement, Komando Jihad. Meeting at his hostel the next morning, Tinguely proudly wore a Japanese robe he said was a gift from a leftist Japanese friend. And during a 30 April lunch, he boasted he was not afraid to die and that he hated the CIA with a passion.

Such fighting words aside, Tinguely spent most of his time chasing girls and lounging among the European backpacker community. During the first two weeks of May, he left Jakarta for Bali with an Indonesian female companion and some French acquaintances. During the trip, the military's surveillance team kept him in sight. But rather than watching from the shadows, the military's idea of surveillance came up short on discretion. When Tinguely met Hans back in Jakarta, he reported that government "gangsters" had harassed him at his hotel, had rifled through his luggage, and threatened his girlfriend.

Despite such proverbial heat, Tinguely was game for more. On 24 May, he ventured to the immigration office in Menteng with the intension of extending his thirty-day visa for a second month. Stretching credibility to the limit, Hans showed up on the pretext that he, too, was extending his visa. But as the two met, the dejected Swiss national said his extension had been rejected and he needed to leave Indonesia within forty-eight hours. Watching him until the end, an ostensibly sympathetic Hans met him for coffee the following morning before a Satsus Intel team at the airport confirmed he boarded a

Singapore Airlines flight that afternoon for Frankfurt via Bangkok.

Upon Tinguely's departure, hearty congratulations were passed around Bakin and Moerdani's military intelligence unit for expelling what they deemed was a likely member of the Baader-Meinhof Gang, the JRA, or a combination thereof. To be sure, the Swiss national made no attempt to sugarcoat his radical sympathies. And Japanese language articles found in his luggage (not translated until 1 June) were of the same extreme political orientation. But his boasting to virtual strangers like Hans hinted that he was more of an ideological groupie than a true terrorist operator. In the hypersensitive political environment of Indonesia, such indiscretion made Tinguely guilty of felonious stupidity, probably nothing more.

1   In 1974, Satsus Intel also contemplated surveillance against India. Though the world's largest democracy, New Delhi had signed a friendship treaty with Moscow in 1971 and there were concerns that Indian diplomats might be in contact with Soviet intelligence officers in Indonesia. The planned coverage against India, however, was never executed.

2   Bakin Case File, "Iraq." Egypt had long been sympathetic to the Soviet Union, but did not sign a formal treaty of friendship with Moscow until 1971.

3   Bakin Case File, "Panitia 9."

4   One of the few accomplishments of the Committee of Nine was to hold a meeting on 28 October 1973 to organize a fund-raising drive among Arab Indonesians for the Arab participants in the Yom Kippur War. Ibid.

5   Ibid.

6   Bakin Case File, "CP 119 Arab Report."

7   Bakin Case File, "International Terrorism."

8   As reflected in documents passed between the two organizations, Zebra was also Bakin's codename for the CIA. This was chosen because the stripes found on the U.S. flag.

9   Bakin Case File, "Zebra."

10 In October 1979, as part of a VIP protection course, the CIA conducted a vehicle ambush assessment for Bakin's new headquarters compound under construction in Pejaten, South Jakarta. Bakin officially moved to the Pejaten site in 1980, and remains there to this day.

11 One of the courses given during 1980, "Incident Management," was conducted by William Buckley. Four years later, while serving as station chief in Beirut, Buckley was kidnapped by Islamic extremists and murdered.

12 Bakin Case File, "Tradecraft."

13 Bakin Case File, "JRA."

14 BPF, "Takahashi Taketomo."

15 Bakin Case File, "JRA."

16 There was also concern about links between international terrorists and left-leaning South Moluccan separatists who had sought sanctuary in Holland. In October 1976, a Dutch terrorist detained in Israel revealed that, when she was trained by the PFLP in Lebanon, a South Moluccan had been in her contingent. Bakin Case File, "International Terrorism."

17 Bakin Case File, "JRA."

18 Bakin Case File, "Pemilu."

19 BPF, "Hugo Tinguely."

20 On the CIA memo detailing the threat to the Golkar rally, Bakin officials penciled on the bottom biographical details of Hugo Tinguely. Bakin Case File, "Pemilu."

21 BPF, "Hugo Tinguely."

CHAPTER NINE

KOMANDO JIHAD

T he overwhelming majority of Indonesians are Muslim. For most, theirs is a moderate, tolerant take on Islam, often liberally overlaid with elements of mysticism, Hinduism's stratification, and other local traditions.

But Indonesia has also seen its share of Islamic extremists. One of the most serious challenges was from a movement known as *Darul Islam*, a reference to the Medina community founded by the Prophet Mohammed.[1] As it was originally conceived, Darul Islam was, in many respects, a social reaction during the mid-twentieth century by the people of West Java to the rest of that island. Culturally and linguistically, West Java's ethnic Sundanese majority had historically labored in the shadows of the more powerful Javanese kingdoms further east. Eager to differentiate themselves, the Sundanese came to shun the heavily stratified, Hindu-influenced societies – and resultant class conflicts – favored by the Javanese. While this made them less receptive to the precepts of communism (which eventually allowed the PKI to make deep inroads in places like rural Central Java), many instead embraced Islamic piety as a means of expressing an Indonesian identity.

Founding the Darul Islam movement was an ethnic Javanese named Sekarmaji Marijan Kartosuwiryo. Born in 1905 and an early member of the Islamic League – a nationalist organization formed at the start of the twentieth century – Kartosuwiryo had risen to become its secretary general by 1931. Nine years later, opportunities for him and the league mushroomed following the Japanese occupation of Indonesia during World War II. After initially persecuting nationalists across Southeast Asia, the Japanese reversed themselves and encouraged the growth of religious organizations and independence movements – even to the point of training indigenous armies – as a means of currying local favor and frustrating attempts by the Allies to reassert colonial domination in Asia.

Wearing religious and political hats, Kartosuwiryo appealed to the Japanese on both counts. Stoking his activism, the Japanese allowed him to set up a four-hectare training camp in West Java for a fledgling militant Islamic wing. By the time World War II ended, and renewed hostilities against the Dutch looked set to begin, his loyalists had a significant armed presence across the Sundanese heartland in West Java.[2]

During the war of independence that followed, Kartosuwiryo's partisans fought dozens of pitched battles against the colonialists.[3] In doing so, they formed a loose alliance with the nationalist guerrillas that had also taken up arms across Java. Neither faction lost sight of the fact that theirs was a marriage of convenience: whereas the nationalists were fighting for an independent, secular state, Kartosuwiryo's religious warriors made no secret that they envisioned a non-secular Indonesia ruled according to Islamic law.[4]

Midway through the war, Kartosuwiryo caught a lucky break. When the Dutch agreed to a ceasefire, the 35,000-strong nationalist guerrilla army in West Java conducted a long march into Central Java to regroup. But after the ceasefire collapsed and the nationalists moved back toward their home province in August 1949, they discovered Kartosuwiryo's men had expanded their area of operations across West Java during the interim. Pushing his advantage, Kartosuwiryo during the same month formally proclaimed he was head of what he termed the "Indonesian Islamic State" (Negara Islam Indonesia, or NII).[5] The zones of West Java that were under the control of his partisans were known as Darul Islam, a title that became synonymous with the NII movement.

Exhausted by their extended march and again pummeled by the Dutch, the nationalists could offer only a limited response to the Darul Islam challenge. Once independence was granted in December, a response was delayed further by the need to counter a Dutch-inspired uprising near Bandung in January 1950, then by the need to export Java-based troops to confront a secessionist rebellion in the Malukus. As a result, Sukarno formally announced the formation of a republican government that August, and Kartosuwiryo felt sufficiently confident to reject Jakarta's right to rule.

By the following year, Darul Islam had turned West Java into a province aflame. It effectively displaced the government across much of rural West Java and was not above inflicting bloodshed across the provincial countryside. During the last three months of 1951, Islamic guerrillas were accused of killing over four hundred and burning more than four thousand houses.[6]

Over the remaining years of the decade, Darul Islam would mushroom across the archipelago as affiliated chapters took root in places like Aceh, Central Java, and South Sulawesi. The movement would also attract strange bedfellows. The U.S., looking to snipe at the mercurial Sukarno, indirectly offered aid to Darul Islam's Aceh chapter as part of the CIA's short-lived 1958 paramilitary program in support of anti-communist rebels on Sumatra and Sulawesi.[7]

But by the early sixties, the Darul Islam movement was beginning to fray. This occurred for several reasons. First, Darul Islam was never a coordinated movement; rather, it was an umbrella for disparate, ethnically-diverse chapters that generally sympathized with each other, but never synchronized their operations. Second, Darul Islam never gained significant external support. Third, the Indonesian armed forces were growing more competent and were eventually able to perfect effective counter-insurgency strategies. Fourth, the Acehnese proved opportunistic and, after extracting several political concessions, coasted toward a separate settlement in 1962. Fifth, the Darul Islam foothold in Central Java never gained widespread appeal, due in large part the fact that Darul Islam's underlying opposition to Javanese chauvinism rang hollow in the Javanese heartland.

With the exception of the South Sulawesi chapter, which sputtered through 1965, Darul Islam was effectively defeated with the capture of Kartosuwiryo in 1962.[8] When most in his high command were either killed or accepted a government amnesty the following year, the movement, for all intents and purposes, appeared to be dead.

Ironically, some in the army – who had just spent the previous decade hunting down religious extremists – now began to find a common cause with their vanquished Darul Islam foe. This was because both were united in their opposition to the PKI: the army abhorred the Communist party because it was a dangerous political opponent; the Islamic right hated the communists because of Marxism's atheistic precepts.

With a reputation for unorthodox thinking, Ali Moertopo's Opsus was quick to explore synergy with religious extremists. By early 1965, Opsus officer Sugiyanto had established ties with Danu Mohammad Hasan, a top Darul Islam commander from West Java who had accepted the earlier government amnesty. The relationship soon provided Opsus with unexpected dividends. "I was acting as Danu's handler," recalls Sugiyanto, "and in March 1966, we used him and his men to hunt down members of the BPI that were hiding in Jakarta."[9]

The rest of Darul Islam's first generation remained suitably contrite for a time. But by 1968, veterans from the movement were growing restless. That year, the son of Darul Islam founder Kartosuwiryo, Dodo Mohammad Darda bin Kartosuwiryo, presided over a meeting attended by many of his father's former lieutenants. Behind closed doors, they declared their intention of resurrecting the Darul Islam vision of a non-secular Indonesia ruled according to Islamic law. Among themselves, they adopted the name *Komando Jihad* ("Holy War Command").[10]

For its first year, Komando Jihad was nothing more than a talk shop. Adah Djaelani, Kartosuwiryo's onetime protégé, was named overall head of Komando Jihad. Under him – on paper – Indonesia was divided into seven area commands that mimicked the former Darul Islam organizational chart. Of the seven, the only one of substance was Area Command 3 covering West Java, which was to be commanded by Opsus informant Danu.

It was through Danu that Opsus quickly received news of the initial Komando Jihad tryst. But while the New Order normally was notoriously thin-skinned toward dissent, Opsus saw opportunity in the revived religious right. This was because Ali Moertopo was already looking to identify constituent blocs that would stump for Golkar – the New Order's political machine – ahead of the 1971 polls. In the hope that the top figures in Komando Jihad might be able to deliver the votes of their sympathizers, they became an Opsus target.

Handling the Komando Jihad project was Pitut Soeharto. Pitut was uniquely qualified within Opsus to court the extremists. Born in East Java, as a teen during the war of independence, he had rushed to enter the fledgling nationalist forces. As the closest unit was comprised of military engineers, he signed up as a trainee. But before learning the basics of engineering, his platoon was thrown into battle – not against the Dutch, but rather against the communists that had seized control of Madiun.

The skirmish that followed was decisive. Rushing communist lines, all of Pitut's fellow platoon members were either immediately killed or executed shortly thereafter. Alone, Pitut managed to escape back to nationalist territory. This was a defining moment in his life and forged an unshakable hatred of the PKI.

After the revolution, Pitut enrolled in law school. Graduating in 1957, he re-entered the military and was accepted into the army's intelligence school. Seconded to the Ministry of Foreign Affairs, he spent the last two years of the decade in Singapore as vice consul. Returning to Indonesia – with the rank of lieutenant colonel – he was assigned as Deputy Minister for Land Transportation, Post, Telecommunications, and Tourism.

Behind this wordy title, Pitut had an unusual mandate. When Darul Islam rebels were offered amnesty in 1963, their surrender ceremonies involved issues linked with land transportation. As this was part of his deputy ministerial portfolio, he attended multiple ceremonies across West Java. Not only did he meet most of the movement's repentant leaders, but he commiserated in their common opposition to communism.

In January 1964, Pitut's vocal anti-communism proved costly. His politically incorrect rhetoric was reported to senior government officials, who not only ran him out of the ministry but, after appealing to his military commanders, had him officially demoted from colonel to captain.

The feisty Pitut took the demotion in stride. But when they moved to place him in detention, he drew the line and fled the capital. As he hailed from East Java, it was to there that he ran. And as he had befriended much of the Darul Islam leadership – and knew they shared his strident anti-communism – he sought sanctuary in the home of a former Islamic extremist living in the town of Gresik. From there, they bundled him off to South Sulawesi, where they kept him shielded among rebels that had yet to rally to the government.[11]

Six months later, Pitut re-established contact with colleagues in the military and received assurances he would not be further sanctioned for his insubordination. His surrender proved timely: immediately after he came in from the cold, the attempted PKI coup threw the communists on the defensive. In a bit of poetic justice, he was reassigned to the army's combat engineers and charged with rooting out communist sympathizers.

After almost three more years of anti-PKI operations in his native East Java, Major Pitut received unexpected orders, signed by Ali Moertopo: he was told to immediately report to Opsus. Moertopo had apparently done his homework and knew of Pitut's past history with the Darul Islam ralliers. Capitalizing on this background, Moertopo handed the major a challenging assignment: split Komando Jihad and entice the movement's more moderate elements into Golkar.

In 1969, Pitut made his first approach toward the regrouped extremists. It was not a penetration operation in the classical sense. Rather, following from introductions made by Danu, the major openly attended Komando Jihad meetings using his real name and rank. To do otherwise would have been folly: most already knew him, or knew of him, from the 1963 surrender ceremonies.

The major also made no secret of his intent to bring them into the government fold. To do this, he had an unorthodox weapon. With agreement from Pertamina, the state-owned oil and gasoline company, Pitut was able to secure kerosene distribution rights for portions of Java. Key distribution slots were offered to Komando Jihad leaders, who could then pass local distribution positions to sympathizers. The quid pro quo: bring in the votes for Golkar.

Two Komando Jihad figures were quick to take up Pitut's offer. The first, Danu, had already been proving cooperative for most of the decade. The second, Ateng Djaelani, showed strong entrepreneurial skills and was ultimately placed in charge of the kerosene network allocated to Opsus.

When elections were finally held on 3 July 1971, Golkar emerged victorious. Pitut, who had just been promoted to lieutenant colonel, had only been partially successful in his attempt to woo Komando Jihad moderates. "Of the twenty-six core leaders in the movement," he later stated, "only about a third were cooperative."[12]

Although the vote had concluded, the Opsus lobbying effort directed at Komando Jihad continued. During secret meetings in 1972 and 1973, all attended by Pitut, the movement's leaders mapped out efforts to realize chapters outside of West Java. In Aceh, contact was established with the former Darul Islam chief in that region, Daud Beureuh. Representatives were also dispatched to South Sulawesi and Kalimantan. Despite this push, however, no presence of any substance ever took root outside of Java – in part, because extremists on the outer islands were irate that Ateng Djaelani was not generous with his Pertamina concessions.[13]

By the following year, meanwhile, Opsus had been fully incorporated under Bakin's Deputy III. Promoted to colonel, Pitut retained the Komando

Jihad portfolio.[14] His efforts to seal the movement's cooperation were growing more difficult by the year. During a 1974 restructuring, informant Danu was promoted as commander for all of Java. But Haji Ismail Pranoto (better known as Hispran) and Dodo Mohammad Darda bin Kartosuwiryo, both hard-liners who refused Pitut's entreaties, were chosen as deputy commander and chief of staff, respectively.[15]

Of equal concern were the activities of an Islamic extremist cell roaming Sumatra. That seven-man band, calling itself *Momok Revolusioner* ("Revolutionary Ghost"), hailed from a younger generation that had no links to either Darul Islam or the Java-centric Komando Jihad. They were violent, setting off a string of explosions at theaters, bars, and churches in Medan, as well as a Baptist church and mosque in West Sumatra. Worse, from the government's perspective: pamphlets left behind by the group were rife with communist rhetoric.[16]

On the surface, Islam and communism were polar opposites. In most cases where socialism had made gains in the Islamic nations of the Middle East, it was because they came down on that side in the Cold War. But an exception was found in Libya, where a bloodless coup in September 1969 saw King Mohammad Idris al-Sanousi usurped by a group of army officers. Renamed the Libyan Arab Republic, the new government was anything but republican: led by a Revolutionary Command Council under Moammar al-Gadhafi, membership in opposition political parties was decreed punishable by death.

Libya quickly came to be synonymous with Gadhafi's idiosyncratic view of himself and his self-appointed world role. Born of humble origins, he had been profoundly influenced by the fiery nationalist sentiment of Egyptian President Gamal Abdel Nasser as well as the resounding Arab defeat in the 1967 Six-Day War. These factors led to Gadhafi's apocalyptic vision of leftist pan-Arabism and Islam locked in a mortal struggle with what he termed the "encircling, demonic forces of imperialism and Zionism." More than just words, he began using oil revenues (Libyan oil distribution was nationalized in 1970) to promote his ideology; this included support for select subversives, including Muslim rebels from the Moro National Liberation Front (MNLF) in the southern Philippines.

In 1974, Gadhafi turned part of his attention toward Indonesia. Early that year, the CIA passed information to Bakin that an undetermined number of Indonesian students – some from Java, others from Aceh – had traveled to Saudi Arabia on the pretext of a religious pilgrimage, then had made their way to Libya for schooling. Some were apparently attending bona fide religious courses at the Institute of Dakwah Islamiyah in Tripoli. But others were reportedly receiving a paramilitary tutorial similar to what had been extended to the MNLF.[17]

With Indonesian embassies across the Middle East placed on alert, proof positive of the Libyan connection came on 22 July from Saudi Arabia. Ten days earlier, read an embassy cable forwarded to Bakin, five Indonesian students had arrived in Jeddah from Tripoli; Satsus Intel was ordered to put them under surveillance upon their arrival in Jakarta.[18]

To gather more details on the Libyan training, Colonel Pitut rushed to the Middle East. Having already frequented the region by tagging along on Pertamina delegations, he had established a number of Libyan contacts. One was a high-ranking member of Libya's Revolutionary Command Council who was partial toward Beirut's famed nightlife. Rendezvousing in that city, Pitut was not only able to secure entry to Tripoli but even visited one of the centers that hosted the Indonesian contingent. After confirming that the training regimen was indeed paramilitary in nature, the Libyan embassy in Jakarta was ordered closed in 1975.[19]

The closure barely had an effect. The Libyan embassy in Kuala Lumpur coordinated the passage of further Indonesian contingents to Tripoli every six months. They continued to be a mix of Acehnese and Javanese; the latter were recruited not from Komando Jihad but rather from mainstream Muslim grassroots organizations.[20]

At that point, bedfellows grew stranger still. Beginning in 1975, Anton Ngenget, a former PKI member turned government informant, had been reporting that members of the Soviet consulate in Surabaya were encouraging underground PKI remnants to foster contact with Komando Jihad. The Soviets, said Ngenget, predicted an ultimate showdown between the secular Indonesian government and the religious right. Ahead of this confrontation, Moscow was reportedly willing to provide military aid (via submarine) to Libyan-trained "progressives," who in turn would share their cache with Komando Jihad.[21]

In hindsight, the nexus between Soviet aid, Libyan-trained progressives, and Komando Jihad never developed beyond the musings from Surabaya. At the time, however, the government was especially sensitive to any threats – no matter how unlikely – given the upcoming 1977 national elections. This time around, the New Order had reduced the number of recognized political parties down to just three: the government's own political machine, Golkar; the Muslim-oriented United Development Party (*Partai Persatuan Pembangunan*, or PPP); and the secular catch-all Indonesian Democratic Party (*Partai Demokrasi Indonesia*, or PDI). Suharto was determined to receive – or orchestrate, if need be – an overwhelming public mandate via Golkar.

Just as Opsus had done prior to the 1971 polls, Bakin's Deputy III again tried to mobilize Komando Jihad votes. But this time around, not all would be going to Golkar. Longtime informant Danu, for one, hinted he would throw his weight behind the PPP. While that would not contribute to a Golkar landslide, the fact that he was favoring elections, rather than violence, was welcomed by Bakin.

For the rest of Komando Jihad, the New Order had run out of patience. In January 1977, four months ahead of the polls, security officials went on the offensive and eventually detained 185 persons by mid-year. All these arrests took place on Java: 105 were in Jakarta, 38 in West Java, 19 in Central Java, and 23 in East Java. A separate series of raids in Sumatra netted the *Momok Revolusioner* cell over the next two years.[22] Although a handful of extremists were still on the lam (including informant Danu), Komando Jihad was no more.

At the same time Komando Jihad was being defanged, Bakin was moving against other domestic challenges during the run-up to the 1977 polls. One operation, codenamed *Kilat* ("Lightning"), concerned the restive territory of East Timor. Ever since the overt invasion of Timor of December 1975, military intelligence – not Bakin – had established a monopoly over the Timor theatre. But in March 1977, after Jakarta received word that the first U.S. congressional delegation was scheduled to visit Timor the following month, Bakin was hurriedly brought into the picture.

The delegation greatly concerned the Indonesian government from the start. Even under the best conditions, U.S. legislators on fact-finding trips can be highly demanding visitors. Worse, from the Indonesian perspective, the delegation slated to visit Timor was far from friendly: led by Congressman Lester Wolff, chairman of the House Subcommittee on International Assistance, it had already conducted highly-critical hearings highlighting reported human rights abuses in Timor.

Indonesia's normal reaction to such delegations was to closely stage-manage the visits with chaperones from the Ministry of Foreign Affairs and the military. But this time around, Satsus Intel would keep track of what the delegates said behind the scenes – and if they attempted to contact any sources away from their escorts. For obvious reasons, the Kilat surveillance operation was to be kept secret from the CIA liaison officers working with Bakin's spycatchers.

On 12 April, the Congressional delegates landed at Jakarta's Halim airbase aboard a U.S. Air Force jet. From the moment they disembarked, Satsus Intel gave special attention to John Salzberg. The senior staffer on the delegation, Salzberg had played a prominent behind-the-scenes role during the earlier critical hearings on Capitol Hill. Not only did Satsus Intel place a listening device in his hotel room, but – shades of the 1975 operation against Portuguese Major Soares – had his water spiked with a powerful laxative in the hope that stomach cramps would cause him to briefly leave his room and allow his briefcase to be searched.

But just as during the Soares operation, the spiked water did not have the desired effect. As Satsus Intel operators listened to Salzberg's room microphone from the floor below, they heard the staffer repeatedly visit the bathroom. The dosage was apparently not sufficient for him to seek medical attention, and the Satsus Intel flaps and seals team (including a photographer and another member proficient in picking locks on attaché cases) was never called into play.[23]

For his part, Salzberg was not aware of the extra attention he had attracted.[24] On the following day, he and three other Americans landed in Dili for a highly-orchestrated one-day tour. Back in Jakarta by 14 April, they were again tailed by Satsus Intel until boarding a flight out of Indonesia later that day. None of the delegates had their opinions changed by the Timor jaunt; to the thinking of the Indonesian government, however, the lack of heated dialogue just one month before the election was seen as a mark of success.

Another pre-election challenge tackled by Bakin came from within the military. Ishak Djuarsa, an outspoken major general from West Java, by 1970 had grown tired of Suharto's uncontested lock on the presidency. As an alternative, he favored the Republic's highly-respected former vice president, Mohammad Hatta. After assuring the 68-year old Hatta during a November meeting that his age should not be a factor – octogenarians were running China, he noted – Djuarsa received Hatta's pledge that he would announce his candidacy ahead of the 1971 polls.

Very quickly, whispers of Hatta's contemplated presidential run reached Suharto. Although Hatta was soon talked out of the idea, Djuarsa's endorsement was not forgotten or forgiven. In an effort to banish him from the Jakarta political arena ahead of the polls, the general, in February 1971, was conveniently sent to Cambodia on an extended Kopkamtib assignment to coordinate assistance to the Phnom Penh regime.

Not until 1974 did Djuarsa finish his Cambodian tour and return to Jakarta. Picking up where he left off, he held a birthday bash for Hatta that August. Figuring that the general was trying to lobby Hatta for yet another presidential bid, the New Order leaders again sent Djuarsa packing as the new ambassador to Cambodia in February 1975. When that country fell to the Khmer Rouge in April, the general stayed in Thailand for a time before being bundled off in early 1976 as the ambassador to Yugoslavia.[25]

By that time, all eyes were fixed on the upcoming 1977 elections. Although the restive Djuarsa was out of the country, and Hatta had not committed to make a stab at the presidency, the Suharto regime was still deeply concerned that the two might still make waves during the run-up to the polls. These concerns deepened when Bakin received word of a bizarre plot involving a government bureaucrat named Sawito Kartowibowo.

Sawito was a most unlikely threat to the president. A mid-level official at the Ministry of Forestry, he had built a sizable following for his blend of aesthetic mysticism, yoga, and (still in its infancy as a sport) aerobics. But as Yoga Sugomo reported to Suharto in September 1976, the bureaucrat was involved in far more than calisthenics and meditation. As proof, the Bakin chief produced copies of a series of proclamations Sawito had penned between February and July. The last, dated 17 July, was a missive about his countrymen's collective health entitled "Toward Happiness." The implication, though far from specific, was that Indonesia might be a better and stronger country, given political change. Several prominent Indonesians had signed the treatise, including three senior religious leaders and Hatta.[26]

At another time in Indonesia's history, Sawito's mild affront would probably have been ignored. But in the sensitive pre-election atmosphere under the New Order, the letters begged a crackdown. Because of his advanced age, Hatta was spared. But the rest of the signatories were hauled in for questioning; Sawito was sentenced to eight years in prison.

Intuitively, Bakin felt Ishak Djuarsa was somehow involved in the Sawito case. In an operation codenamed *Cakrawala* ("Heavens"), Satsus Intel was assigned with watching his Jakarta residence beginning in late September.

Then on 30 September, Djuarsa received a telegram in Belgrade to report immediately back to Indonesia. Boarding the next available KLM flight, he arrived in Jakarta two days later. A Bakin representative met him on the tarmac and escorted him to a double suite at the beachside Horizon Hotel. A Satsus Intel team, meantime, secretly opened his two pieces of luggage (one at the airport, the other at his hotel room) and searched the contents.

Their haul was disappointing. Among the documents in Djuarsa's possession were photocopies of the Sawito letters (Djurasa himself was not a signatory), as well as a dull 11 September correspondence from Hatta in which the latter requested some books on the Yugoslavian economy.[27]

Though it had found no smoking gun, the New Order wanted Djuarsa muzzled through the election. On orders of military intelligence chief Benny Moerdani, the major general was placed under house arrest for nineteen months – sufficient to last through the 1977 polls and 1978 presidential selection. With no challengers willing to step forward, Suharto received a unanimous nod for another term.

1   Derived from the Arabic words *Dar Al Islam*, it literally translates as "House of Islam" or "Realm of the Faith." It more broadly refers to a nation, state or zone ruled according to Islamic law.
2   Although Kartosuwiryo was himself an ethnic Javanese, one of his wives was Sundanese and the vast majority of the movement's early membership was Sundanese.
3   The Islamic partisans on Java, all nominally under Kartosuwiryo's leadership, went by various names and usually operated as autonomous district-level bands. In the Tegal area of West Java, for example, they were known as *Mujahidin* ("Warriors of Jihad").

4   Early in the independence struggle, Kartosuwiryo participated in a debate over the wording of the 1945 constitution being championed by the nationalists under Sukarno and Mohammad Hatta. Kartosuwiryo and his top followers eventually gave tacit support to a secular state as laid down in the constitution; however, they continued to harbor the conviction that Indonesia would eventually become an Islamic state after the defeat of the Dutch.

5   Kartosuwiryo's written proclamation, which amounted to one long sentence, was dated 7 August 1949. It merely stated that Indonesia was an Islamic state ruled according to Islamic law.

6   During the first three months of 1952, Darul Islam partisans were accused of killing 428 persons and burning 3,052 houses. *Sejarah TNI, Jilid II* (Jakarta: Markas Besar Tentara Nasional Indonesia, 2000), p. 82.

7   Details of the CIA's assistance to rebel Indonesian troops can be found in Kenneth Conboy and James Morrison, *Feet to the Fire* (Annapolis: Naval Institute Press, 1999).

8   In yet another example of strange bedfellows, the British government began sending covert military aid to Darul Islam's South Sulawesi chapter during 1964, this as part of an attempt to divert Indonesian attention from Kalimantan during Confrontation. Details can be found in the Indonesian government publication entitled *Why Indonesia Opposes British-Made "Malaysia"* (Djakarta: Government Printing Office, 1964), pp. 71-73.

9   Sugiyanto interview. At that time, the intelligence services were tracking down former BPI operatives and interrogating and jailing them.

10   The Arabic term *jihad* (literally, "striving") is open to interpretation. Moderates see jihad as a call to achieve higher moral standards, with violence not necessarily implied. A more extreme – and commonly held – interpretation, however, defines jihad as an injunction for military action by the pious against non-believers and all others not sharing in their militancy. There has been some question as to whether the Darul Islam successors used the term Komando Jihad, or if this was an inflammatory term coined by the Indonesian government. According to Pitut Soeharto, the Opsus officer who attended most of their meetings, the name was used from the start among the movement's members. Gaos Taufik, a Darul Islam leader based in North Sumatra, also says that the name was used within the movement. Pitut Soeharto interview; interview with Gaos Taufik, 23 July 2003.

11   Pitut spent most of his time in South Sulawesi with Andi Sele, a warlord who was opposed to the regional military commander. The Darul Islam chapter in South

Sulawesi was led by Kahar Muzakkar, who also had a personality conflict with
the regional military commander. Muzakkar was eventually killed by government
troops in February 1965.

12   Pitut Soeharto interview.

13   Taufik interview.

14   Pitut was named head of the Opsus Directorate under Deputy III.

15   Kopkamtib report entitled "Informasi Khusus" dated 2 February 1977, found in
Bakin Case File, "Pemilu."

16   Taufik interview; Bakin Case File, "Darul Islam."

17   Pitut Soeharto interview.

18   Bakin Case File, "Libya."

19   Pitut Soeharto interview.

20   When the first Acehnese received paramilitary training in Libya, the separatist
movement in Aceh had been in remission for more than a decade. It was not until
early 1977 that the Free Aceh Movement (*Gerakan Aceh Merdeka*, or GAM)
resumed its battle with the central government.

21   Ngenget was an informant for Kopkamtib's intelligence task force , though his
reports were shared with Bakin. BPF, "Anton Ngenget."

22   *Momok Revolusioner* never received any foreign support. "They were leftists,"
said one Darul Islam veteran, "because its members were young, and such politics
were fashionable among students." Gaos Taufik interview.

23   Bakin Case File, "Kilat."

24   Interview with John Salzberg, 20 May 2003.

25   Interview with Ishak Djuarsa, 10 May 2003.

26   *Memori Jenderal Yoga*, p. 257.

27   BPF, "Ishak Djuarsa."

CHAPTER TEN

EMASCULATION

T he latter half of the seventies was a time of profound change in Bakin, much of it personality-driven. Back in February 1975, Ali Moertopo had been promoted from Deputy III to the number two slot of Bakin deputy chief. But even though he was sent up, he was not opposed to meddling in his former portfolio. Recalls Aswis Sumarmo, one of Moertopo's replacements:

> Deputy III was very messy when I got there. Several of the top officers, including Pitut [Soeharto], bypassed me and still reported to Ali as deputy chief.[1]

This situation persisted through March 1978, when Moertopo was tapped as the new Minister of Information during a cabinet shake-up. Leaving Bakin with him were longtime Opsus stalwarts Pitut and Sugiyanto, purging the agency of Moertopo's key accomplices.

In as the new Bakin deputy chief was Major General Benny Moerdani. Moerdani's personal stock in Suharto's eyes was fast on the upswing – partly because of his undisputed cunning in intelligence matters, partly because Suharto favored Christians like Moerdani in sensitive slots as they had a vested interest in preserving the New Order status quo.[2] Over the previous four years, Moerdani had been patiently consolidating all military intelligence functions under his direct control within the Ministry of Defense and Security. This came at the expense of Kopkamtib, which no longer retained the same clout after General Sumitro's undignified exit.

Retaining his multiple hats in military intelligence, Moerdani's influence on Bakin was immediate – and not favorable. Straddling both military and civilian intelligence organizations, he had the inside track on all unfolding intelligence assignments. Given the choice between steering choice projects to either military intelligence – where he dominated the limelight – or Bakin – where he sat second chair to Yoga – he invariably wrested the best cases for the former.

Wanting more, Moerdani's opportunity came in 1981. Two years earlier, in February 1979, the Imperial Iranian government imploded and was replaced by an Islamic revolutionary regime under the Ayatollah Khomeini. This was the first successful Islamic revolution in modern times and, although the Iranians were Shiite Muslims (as opposed to Indonesians, who are almost exclusively Sunni), the rise of Khomeini had ripples across the archipelago.

Among those who felt inspired was an Indonesian named Imron bin Zein. Born in 1950 in West Sumatra, Imron at nineteen had ventured to Saudi Arabia in a futile attempt to pursue a religious education. Unable to gain university admission, he stayed in the kingdom for more than half a decade working odd menial jobs.[3]

Not until 1977 did Imron return to his native Sumatra. Shifting to Jakarta two years later in search of better employment, he could only eke out a living as a street vendor. While surveying other job prospects, he began to network with other Indonesians who had worked in the Middle East. Among them was a Sundanese student named Salman Hafidz. Much like Imron, Salman had ventured to Saudi Arabia in 1975 to study Islam but ended up spending no time in a classroom. As fellow Indonesian laborers, the two grew close over the following year. After that, Salman left the kingdom to backpack from Egypt to Pakistan; when cash ran low, he would seek out temporary work as a clerk.

Back in Jakarta by the opening of 1979, Salman quickly linked up with Imron. For a time they ran in business circles: Salman took a job at an insurance company; Imron found some success in exporting turtle eggs to Singapore. But by early 1980, Imron found something far more profitable. Making much of his extended stint in Saudi Arabia – which won him added respect within certain religious circles – he began to build a following by preaching the conservative, intolerant strain of Islam common in the kingdom.

By the second half of 1980, Imron's stint as a militant preacher was showing dividends. In Bandung and the neighboring town of Cimahi, he had nurtured sizable congregations; smaller groups were taking shape in Surabaya and Jakarta. Though there were ethnic Sundanese and Javanese among his acolytes, many hailed from North and West Sumatra. Many, too, were young university students or persons, including Salman, who had spent time in Saudi Arabia.

Given the hard-line brand of Islam he was preaching, Imron was predisposed against Indonesia's secular state. Taking inspiration from the Iranian revolution, during the second half of 1980, he decided to launch a quixotic campaign to overthrow the New Order and establish a non-secular regime.[4] To accomplish this, Imron had his followers launch a series of attacks – mostly against mainstream Islamic targets – in both Jakarta and West Java.[5]

During the early morning hours of 11 March 1981, the Imron group staged its boldest paramilitary attack to date. In a bid to obtain weapons, he ordered Salman to lead fourteen other members in attacking a police post in Bandung. Overwhelming the post's four police officers, they made off with two Colt pistols.[6]

The government's reaction to the Bandung attack was swift. Within days, it had arrested several dozen of Imron's followers (most were sympathizers who had not actually participated in the raid). But Imron himself escaped and was far from conceding defeat. Near month's end, he laid out plans to hijack a Garuda airliner and swap the hostages for his jailed colleagues. Five members were chosen to carry out the hijacking: an Indonesian of mixed Arab parentage who had studied in the Middle East, two from North Sumatra, one from West Sumatra, and one from Jogjakarta.

Three days before the end of March, the five put their plan into effect. Commandeering a Garuda DC-9 on its way from Palembang to Medan, they had the plane fly to Bangkok, Thailand. Once on Thai soil, the hijackers issued a series of demands. Highest on their list was the release of 80 extremists, including some from Komando Jihad and those that had been detained following the Bandung raid. They later demanded $1.5 million in cash and safe passage to an unknown destination, thought to be Libya.

What happened next was a pivotal event for Bakin. Yoga Sugomo was fast to arrive in the Thai capital with a negotiating team, but it was his deputy, Benny Moerdani, who quickly seized the spotlight. Acting in his capacity as military intelligence chief, Moerdani was flanked by a crack hostage rescue team drawn from the army special forces. The subsequent rescue operation was successful, with Moerdani – and the military – correctly receiving the most kudos. Yoga's contribution, by comparison, earned far less praise.

In the weeks after the hijacking, suspicions proliferated and conspiracy theories abounded. A news report from Thailand, later discounted, claimed the five terrorists who seized the plane were remnants of Komando Jihad.[7] There was also a report from CIA agent Friendly/2 that an Imron follower had been a conspicuous consumer with mysterious sources of funding.[8]

Reviewing this initial information, Moerdani intuitively smelled a covert government hand in the hijacking. He could be forgiven for such suspicion: even though Ali Moertopo was theoretically out of the special operations business, rumors of his continued dabbling were widespread. It was also hard to overlook Opsus' long relationship with the extreme religious right. Calling in Deputy III Aswis Sumarmo, Moerdani minced no words. "Tell Pitut to stop it," he growled, "or I will have him arrested."[9]

Confronted, Pitut denied any link to Imron. But whether because he doubted the denial, or whether because he wanted an excuse to expand the responsibilities of his coddled military intelligence, Moerdani turned against Bakin. In May 1981, two months after the Bangkok hijacking, Bakin underwent a major reorganization that more closely resembled emasculation. From seven deputies, Bakin was cut to just four. Removed in its entirety was Deputy III for Conditioning; the mandate for penetrating and wooing key elements of society was instead shifted to Benny's burgeoning military intelligence empire.

As his agency hemorrhaged, Yoga looked impotent. By contrast, Moerdani was still on the fast track and, in 1983, was named commander of the entire armed forces. Among Moerdani's first orders of business concerned intelligence. Ceding his title as Bakin deputy chief, he used the opportunity to give military intelligence an extra push.[10] The existing Strategic Intelligence Center was now expanded into the Strategic Intelligence Agency (*Badan Intelijen Strategis*, or Bais); given its added bureaucratic clout – as well as its stated strategic mandate – the new agency absorbed many of the investigatory and enforcement powers of Kopkamtib. And with military attachés worldwide now reporting to Bais, its international outreach was equally formidable.

Against the rising fortunes of Bais, Bakin spent the early eighties trying to defend its dwindling turf. One area where it showed slight gains was in its overseas presence. Special attention was given to the Middle East, where Bakin had established three new posts during the previous decade.[11] Offering training assistance was Israel, which had been dispatching occasional instructors for Satsus Intel since 1970. In early 1983, a single Israeli advisor was sent to Jakarta to give a month of intensive tradecraft instruction to five select junior officers being primed for overseas slots.

For three of these officers, a unique training opportunity was yet to come. That July, the first Bakin candidate ventured to Israel for an additional six weeks of instruction in agent handling. The following month, the two remaining officers rotated through the same course. Their intensive regimen of instruction stressed improvisation. Remembers one:

> On fifteen occasions, the trainer took me to a luxury hotel and then singled out a single stranger in the lobby. I was given five minutes to think up a cover story, introduce myself to the target, and convince that person to meet me again in the lobby at seven o'clock that evening. If the target was waiting that night, I passed. When the target was an Arab, I was always able to establish rapport and make a successful introduction within five minutes.[12]

Bakin made prompt use of its Israeli-trained contingent. One graduate opened a new Bakin post in Egypt during late 1983. Another took over the Bakin seat at the Indonesian embassy in Saudi Arabia. For the first time, these officers were authorized to begin recruiting agents and other covert intelligence-collection tasks; previously, Bakin's overseas representatives limited themselves to little more than open source collection from media sources.

Closer to home, Bakin enjoyed no such gains. Although it theoretically had offices in every province, in reality, it was conspicuously absent from the most critical parts of the country. In East Timor, which was suffering Indonesia's most serious insurgency, Bakin was completely shut out in favor of a strong Bais presence.[13] In Irian Jaya, which had suffered a separatist insurgency since the sixties, Bakin was again wholly eclipsed by Bais. And in Aceh, where armed separatism broke out in 1977, Bais alone was allowed to post personnel.[14]

In the domestic political arena, too, Bakin was trumped. Its conditioning mandate gone, among the agency's only contributions in the lead up to the

1982 election was to passively monitor political rallies and to publish a classified but otherwise unremarkable guide for all governors that outlined the political challengers to Golkar.[15] And although Bakin retained a directorate for "counter-subversion" – the New Order term for anyone that strayed from the Suharto line – a nearly identical body within Bais was far more prominent and aggressive in keeping loyalties under wraps.[16]

One of the few areas where Bakin held its own was in counter-intelligence against foreign spies. It kept its edge in part due to new surveillance equipment courtesy of the CIA. This was long overdue, since Satsus Intel's original Sony Type TC-800 recorders had been in steady use since 1969. In late 1979, a new generation of taps and recorders was finally introduced; the latter for the first time featured smaller and more compact cassette tapes.

As before, communist nations were the chief targets of Indonesia's spycatchers. Also as before, top favorites included Vietnam and North Korea. In the case of Vietnam, Satsus Intel continued its stakeouts and teltaps against embassy personnel. Compounding the normal concerns about Hanoi was the fact that its pro-Soviet government was showing aggressive tendencies across mainland Southeast Asia. After bullying neighboring Laos into submission, it had toppled the genocidal Khmer Rouge and occupied Cambodia. This sparked a brief but bloody border war with China in early 1979, which was angered at Hanoi for overthrowing its ally in Phnom Penh.

By late 1979, the Vietnamese regime was also breeding significant disillusionment at home. Between failed socialist economic policies, prejudice against citizens of ethnic Chinese origin, and an unpopular draft to fight against resurgent Cambodian guerrillas, tens of thousands of Vietnamese began fleeing their country by sea. Many ended up in refugee camps in Thailand and the Philippines. And about 8,000 reached the Indonesian archipelago, where most were steered to a ten-hectare complex on Galang Island near Singapore.

This pool of Vietnamese exiles held appeal for the CIA. Potentially included among their number were persons who might have information about missing Americans from the Vietnam War. Also among the refugees might be deserters from the communist army, who could have useful insights about Vietnam's current military setup. To tap this source of information, the CIA sent debriefers to the refugee settlements in Thailand and the Philippines. Plans were also developed in 1979 to initiate a similar program on Galang, but bureaucratic delays in Washington caused the operation to be stillborn.[17]

In December 1981, the CIA looked to try again. Proposing a four-week program in a memo to Bakin, the station chief suggested sending a single U.S. officer to Galang to interview Vietnamese refugees; high on the list of targets would be former servicemen who had recently served in Cambodia. The chief specifically suggested that the person dispatched to Galang be the same ethnic Vietnamese officer who had served prolonged tours in Jakarta during the seventies while working on the NLF wiretap operation.

Reviewing the proposal, Bakin thought it had merit. In particular, the Indonesians were concerned as to whether or not Vietnamese government intelligence agents had infiltrated Galang, a tactic Hanoi had used in other overseas refugee communities.[18] Following quick approval, planning lasted through January 1982. On 12 February, the CIA's Vietnamese officer arrived on Galang and immediately began interviews. His identity was kept secret from both the refugees and the local Indonesian authorities. Fluent in Indonesian, he was given an Indonesian alias and claimed to be a staff member from the Indonesian embassy in Hanoi.

Four weeks and 98 interviews later, the Galang debriefings were concluded. Twenty persons, mostly enlisted men from the communist Vietnamese army, were deemed of sufficient value for more in-depth sessions. One of them, a 25-year old corporal named Ho Ngoc Minh, detailed coastal exercises with Soviet military advisors. Others provided information on the amount of Soviet oil delivered to Vietnam from Vladivostok or via Singapore. Still others shed light on the use of the Vietnam News Agency as a cover for intelligence operations.

Even more revealing was a 25 February interview with a 35-year old doctor named Ton That Phuoc. Serving on the staff of a mental hospital near Saigon prior to 1975, he had repeatedly met with an American patient named Paul Horton over the following year. An agricultural expert who had worked for a volunteer agency, Horton had steadfastly refused to leave after South Vietnam's fall. Information on Horton was quickly forwarded to Washington, where it was entered into the database on Americans missing in Indochina.[19]

One year later, in January 1983, the CIA and Bakin decided to restart the interviews with a new batch of Vietnamese boat arrivals. Over the next two months, 45 detailed briefings were completed; of these, a dozen were with army deserters and another eighteen with paramilitary troops. Among the details gleaned was order-of-battle information about border guard formations along Vietnam's southern coast, insights into persecution of Buddhist clergymen, and data on Vietnamese trade with Cuba. Another result: a 44-year old ethnic Vietnamese, born in the United States and thereby an American citizen, was tracked down and sent to the U.S. embassy for processing.

Satsus Intel's other perennial favorite was North Korea. Though a decade had passed, the North Korean diplomats stationed in Jakarta during the early eighties were little different than their comrades of the seventies. As before, they were cloistered and extraordinarily suspicious of outsiders. Nearly all lived commune-style at the embassy residence, leaving the premises only in pairs to guard against defection or unauthorized fraternization.

While these factors made them among the hardest targets for Satsus Intel to track, a unique break came in February 1982. That month, two diplomats approached CIA agent Friendly/2 – one of the few seemingly sympathetic Indonesians with whom the North Koreans maintained regular contact – and requested his help in renting a house that would be shared by both families.[20]

This piqued the interest of both the CIA and Bakin. Not only was this one of the rare occasions when the Koreans were leaving the confines of their embassy residence, but these two diplomats were of particular interest. The first, Kwon Won Hyong, 42, was a graduate of Pyongyang's College of International Relations and had spent several years in China before arriving in Indonesia the previous August. Fluent in Mandarin, he knew little English or Indonesian. Linguistic deficiencies notwithstanding, he was listed as a first secretary (trade) and thought to be an intelligence officer.

The second, Kim Un Bong, 37, graduated from the North Korean College of Foreign Languages. Conversant in Indonesian, he was listed as a third secretary. Like Kwon, he was strongly suspected of being an intelligence officer.

On 22 March, after the Koreans signed a lease for a house suggested by Friendly/2, the CIA and Bakin began planning a joint technical operation. Time was of the essence, as the house was being renovated prior to occupation and both diplomats had notified the Ministry of Foreign Affairs they would be going to Bangkok for a week beginning 25 March. To exploit this window of opportunity, both intelligence agencies planned to install bugs on the day after the diplomats' departure to Thailand. Their operation was to be codenamed *Nyamuk* ("Mosquito").

At that point, Murphy's Law made a rude introduction. Rather than being absent for a full week, the Koreans changed their itinerary: they were now to depart on 24 March and return just two days later. But electing to proceed as planned, the joint entry team assembled at a Menteng hotel at 2030 hours on 26 March, then headed for the targeted house two hours later. Covering the front windows with sheets, CIA technicians using headlamps climbed a ladder into the crawlspace above the ceiling and installed two woodblocks by midnight. Despite a second spell of Murphy's Law – one of the woodblocks was defective and had to be replaced – both devices were working at month's end.[21]

By 4 April, the Nyamuk bugs were transmitting signals as the two diplomats, their wives, and two small children settled into their new house. The audio voyeurism revealed little during the first month. Examples:

5 April: Child singing at top of lungs and crying.

23 April: Wives dwell on making *kimchi*.

24 April: Sounds of persons assembling an unidentified electronic device.

25 April: The electronic device turns out to be a radio; both families gather to listen to the repeat broadcast of Kim Il Sung's birthday celebrations.

The May results were similarly benign, with one exception. On the last day of that month, one of the wives picked up the telephone and, perhaps by force of habit, answered, "Sosong Trading Company." This was a significant slip, as Sosong was long a cover for the North Korean intelligence service.

Over the next four months, the teltap results sometimes bordered on the bizarre. Confirming the cloistered, suspicious nature of the North Korean regime, the embassy's party secretary called the house on the afternoon of 2 June and warned the wives never to venture outdoors because they might be "attacked." The wives were further instructed to call and report everyday to the embassy. He then asked which volumes of Kim Il Sung's select works were readily available at the house. "Volumes 1, 2, and 6," was the dutiful response.

Other items picked up by the teltap were more mundane:

> 27 June: Kwon Won Hyong complains that his underwear smells bad, urges his wife to soak them for a few more hours before washing. She agrees.
>
> 10 July: Wives complain about Indonesia.
>
> 12 July: One of the wives complains that her husband drinks too much beer.
>
> 6 September: Kwon Won Hyong's daughter cries loudly. Her parents try to appease her, but she continuously wails.
>
> 8 September: Wives discuss growing bean sprouts; two children sing a Korean song.
>
> 9 September: Kwon Hon Hyong complains that food served at breakfast seems to be left over from yesterday. Wife tells husband not to complain.

What the bugs did not reveal was that both Kwon and Kim were involved in extracurricular activities that had nothing to do with espionage. Taking advantage of their trade portfolios, the pair concocted a lame scheme to massively inflate the bill for $650,000 in railroad ties imported by Sosong to Indonesia, then use the difference to purchase a pair of pricey BMW sedans for themselves. Taking stationery with embassy letterhead, they then prepared export forms for the two cars to be shipped to North Korea without paying duty. The CIA and Bakin knew of the plot because, once again, Friendly/2 acted as middleman during the transaction.

Not surprisingly, the ploy soon began to fall apart. In November, both diplomats were called to Pyongyang for questioning about the suspicious railroad tie deal. Soon afterwards, the paperwork for the car purchase came to light and Kim alone was called back to Jakarta for further interrogation. Finding opportunity for a brief, private rendezvous with Friendly/2, Kim listened as the CIA agent pointed out that his career, and almost certainly his freedom, was nearing an end. "Defect," urged Friendly/2. "Save your own skin." Torn, the tainted diplomat ultimately elected to return to Pyongyang's tender mercies.[22]

In addition to Vietnam and North Korea, there were two new foreign threats. Ever since the 1979 Iranian revolution, Indonesia had been uneasy with the new Islamic regime in Teheran. Not only were the Iranians aggressively exporting their revolution to many parts of the world, but their Shiite take on Islam clashed with the Indonesian Sunni majority.

Bakin's approach toward Iran was two-fold. For one thing, the agency tried to keep track of all Indonesian students partaking in religious study in Iran. As of 1982, five were known to be studying in the holy city of Qom. By 1984, that number had risen to eighteen; most of them were from Surabaya and had prior association with conservative Islamic groups.

For another thing, Bakin kept the Iranian embassy under scrutiny. As of 1982, information provided by foreign counterparts indicated that Iranian diplomats in Jakarta were distributing thousands of free copies of a militant magazine called *New Jerusalem*, giving weekly sermons at their embassy, and on at least one occasion subsidized an Indonesian delegation attending an overseas conference sponsored by Teheran. To keep track of such activities, Satsus Intel in 1984 organized special Iranian coverage with nine teltaps. They also began a comprehensive letter-scanning operation; stationery from the embassy, noted the censors, was printed with the decidedly-undiplomatic letterhead "Wishing the Oppressed Victory over Oppressors."

For all their bluster, however, the Iranians made little headway in Indonesia. Apparently unable to surmount the Sunni-Shiite divide, their diplomats had difficulty attracting followings for their magazine and weekly religious meetings. And while the censor campaign netted plenty of cordial letters posted by Indonesians, no evidence was uncovered during the early eighties of intelligence or paramilitary plots.

The other new threat watched by Bakin, albeit briefly, was Yugoslavia. Despite their political differences – Indonesia was unapologetically anti-communist, Yugoslavia was following an independent socialist line – the two nations long had cordial ties as prominent co-founders of the non-aligned movement. And aside from a brief teltap of the Yugoslavian military attaché's residence in 1979, its diplomats in Jakarta did not fall under the same cloud of suspicion as those from the Soviet bloc.

On 11 July 1981, however, came word of an impending Yugoslavian intelligence operation on Indonesian soil. The tip came courtesy of the CIA, whose overseas stations had pieced together an imminent plot to kill a Croatian living in Australia; planning for the murder was to take place in Indonesia.

The background to the assassination was grounded in Yugoslavia's complex ethnic composition. In the thirties, Croats intent on creating an independent nation murdered the Yugoslavian king during a state visit to France. The hounded separatist leaders then took refuge in Germany, where the Nazis nurtured them and, following the Axis invasion of Yugoslavia in 1941, sponsored creation of an independent, subservient Croatia.

What came next was a dark period in Yugoslavian history. Embracing the Nazi concept of a final solution, Croat fascists executed tens of thousands of Jews, as well as sizable numbers of Serbs and Gypsies. They also battled socialist partisans led by Josip Broz Tito, who had the backing of the Allies.

Following the Allied victory in World War II, Tito assumed control over a reunited Yugoslavia. Many of the Croat fascist leaders had already taken their exit, seeking refuge in places like Argentina and Spain. This did not deter the Yugoslav government, which dispatched agents to track down – and often kill – the Croats that had avoided justice. Few foreign nations protested the assassinations because they wanted to maintain cordial ties with Tito, and because they had little sympathy for fascists on the lam.

Hardly taking this lying down, the neo-Nazi exiles struck back. Several assassinations of Yugoslavian diplomats were planned and carried out; in 1971, for example, Croats raided the Yugoslav embassy in Sweden and murdered the ambassador. They also used a bomb to down a Yugoslavian passenger jet over Czechoslovakia that same year.

The most daring Croat counter-strike took place in 1973. Drawing from their large diaspora in Australia, paramilitary training was conducted in the outback. Nineteen armed men then made their way to Europe and crossed into Yugoslavia with the intention of sparking a Croat rebellion. Predictably, the raid fizzled almost immediately; all nineteen were quickly killed or captured.

Since then, Yugoslavia paid special attention to Australia's Croat exiles. Apparently going on the offensive, the CIA's July 1981 information indicated that the Yugoslavian intelligence service was targeting a prominent member of that community for assassination. To carry out the act, they intended to send a case officer named Ilijas Ganic to Indonesia; there he was set to brief a Yugoslavian-born Australian citizen named Maric, who would then return to Australia to commit the deed.

By 16 July, the CIA, in concert with Australia's domestic intelligence service, had compiled more information about the upcoming Indonesian tryst. Maric would be departing from Australia on 19 July and was booked at Hotel Indonesia. He would be staying for a total of five days, part of that time possibly in Bali. Meanwhile, a trace conducted on Ganic revealed that he had ventured to Southeast Asia once before under the guise of an engineer.

Concerned over the meeting of assassins on its turf, Bakin agreed to keep the Yugoslavians under surveillance. Operation *Kangguru* ("Kangaroo") took shape beginning on 17 July, with Satsus Intel officers visiting Hotel Indonesia and installing woodblock bugs in a pair of adjacent rooms. In addition, a flaps and seals specialist was placed on standby.

As expected, Maric landed in Jakarta in the early evening of 19 July and made his way to the airport's immigration counter. When he presented his passport for inspection, the immigration official gave a signal to a waiting Satsus Intel officer disguised as a fellow passenger. That officer was holding an attaché case fitted with a Robot camera that could be secretly triggered by a thumb switch; provided by the CIA, the Robot's high-quality lens offered a wide angle photograph of outstanding clarity.[23]

As Maric made his way past immigration and customs, Satsus Intel captured him on film. Unfortunately, when they collected a copy of his entry form, they saw he had noted that Hotel Sahid Jaya was to be his intended residence. Seeing this, the airport team called headquarters and told them to yank the woodblocks at Hotel Indonesia. Meanwhile, others in the surveillance operation kept track of Maric as he met a second Caucasian – presumably Ganic – and together rode a taxi to the Sahid Jaya.

More surprises followed. As the two entered at the hotel lobby, a third Caucasian was awaiting them; the CIA information brief had not anticipated a third person. Maric took a room on the ninth floor; the other two got adjoining rooms on the third.

Pausing to assess the situation, Satsus Intel poured over the hotel registration forms. The third person waiting in the lobby was Ivan Karamajic, a Yugoslav citizen who had entered Indonesia with Ganic. Like Ganic, he claimed to be an engineer working for the Yugoslavian construction giant Energoinvest.

At 2130 hours, all three Yugoslavians descended to the lobby and took a taxi toward the Chinese quarter. While one Satsus Intel team kept tail, another entered the adjoining rooms and installed the two woodblocks recovered from Hotel Indonesia. A listening post was established across the hall.

Regarding Maric's room on the ninth floor, the listening post was too far away for good reception. As an alternative, a CIA snake eye – a tiny microphone on the end of a flexible probe – was inserted under the connecting door from the neighboring room.

By 2240 hours, the three targets returned from dinner and headed to their rooms. The bugs immediately began to pick up suspicious talk. As the two Yugoslavians on the third floor gathered for a late-night discussion, one mentioned that Maric had walked through customs with a clenched fist, a secret signal that he had not attracted suspicion – odd behavior for purported engineers.

Unfortunately for the CIA and Bakin, there were no further revelations over the following two days. Late on 21 July, two days ahead of schedule, Maric boarded a Garuda flight for Sydney via Bali. As he had not violated any Indonesian laws, his departure went unimpeded.

Later that night, however, the two remaining Yugoslavians again raised eyebrows during a late-evening conversation. "There is no problem," said Ganic cryptically. "He will do it. He only needed to be briefed."[24]

Still later that night, those in the listening post heard Karamajic return to his room with an Indonesian female companion. Straining to discern words over the sound of the television, they heard the girl say, "Money is not everything; I should like the man." What came next was the sound of prolonged lovemaking. "It was the most enjoyable surveillance operation of my career," a Satsus Intel veteran said later.[25]

The next day, the two Yugoslavians went shopping. Curiously, the only item they purchased was a Bushnell rifle telescope. This was suspicious activity, but again, not a violation of Indonesian law.

That evening, Karamajic once more took a girl to his room. After a quick round, she asked for payment before leaving. But when the Yugoslavian offered a paltry amount, she began to complain bitterly. To appease her, he promised to pay her 1 million rupiah – a small fortune at that time – if she returned the following morning after he visited his safety deposit box. Though she agreed, Karamajic obviously had no intention of paying: shortly after sunrise on 23 July, both Yugoslavians checked out and took a flight to Bali.

For two more days, Ganic and Karamajic were tailed while lounging in

Bali. As they swam at the hotel pool, their rooms were searched. No incriminating items were uncovered, and the pair was apparently unaware of the Bakin surveillance when they boarded a flight home on 25 July. Kangguru concluded on this anticlimactic note, with no evidence that any Croat neo-Nazi was ever assassinated in Australia.

1   Sumarmo interview.

2   Lowry, *The Armed Forces of Indonesia*, p. 57.

3   Originally born with the single name Harmon, he changed his name to Imron bin Zein while living in Saudi Arabia. B. Wiwoho, *Operasi Woyla*, (Jakarta: PT Menara Gading Nusantara, 1981), p. 175.

4   Media reports from Indonesia later claimed Imron penned a laudatory letter to Iran's Ayatollah Khomeini claiming he headed an Indonesian Islamic Revolutionary Council. There is no evidence in Bakin archives that such a letter was ever posted.

5   By the end of 1980, some of their attacks were against non-religious targets. On 29 December 1980, for example, a member of Imron's group who worked as a security guard at the Jakarta Hilton unsuccessfully attempted to set that establishment ablaze.

6   Imron had been able to obtain two firearms prior to the police post raid: one Garand rifle had been stolen from the army's Logistics Training Center, and one pistol had been stolen from an army colonel whose son was a Imron follower. Bakin Case File, "Pembajakan Garuda."

7   *Bernama*, the Malaysian news agency, made the initial Komando Jihad claim; this was repeated by the French press agency. See *Foreign Broadcast Information Service*, Far East edition, 30 March 1981, p. J8.

8   Friendly/2 had witnessed Mahrizal, later one of the Garuda hijackers, purchasing several expensive Rolex watches in Singapore. But according to Salman Hafidz, both Mahrizal and Imron were partners in exporting turtle eggs to Singapore; this probably accounts for Mahrizal's shopping trip to the city-state. Subandi interview; Bakin Case File, "Pembajakan Garuda."

9   Sumarmo interview.

10 On 25 March 1983, Major General Roedjito – the same officer who two decades earlier had spearheaded intelligence operations during the West Irian campaign – was named the new Bakin deputy chief.

11 In 1974, a Bakin officer was posted to Turkey. Three years later, a representative
    was deployed to Iran. Another two years after that, Bakin opened a station in
    Saudi Arabia.

12 Interview with BIN official, 10 June 2003.

13 During the eighties, Bakin's only operation pertaining to East Timor came in
    1984 when the agency surreptitiously opened all letters going to the province from
    foreign nations. After twelve months without uncovering any suspicious activity,
    the letter-opening campaign was halted. Bakin Case File, "Tim Tim."

14 Bakin maintained an exceedingly thin file on Aceh, most of it concerning the
    overseas movements of Acehnese separatist leader Hasan Tiro. In September 1973
    and again in early 1974, Tiro, who had been in self-exile in the United States since
    the fifties, contacted the Indonesian embassy in Washington and requested a visa
    to visit his family. Bakin reviewed the requests and offered no objections, though
    surveillance was placed on Tiro when he entered Medan in 1974 and Jakarta in
    September 1976. Later in 1976, Tiro ventured to Aceh and, by early 1977, he had
    created GAM. When the military moved in to quell GAM, Bais monopolized all
    intelligence operations in Aceh from that time forward. BPF, "Hasan Tiro."

15 The classified 183-page guide, dated 6 March 1982, was titled *Intern Parpol dan
    Organisasi/Kelompok yang Bergerak di Bidang Politik* ("Domestic Political Parties
    and Organizations/Groups that are Active in Politics").

16 One group of dissidents that caused the New Order special concern was the so-
    called Petition of 50, a collection of fifty former government officials who beginning
    in May 1980 declared their opposition to the Suharto regime. While none were
    arrested, all were continuously harassed. Some of the more vocal members of the
    group were singled out for Satsus Intel surveillance. This included General Ali
    Sadikin, the popular former governor of Jakarta, whose residence phone was
    occasionally tapped between 1983 and 1985. Interview with Ali Sadikin, 30 June
    2003; BPF, "Ali Sadikin."

17 The cancelled 1979 operation on Galang was codenamed *Pelangi* ("Rainbow").
    This was a recycled codename, as Bakin had also used *Pelangi* as the crypt for a
    1975 surveillance operation against the Soviet embassy.

18 In hindsight, the 1982 Galang interviews did not turn up details on any infiltrations.
    Years later, however, Bais discovered that a Vietnamese intelligence officer had
    spent time on Galang disguised as a refugee during the late eighties. That officer,
    ultimately promoted to colonel and serving as Vietnam's defense attaché in Jakarta,
    joined a delegation of military attachés who visited Galang in 2000. By coincidence,

an Indonesian mechanic who had once worked at the refugee camp immediately recognized the colonel and publicly reminded the Vietnamese officer they had worked together in the motor pool – much to the embarrassment of the colonel.

19   Bakin Case File, "Pulau Galang."

20   By May 1978, Friendly/1's access to communist targets of interest was fast dwindling. The CIA was torn: while no longer interested in handling him, it was afraid to terminate its relationship over fear that those with long memories in Kopkamtib might step in to make an arrest. After some backroom guarantees, the CIA cut ties to Friendly/1 in July. This left Friendly/2 as the only agent shared between the CIA and Bakin. BPF, "Munaf (F1)."

21   Bakin Case File, "Nyamuk."

22   Subandi interview.

23   The CIA provided Satsus Intel with two Robot cameras. One was concealed inside an attaché case; the other was disguised inside a small gift-wrapped package.

24   Bakin Case File, "Kangguru."

25   Benny S. interview.

CHAPTER ELEVEN

HARD TARGET

A s much as countries like Vietnam and North Korea – known in CIA parlance as "hard targets" – continued to concern Bakin, none compared to the angst generated by the hardest of targets, the Soviet Union. By the late seventies, Russia's spies in Indonesia were unparalleled in terms of numbers and aggressive tactics during recruitment overtures.

Some of their techniques were as innovative as they were brazen. On at least three occasions, for example, they intentionally rammed their vehicles into cars being driven by Bakin personnel; apologizing profusely, they offered to generously pay for all damages. The catch: they asked for contact details, including home phone numbers.[1]

Another bold tactic involved the relatively new practice of handing out business cards. On 29 November 1980, 36-year old Alexandr Pavlovich Finenko, the Aeroflot station manager in Jakarta, had ventured into the waiting room at an eye clinic behind Hotel Indonesia. Frequented by military personnel, one of the patients that day was Lieutenant Colonel Sukerman. An officer with the East Java military command, Sukerman noted the Russian was handing out name cards to everybody in the waiting room under the pretext of looking for language tutors. When he finished his examination fifteen minutes later and prepared to leave, the officer was approached by Finenko. Accepting a card for himself, Sukerman naively offered his telephone number in return.

Predictably, Finenko had enticed Sukerman out for dinner by week's end. Looking to prolong the relationship, he phoned the officer several additional times. One of those calls, on the evening of 27 January 1981, was from Finenko's home phone. As this was subject to a Satsus Intel teltap, Bakin was soon able to identify Sukerman as the recipient.[2] After placing the lieutenant colonel under surveillance for several months, he was finally brought in for questioning on 8 June. Though no charges were filed – Sukerman had not yet broken any laws – the case did serve to cast a pall of suspicion over Finenko. Because Soviet military intelligence had used Aeroflot as a cover in several other countries, Bakin, from that point forward, considered him to be a likely GRU officer.[3]

But while Finenko had engaged in highly suspicious activity, Satsus Intel at the time was inundated by targets and did not have the capabilities to keep the Aeroflot manager under anything more than routine teltap surveillance. On the evening of 21 January 1982, almost one full year after the suspect call to Sukerman, Finenko was recorded having a cryptic conversation with an unidentified Indonesian female (UIF) and an unidentified Indonesian male (UIM):

UIF:	*Hallo.*
Finenko:	*Selamat malam.* [Good evening.]
UIF:	*Selamat malam.* [Good evening.]
Finenko:	*Papa ada?* [Is Papa there?]
UIF:	*Dari siapa?* [Who is this?]
Finenko:	*Papa ada di rumah?* [Is Papa home?]
UIF:	*Ada.* [He's home.]
Finenko:	*Bisa panggil?* [Can you call him?]
UIF:	*Ya.*
UIM:	*Hallo.*
Finenko:	*Selamat malam.* [Good evening.]
UIM:	*Selamat malam.* [Good evening.]
Finenko:	Thank you very much.
UIM:	You are welcome.
Finenko:	How is everything?
UIM:	Ok, all right.
Finenko:	Do you remember next meeting?
UIM:	Pardon me?
Finenko:	Do you remember next meeting?
UIM:	When?

Finenko: *Ah…tanggal 4.* [Ah…the fourth.]

UIM: 4 February…ya.

Finenko: *Tahu mana?* [Do you remember where?]

UIM: *Di mana?* [Where?]

Finenko: *Jawa Tengah.* [Central Java.]

UIM: *Jawa Tengah, ya, ya.* [Central Java, yes, yes.]

Finenko: *Ya, sampaikan salamya.* [Yes, until then stay well.]

UIM: *Ya.*

Finenko: *Terima kasih sekali lagi, selamat malam.* [Thanks again, good night.]

Because of the backlog in transcribing the dozens of Satsus Intel bug readouts, this 21 January conversation had yet to analyzed when a second call was placed by Finenko two evenings later:

UIM: *Hallo.*

Finenko: *Selamat malam.* [Good evening.]

UIM: *Selamat malam.* [Good evening.]

Finenko: *Apa kabar?* [How are you?]

UIM: *Baik. Bagaimana?* [Good. How are you?]

Finenko: *Ah..sedikit kurang baik.* [Ah…not too good.]

UIM: *Huh?*

Finenko: *Tidak kelihatan.* [I can't see them.]

UIM: *Semua?* [All?]

Finenko: *Semua, ya.* [All, yes.]

UIM: *Huh?*

Finenko: *Perlu tambah lampu.* [You need to add another lamp.]

UIM: *Oh, perlu tambah lampu.* [Oh, I need to add another lamp.]

Finenko: *Itu lampu kira-kira 60 centimeter dari material.* [The lamp has to be about 60 centimeters from the material.]

UIM: *Tambah satu lampu lagi.* [Add one more lamp.]

Finenko: *Eh.* [Right.]

UIM: *Ya.*

Finenko: *Sekali lagi, ya?* [One more time, yes?]

UIM: *Bisa, bisa.* [I can, I can.]

Finenko: *Dan 4 Februari?* [And 4 February?]

UIM: *Ya, ya, saya bawa.* [Yes, yes, I will bring.]

Finenko: *Terima kasih.* [Thank you.]
UIM: *Kembali.* [You are welcome.]
Finenko: *Selamat malam.* [Good night.]
UIM: *Selamat malam.* [Good night.]

It was another three days, on 26 January, before the first of these calls was transcribed and circulated between Bakin and the CIA. Though it was a major violation of tradecraft, Finenko appeared to be speaking in rather open terms with an indigenous agent. A quick check showed that the Aeroflot manager, who had arrived in Indonesia in February 1978, was scheduled to end his tour in just over two weeks. Bakin officers surmised that, with little time remaining, Finenko had grown careless in order to rush the turnover of his agent to a new Soviet handler.

By the next day, 27 January, Satsus Intel had been able to trace the recipient of Finenko's call. Yohanes Baptista Susdaryanto, a 48-year old Catholic from Central Java, was a lieutenant colonel in the Indonesian navy. A hydrographic specialist trained in the U.S. during the early sixties, he had worked at the navy's hydro-oceanographic service for all of the previous decade. He lived with his wife and three children in Tanjung Priok, a district near Jakarta's port.

Three days later, Susdaryanto's home and office phones had taps in place. In addition, the readout from the 23 January phone call had been transcribed and analyzed. Judging from this second exchange, the navy officer had probably made a dead drop of film shortly before the first call. But as the film had been underexposed, this prompted Finenko to ring again. Susdaryanto would apparently be bringing new rolls of film to their scheduled meeting on 4 February at Jawa Tengah, a restaurant on Jalan Pemuda in East Jakarta.

All of this put Bakin in a bit of a bind. When General Yoga was briefed on the case, he feared potential blowback in having his agency take the lead in a high-profile arrest of a military officer. "Don't get directly involved," he warned his deputy in charge of foreign operations. "Give it to Benny."[4]

General Moerdani, as was his style, did not duck the challenge. Putting on his military intelligence hat, he handed the assignment to the Kopkamtib intelligence task force headed by Brigadier General M.I. Sutaryo. But as he pragmatically recognized the superior surveillance abilities of Satsus Intel – especially during its good showing alongside his own men during the 1977

Tinguely case – Moerdani invited the Bakin spycatchers to participate alongside Sutaryo's unit. Their joint operation was codenamed *Pantai* ("Beach"), a reference to Susdaryanto's residence near the port.

With time running short, the Pantai task force huddled on 1 February to plan its course of action. It agreed that the navy was not to be informed, as word might leak to the targeted lieutenant colonel. It also agreed that, with Finenko on the eve of returning to the Soviet Union, it did not have the luxury of planning a complex doubling or disinformation campaign. Rather, it would place Susdaryanto under continuous surveillance over the next three days and arrest him on the morning of his scheduled tryst. If possible, he would be enticed into keeping his meeting with Finenko; if the naval officer could be witnessed handing classified material to the Russian, this was grounds for arresting the Aeroflot manager. And since the Aeroflot manager did not have diplomatic immunity, he would be subject to the death penalty.

According to plan, Satsus Intel had operatives positioned along Jalan Menteng in Tanjung Priok on the morning of Thursday, 4 February. At 0635 hours, they watched Susdaryanto, his chauffeur, and an elderly Indonesian male get in the subject's Daihatsu jeep. Eight minutes later, as the jeep slowed along Jalan Raya Pelabuhan to make a turn, Kopkamtib vehicles boxed in Susdaryanto's vehicle near the curb. A military police van immediately pulled alongside; all three occupants of the jeep were loaded into the van, which sped off in seconds.

In custody, Susdaryanto wilted. Quickly admitting to acts of espionage, he agreed to keep his scheduled meeting with Finenko that evening. He also agreed to carry two rolls of film, which would be hidden inside a Pepsodent toothpaste box.

At 1800 hours, Satsus Intel operatives were in place in front of Jawa Tengah. Hidden in the back of the restaurant was a team of troops ready to make an arrest. And sitting at one of the tables was Major Jacob Sutardi, the Satsus Intel deputy commander; he had taken along his wife and three children, all unaware of what was about to unfold.

One hour later, a Japanese compact car passed by the front of the restaurant. Coming to a halt 200 meters down the road, a Caucasian male exited the vehicle and entered the restaurant. He was directed to a table a few meters from Sutardi and his family.

A few minutes after that, Susdaryanto's jeep pulled into the front of Jawa

Tengah. As he entered the restaurant, the navy officer was in for a surprise. The waiting Russian was not Finenko but Lieutenant Colonel Sergei Egorov, the Soviet assistant military attaché. In hushed tones over bottles of Anker beer, the 38-year old Egorov, who had been in Indonesia since August 1980, explained that he would be taking over as Susdaryanto's case officer.[5]

Egorov quickly showed himself to be a tough taskmaster. As the pair chatted for the next hour, the Russian officer rattled off a litany of demands. He began by asking for physical data on the Makassar Strait. Then he asked whether the U.S. had an early warning system at sea; if so, Susdaryanto was to try to get details. After that came a request for biographical data on key naval officers. He stressed the need for Susdaryanto to seek out better documents than in the past.

Tuning to administrative matters, Egorov handed over radio frequencies that Susdaryanto would use over the coming year and an envelope with a stipend of 300,000 rupiah.

All the while, the Pepsodent box filled with the film canisters remained on the table. In order to arrest the Russian for espionage, he needed to take custody of the film. From the neighboring table, Major Sutardi kept track of the toothpaste box from the corner of his eye. Noticing his diverted attention, Jacob's wife began to complain. Juggling his wife's concern and the subjects' actions, the major finally saw the Russian pick up the box and place it in his bag.

"Arrest him!" Jacob screamed as he rose to his feet. Bursting from the back of the restaurant, troops smothered Susdaryanto and Egorov. They were placed in separate vans and hauled off to detention.[6]

In shackles at the military police brig, Egorov's identity was soon confirmed. Though he had diplomatic immunity, the Indonesian authorities delayed his release for several hours. When he failed to return home that night, the attaché's wife contacted colleagues at the Soviet embassy. Fearing the worst, Finenko was recorded making a nervous call to Susdaryanto's house early the following morning. As with the rest of her family, Susdaryanto's daughter was unaware of the previous evening's developments:

Finenko: *Mama ada?* [Is your mother home?]
UIF: *Ini dari siapa?* [Who is this?]
Finenko: *Kawannya. Bapak Sus di mana?* [A friend. Where is Susdaryanto?]

UIF: *Sedang keluar kota.* [He's out of town.]

Finenko: *Kapan papa berangkat?* [When did your papa leave?]

UIF: *Kemarin siang.* [Yesterday noon.]

Finenko: *Kapan akan pulang...pergi ke mana? Ke Bogor?* [When will he return...where did he go? To Bogor?]

UIF: *Tidak tahu.* [I don't know.]

Finenko: *Nanti malam akan menelpon lagi.* [I will call again tonight.]

By noon on 5 February, everything became clear when Egorov was released and the Soviet ambassador was summoned to the Ministry of Foreign Affairs. For activities inconsistent with his diplomatic status – doublespeak for espionage – Egorov was declared *persona non grata* and given two days to leave Indonesia. Not revealed to the ambassador was the fact that an arrest warrant had been prepared for Finenko, who did not enjoy diplomatic immunity.

To meet his deadline, Egorov was at Jakarta's international airport at 1800 hours on 6 February to catch a Garuda flight to Singapore. Also queuing at the Garuda counter, trying to attract as little attention as possible, was Finenko and a protocol officer from the Soviet embassy. When Indonesian authorities moved in for an arrest, the protocol officer started a fistfight as a diversion. Both were detained, though the protocol officer was soon released on account of his diplomatic status.

In the meantime, a raid of Susdaryanto's house netted a treasure trove of espionage equipment. Among the items collected was a Grundig *Satelit 2100* radio set, an Asahi Pentax camera mounted on a photographic table, and over a dozen rolls of specialized Fuji SS high-speed film.

Other evidence taken from the house was equally damning. Susdaryanto had retained copies of Soviet instructions for meeting dates and venues, dead drop locations, and lists of questions pertaining to security matters. There were also one-time pads – used for encrypting and decrypting radio messages – as well as a decoded message that read, "Thank you very much for the fruitful business cooperation. Hope it will be successfull [*sic*]."

Against this body of evidence, and facing a death sentence, Finenko was not talking. Going on a hunger strike and claiming he was suffering from acute asthma, he was searched on 10 February and found to have a nail concealed in his pocket. Fearing he might try to commit suicide, an army doctor examined him two days later and found him in good health.

By that time, the Indonesian government had milked the issue for all it was worth. With newspapers headlining anti-Soviet articles the entire week, hundreds of students on 10 February picketed in front of the Soviet embassy. That same day, the authorities ordered the Soviets to close one of their three consulates.[7]

On the morning of Saturday, 13 February, Finenko was unexpectedly taken from the military police brig and rushed to the airport. There, as that morning's Aeroflot flight was ready to depart, he was the last to board. Two days after that, Aeroflot announced a halt to further operations in Indonesia.

Though Finenko was gone, the Susdaryanto saga was just beginning. Starting later that week and continuing through August, the lieutenant colonel underwent intensive interrogation by the military police and Satsus Intel. His revelations shocked them to the core. Back in 1976, a Russian named Vladimir – Susdaryanto never knew his full name, or if Vladimir was an alias – had walked into the navy's hydro-oceanographic office with a broad smile and an open wallet. Claiming he intended to dock Morflot vessels at Tanjung Priok, he said he wanted to buy supplies for his seamen.

Because he spoke English well from his training in the U.S., Susdaryanto handled negotiations with the Russian. Vladimir soon dropped his tone, asking the lieutenant colonel if he could help procure maritime charts. As the maps were not classified, Susdaryanto replied in the affirmative; he also agreed to turn them over at a dinner later that week.

The dinner proved to be a clincher. After asking a torrent of personal questions, Vladimir made clear that he would pay handsomely for maps and any documents that Susdaryanto could obtain. The lieutenant colonel thought for a moment. As Catholics, he and most of his religious peers faced a glass ceiling preventing higher promotion.[8] And given the fact that he had been languishing in the hydro-oceanographic office for years with no clear career path, he quickly justified treason within his own mind. Staring back at Vladimir, he nodded his assent.

For their next meeting, some safety precautions were taken. Boarding a taxi, Susdaryanto drove to a steakhouse in Menteng. Stepping inside, he saw Vladimir already seated in a corner booth. After some small talk, they swapped manila envelopes: Susdaryanto received a wad of rupiah notes; Vladimir received a stack of reports. Finishing dinner, Vladimir departed early to photocopy the pages. Half an hour later, his Volvo passed by the steakhouse, where a waiting Susdaryanto retrieved his documents.

During this initial meeting, the two agreed to rendezvous on the second Thursday of each month at a prearranged venue. In the event one of the two did not show, their alternate date was the third Thursday. Over the course of three more meetings, Susdaryanto brought along a wealth of documents, including the results of oceanographic surveys done in cooperation with Japan, Malaysia, and Singapore, and the U.S. In each case, Vladimir quickly photocopied the pages and brought them back to the restaurant. For his troubles, the lieutenant colonel was paid a total of 600,000 rupiah.

In 1977, Vladimir announced his imminent return to the Soviet Union. During their following meeting at the Jawa Timur restaurant, he brought along his replacement. Introduced as Yuri – Susdaryanto never knew his full name – the new case officer soon injected more safety protocols into their relationship.[9] Instead of borrowing documents for photocopying, for example, late that year he provided the lieutenant colonel with an Asahi Pentax camera. He also provided special film: placed inside normal Fuji SS canisters, the film could only be developed with a secret mix of chemicals; commercial film processing would reveal no images.

With his Pentax, Susdaryanto could now copy the documents at his house without the need to carry them to a meeting. Going one step further, Yuri coached his agent in the use of dead drops. For their purposes, a dead drop was a location that was close to a road and sufficiently tranquil where Susdaryanto could hide a package containing film canisters. Susdaryanto eventually chose two such hiding spots in Jakarta, one at Pulo Mas in East Jakarta and another under a door at an electrical substation in Pluit, North Jakarta.

Very quickly, Susdaryanto put the dead drops to frequent use. On the pretext of pulling by the side of the road to urinate, he would approach one of his two hiding spots and secrete a bamboo tube filled with plastic-wrapped film canisters. In this manner, he left monthly hauls of survey results and other reports issued by the hydro-oceanographic service.

During 1978, Yuri took one further precaution. Turning over a Grundig radio set, he instructed his agent to monitor designated frequencies at a specific time every month. Hidden in Russian broadcasts were simple coded English messages, giving Susdaryanto such information as the time and location of their next meeting.

In September 1979, Yuri finished his Indonesia tour and a handover was made to a third case officer. Alexandr Finenko – who went by the alias "Robert" – quickly bonded with Susdaryanto on account of his easy personality and knowledge of the Indonesian language.

But for all of Finenko's good rapport, he also showed occasional lapses in discretion. Several of his meetings with Susdaryanto, for example, were in high-profile locations like the Hilton. He also had his agent bring along the wife and children for a few of the meetings, including a weekend excursion to a resort in Bogor where he coached Susdaryanto in the use of one-time pads and radio transmissions.

In a further lapse in judgment, Finenko invited Susdaryanto to his residence in early 1981. (Coincidentally, Finenko rented the house next to the former NLF office which was the target of Satsus Intel bugs during the seventies.) While there, he was shown a variety of sophisticated radio gear, which Finenko promised would be supplied to his agent in due course.

But despite these lapses, the pair had yet to attract the attention of the Indonesian authorities through late 1981. That December, the two met in the parking lot of the Jawa Tengah restaurant. After informing his agent that he would be departing Indonesia in February 1982, Finenko pressed Susdaryanto to prepare one last batch of photographed documents under his watch. The Soviet operative was especially interested in the depth and water conditions along the Lombok Strait, which the Soviets were apparently contemplating as an alternate submarine route instead of the Malacca Strait.

Acting as instructed, Susdaryanto shot the film and delivered it to the Pulo Mas dead drop site on 21 January 1982. Perhaps unable to resist the temptation to place a call so close to his departure date, Finenko had phoned his thanks that evening – a final lapse in security which ultimately spelled doom for his prized agent.

In August 1984, after already languishing in prison for more than two years, Susdaryanto went on trial. He had been paid a total of 5 million rupiah by the Soviets over the course of almost six years, and for that the state prosecutors wanted him to serve thirteen years. He was eventually sentenced to ten, less the time already spent in detention.

In the wake of the Aeroflot case, the Indonesian authorities redoubled efforts to keep Soviet diplomats under close watch. Much of this effort was handled by Bakin's Satsus Intel, though part of the burden was given to Kopkamtib's intelligence task force. It was this latter unit, while tailing Third Secretary Aleksei Bobrov on 4 August 1982, which watched him enter into an animated conversation with a young Indonesian male inside the national museum on Jalan Merdeka Barat.

Initially, no red flags were raised by the museum exchange. But on three further occasions over the next month, Bobrov was seen having meals with the same Indonesian. A quick background check of Bobrov indicated no known overseas postings prior to his arrival in Indonesia during August 1981, but he was filling a vacancy left by a departing KGB officer. A background check of the Indonesian, meanwhile, revealed him to be a 23-year old journalism student from Central Java named Mamat; he had no police record or known political affiliation.

Sensing the onset of a Soviet recruitment effort, Mamat was brought in for Kopkamtib questioning on 9 October. Suitably intimidated by the authorities, the university student wrote a long report detailing his contacts with Bobrov to date. It appeared that both Mamat and the Soviet officer had gone to the museum back on 4 August for reasons other than the historical displays: the student was looking for foreigners with whom he could practice English, and the Soviet was apparently trolling for local contacts. Striking up a conversation for half an hour, Bobrov had invited him to a nearby restaurant for lunch. Mamat wasted no time asking if there were positions available at the Soviet embassy; while Bobrov said there were none, he offered to pay for reports on topics like U.S.-Indonesian relations.

Thirteen days later, Bobrov and Mamat had their second meeting. Again, they rendezvoused among the displays at the national museum. During that occasion, Bobrov had asked if the student had any friends in the Ministry of Information. The reason for this, said Bobrov, was because he wanted to obtain copies of a recent press law. Mamat said he did have one acquaintance at the ministry, and would attempt to procure a copy of the requested document.

Mamat's written confession continued. Over the course of their next two meetings, Bobrov gave the student further easy tasks, such as finding copies of books on Indonesia's diplomatic relations. He also encouraged the student to seek work at the Ministry of Foreign Affairs or the U.S. embassy. As a final item, they scheduled their next meeting for 28 October.

So that Kopkamtib could observe where the relationship would lead, Mamat was released and given permission to keep his scheduled 28 October rendezvous. He was forbidden, however, from telling Bobrov about his interrogation.

Two further meetings later, with Bobrov giving his university prospect more simple tasks, Satsus Intel was briefed on the case. Assuming control from Kopkamtib, the Bakin spycatchers tailed both Bobrov and the student through the end of November. At that point, they brought in Mamat for another round of questioning. Judging him sufficiently trustworthy to recruit, they gave him the codename *Kemuning* ("Mock Orange"). The overall case against Bobrov was assigned the crypt *Museum*, a reference to the location where he first befriended the student.

On 9 December, Kemuning held his first lunch meeting with Bobrov as a Bakin agent. The simple tasks continued, with the KGB officer asking him to collect newspaper clippings about Suharto's recent overseas trips. He was also asked to make initial contact with an Indonesian staff member working at the U.S. embassy's library. For his troubles, Mamat was offered a monthly stipend of 40,000 rupiah.

Briefed about the Museum case by Satsus Intel, the CIA weighed in on 21 December. The KGB recruitment of Mamat was taking place along classical Soviet lines, noted a CIA memo to Bakin. Bobrov had made initial contact and an assessment, then slowly cultivated his agent by assigning simple tasks as a test. As the assessment was still ongoing, Mamat had not been asked to do anything illegal thus far.[10]

While the first inclination of Bakin might have been to set up Bobrov for expulsion, the CIA urged otherwise. Through Kemuning, there was good potential for squeezing information out of Bobrov about the KGB presence and its activities in Indonesia. For example, Kemuning could quiz his Soviet handler about how and why he should get information from the U.S. embassy librarian. The CIA suggested that Kemuning not be given any classical training in order to make his conduct appear as unrehearsed as possible; however, they cautioned that Kemuning needed to be monitored to ensure he did not become too attached to Bobrov.

Over the next twelve months, Bobrov and Mamat continued their delicate dance. The tasks from the KGB officer were getting slightly more involved; in January 1983, for example, the student was asked to reconnoiter eight residential addresses used by U.S. diplomats. Meetings were often held more than once a month; about half were car pickups by Bobrov and the other half were "car tosses" where Mamat threw a package of information into an open car window. Perhaps illustrating an indication of the strong potential the KGB saw in Mamat, Bobrov had forsaken his annual home leave in mid-1982 and again in mid-1983.

At the close of 1983, Bobrov finally returned to Moscow for vacation and did not return to Jakarta until March 1984. The following month, he picked up Mamat in a car without diplomatic plates and, for the first time, took him to the home of a Soviet television reporter in Kebayoran Baru. At this safe site, the KGB officer dropped pretenses and asked the student to work for the Soviet Union. The CIA later surmised that Bobrov had given a detailed report on Mamat during his extended home leave, and had been given approval to make a formal recruitment.

Since the KGB had upped the ante, Bakin and the CIA looked to get more innovative. Since Bobrov was scheduled to finish his tour in December 1984, they predicted that he would be under pressure to show solid gains from his agent. The CIA suggested that Kemuning ask for more money and initially appear to be productive, possibly by claiming he had recruited a source in the Ministry of Foreign Affairs. After that, Kemuning was to become more problematic and less cooperative. As Bobrov grew stressed with time running short, Bakin could then explore ways in which he could be manipulated.

As it turned out, however, Bobrov continued his meetings through the remainder of 1984 without showing any apparent rush to obtain results. At year's end, he finished his tour and turned over handling of the agent to Second Secretary Vladimir Yaravoi. A dour case officer trained as a Chinese linguist, Yaravoi made little secret that he wanted reassignment to Beijing.

Behind the scenes, Bakin and the CIA conjured further ways to dangle Kemuning to their added advantage. In March 1985, they agreed to ply him with fake classified documents. After feeding these to Yaravoi for a time, they would then reveal the ruse to the KGB officer. Not only would this put a dent in his ego, but it would also put him in a bad position with his superiors and reduce his chances for a coveted reassignment to China. Demoralized, Yaravoi might be susceptible to recruitment.

Yaravoi, however, was not playing according to script. Still not tasking Mamat to do anything bold or illegal, he was instead asked to continue checking addresses of U.S. diplomats and to befriend local staff at the U.S. embassy.

In November 1985, Mamat, who by that time had graduated and was working as a freelance journalist, was handed over to his third Soviet case officer. Like his predecessors, Attaché Leonid Botchkov pressed the Indonesian to do little more than survey locales around Jakarta. This continued until January 1987 when, during a meeting at a Menteng fast food restaurant, Botchkov seemed ready to ratchet up their relationship to a new level. Not only was Mamat given a series of foreign policy topics to research, but he was also told to start taking English lessons and to cultivate contacts in the Ministry of Information.

During their next scheduled meeting on 19 February, Mamat diligently arrived at the rendezvous point. He was carrying an envelope of documents about the topics requested by Botchkov; all had been vetted by Bakin. He also possessed brochures from an English-language training center. But after waiting an hour without spotting his Soviet handler, Mamat returned home by taxi.

One week later, on their fallback date, Mamat was back at the same restaurant. Again, Botchkov did not show.

As an added fallback measure, Mamat had agreed with his handler to wait on Jalan Langsat at 1900 hours on the first Thursday of the month. Accordingly, on 5 March he spent nearly an hour at the prescribed street corner. Once more, the Soviet diplomat was a no-show.

After briefing his Satsus Intel handlers, Kemuning was ordered to wait for several mornings during April at a street corner near Botchkov's residence. Two days before month's end, he spotted the Soviet diplomat approach in a Toyota; Botchkov, however, sped by without pause.

Persisting, Kemuning was back on the same street corner on the morning of 4 May. This time, Botchkov cracked open a window and tossed out a crumpled piece of brown paper as he passed his erstwhile agent. The paper was torn from a book and featured a drawing of a *langsat*, a small, yellow fruit that comes from the Lansium tree. Assuming this was a signal to go to their Jalan Langsat rendezvous site that evening, he waited nearly half an hour. As before, no one showed.

On that anticlimactic note, Kemuning was ordered by Bakin to stand down. He had played the Soviets for over four years, and had received millions of rupiah during the course of his service. At no point, however, did his KGB handlers give Mamat any illegal assignments or reveal much about their activities.[11]

The entire Bakin campaign against Soviet intelligence, in fact, was rife with question marks and abortive efforts. Through 1989 – when Moscow withdrew from Afghanistan, setting the stage for the Soviet Union's eventual collapse – Satsus Intel had registered no less than 102 cases in which Soviet diplomats engaged or attempted to engage in espionage with Indonesian citizens. Of these, only two – Franky Wena in 1974 and Susdaryanto in 1982 – had resulted in trials that yielded prison sentences. The rest were allowed to float in legal limbo, if that. "There was a sense among many that the Cold War concerned only the Soviets and Americans," reflected one top Bakin officer. "And if an Indonesian was able to trick the Soviets into paying him cash, so be it."[12]

1   During all three of the faux automobile accidents, the Bakin personnel refused Soviet compensation.

2   The number of Satsus Intel teltaps against Soviet targets peaked in 1979 at sixteen. By 1981, the number of Soviet taps had been slightly reduced to thirteen.

3   BPF, "Sukerman."

4   Djajusman interview.

5   Egorov did not reveal his true name to Susdaryanto during the Jawa Tengah meeting; rather, he referred to himself as "Wito."

6   Sutardi interview.

7   The consulate in Banjarmasin, South Kalimantan, was closed as a result of Finenko's arrest. The Soviets were allowed to maintain two other consulates in Medan and Surabaya.

8   Perhaps not by coincidence, anecdotal evidence suggests that a disproportionate number of Indonesians recruited by foreign intelligence services have been Catholic or Protestant. This may be part of a conscious attempt to exploit grievances felt by Indonesia's religious minorities.

9   The identities of Vladimir and Yuri were never conclusively determined by Indonesian investigators.

10 Bakin Case File, "Museum."

11 It was never conclusively determined why Botchkov abruptly terminated contact with Kemuning. The possibility of a mole inside Bakin cannot be discounted.

The existence of such a mole was suggested in October 1979 when former Satsus Intel officer Bram Mandagi was approached in a Jakarta restaurant by two Soviet intelligence officers. In their subsequent failed attempts to recruit Bram, the Soviets tried to sway him by revealing privileged and accurate information about Satsus Intel members – information that could only have been gleaned from an inside source. Mandagi interview; Bakin Case File, "Fatahillah."

12 Djajusman interview.

CHAPTER TWELVE

FREEFALL

On 2 June 1989, an era came to an end. After more than fifteen years, Yoga Sugomo hung up his proverbial cloak and dagger as Bakin's spymaster. Elevated as the new chief was Major General Sudibyo, Yoga's deputy for the previous year. The robust, affable Sudibyo did not enjoy a special relationship with the president like his predecessor. He did, however, have a long history in military intelligence, including a tour in Bais.

As it turned out, Sudibyo's military intelligence background was a double-edged sword. Because of his close, cordial links with the upper echelon in Bais, he was sure to soften inter-service rivalries. But after he introduced fourteen lieutenant colonels to key positions in Bakin, he alienated senior civilian officials in his own agency. Compounding matters was his unapologetic subservience to Benny Moerdani, who, after being elevated to Minister of Defense and Security in 1988, continued to favor military intelligence at the expense of its civilian counterpart. "Benny saw Bakin focused more on analysis," admitted Sudibyo, "like Australia's Office of National Assessments."[1]

This Australian comparison was telling. As the name implied, the Office of National Assessments was a wholly analytical body that depended on information collected by other agencies; it had no operational ability of its own. By holding this up for emulation, Sudibyo saw little problem in further scaling back what little operational capabilities were left in Bakin.

The Indonesian government was comfortable with gutting Bakin due to a growing sense of national complacency. By the close of the eighties, the country's economy was running strong and it enjoyed cordial ties with all of its neighbors. On the domestic scene, none of the nation's simmering insurgencies was seen as particularly problematic: in a classified, multi-volume Intelligence Encyclopedia published by Bakin in 1990, only eight pages were devoted to Fretilin separatists in East Timor; student political activities, by contrast, received 30 pages of coverage.[2]

Even Indonesia's traditional foreign threats no longer inspired the same concern as in the past. The Soviet empire, for one, was visibly fraying along the periphery and seemed destined to place second in the Cold War. Connected to this, Vietnam was talking up a humble withdrawal from Cambodia and seemed less disposed toward military adventurism. Even China, which for years struck a deep negative chord due to its earlier support of the PKI, had embraced capitalism and, in 1990, was allowed to reopen an embassy in Jakarta.[3]

North Korea, alone, was the only remaining communist nation that was still viewed as a potentially dangerous wild card. This was driven home in September 1987 when Third Secretary Kim Chol Min, under random Bakin surveillance, was spotted meeting with a young, bookish Indonesian male. The pair was seen rendezvousing for a second time the following month.

Among Bakin's spycatchers, the two meetings set off warning bells. Formerly known as Satsus Intel, and now going by the name Operational Unit 01 (*Unit Pelaksana* 01, or UP 01), they were struck by a sense of déjà vu: just as the Soviets had tried to cultivate journalism hopeful Mamat, the North Koreans seemed intent on recruiting a student of their own.[4]

A quick background check of the subject proved this to be the case. The Indonesian was a 28-year old born to a Sundanese police officer and a mother from North Sulawesi, and he had been adopted by a Chinese family soon after birth. One year earlier, he had entered the prestigious University of Indonesia as a graduate student-*cum*-teaching assistant.

Taking a page out of the earlier Museum case, UP 01 looked to bring in the student for questioning and possible recruitment as a double agent. On 16 November, he was summoned to a local police post, where UP 01 operatives posing as police officers sat him in a bare room and asked if he had contact with North Korea. Pokerfaced, the student offered a firm denial.

A staredown ensured. Handing him a bowl of candies, the Bakin officers left the student alone to reconsider his answer. When they returned five minutes later, they found him in tears. Given a pen and paper, he was told to detail his contacts to date. It proved to be an amazing tale. Back in 1977, as an energetic young undergraduate, he had knocked on the doors of several embassies – including North Korea's – to acquire material for research papers. Five years later, in 1982, he visited both the North and South Korean embassies to get information for a thesis he was writing on Korean reunification.

Eventually, the North Koreans took closer notice. Having left behind his contact details, the following year the student was paid a surprise home visit by one of the embassy's junior diplomats. North Korea wanted his friendship, he was told, which soon translated into frequent invitations to embassy functions. By 1984, the relationship was upgraded to occasional dinners with Kim Chol Min. Just like the Museum case, the Koreans patiently stoked the student's ego but did not ask him to perform any illegal acts.

By early 1986, Kim Chol Min looked to invest more in the student prospect by inviting him to Pyongyang. As this was an especially sensitive issue for Indonesians, the diplomat offered to take him via China with no suspect stamps in his passport. The student agreed to the plan, and, on 28 September, departed Jakarta for Hong Kong, then crossed into China. Making his way to the North Korean embassy in Beijing, he was received by Kim Chol Min and flown to Pyongyang.

The next eight days made a deep impression on the Indonesian. Plied with hundreds of dollars in spending money, he was chaperoned among Pyongyang's key monuments and garish tourist sites. As he prepared to leave, escort Kim made no secret that he hoped his protégé would pursue a career in the foreign ministry.

The student had apparently enjoyed the attention of the North Koreans over the past five years. But now confronted by UP 01, he agreed almost instantly to work on behalf of the government. As Bakin's newest agent, he was given the call sign *Melati* ("Jasmine").[5]

As it turned out, Melati was recruited just as Kim Chol Min was on his way out of Indonesia. For his next tryst on 28 November, he was met at his house by newly arrived Second Secretary Kim Jong Min. Probably in a reflection of the greater importance they were attaching to Melati, the newest Kim was more senior in rank – and far more demanding. At their opening meeting, he rattled off a list of requirements: Melati was to obtain information regarding the number of athletes and officials Indonesia was planning to send to the upcoming Summer Olympics in Seoul; South Korean business activities in Indonesia; and Indonesian government attitudes toward both North and South Korea. If possible, he was even to get data on U.S. military forces stationed in the Philippines and South Korea. And on top of all this, he was asked to commission an artisan to make a traditional *wayang* shadow puppet – but with the face of North Korean leader Kim Il Sung![6]

For the next six months, Melati had monthly meetings with his Korean case officer. The tasks he was given were time consuming but exceedingly benign, sometimes laughable. Kim Jong Min wanted a photocopy of *Military Technology* magazine, for example, even though it was easily available for subscription.

So benign were the tasks, in fact, that UP 01 began to wonder if Melati was reporting the truth about his interactions with Kim. To put him to the test, Bakin in August 1988 conjured a means of technical verification. Having already known the time and place where Melati was scheduled to hold his next monthly meeting, UP 01 operatives disguised as waiters were waiting. Looking to take advantage of a common practice at many restaurants – especially traditional eateries where hands were used in lieu of utensils – they had concealed a microphone in the large, ornate box of tissues brought to the table after eating had commenced.

Unbeknownst to Melati, a van parked outside the restaurant recorded his every word with Kim Jong Min that evening. The Korean steered their talk to a series of foreign policy issues. Melati, by contrast, spoke about his need for money to pay tuition. When he met with UP 01 representatives later that week and recounted his dialogue, it matched perfectly with the transcript. Melati, they were assured, was not double-dealing.

For the next two years, things barely strayed from this formula. Melati would meet with his Korean case officer, be given easy tasks and sometimes paid a cash bonus, and then report the proceedings to his Bakin handler. In September 1990, however, he took leave of Indonesia for a year of study in England at the University of Birmingham. The Koreans encouraged the move, as they felt it would enhance his chances of landing a berth at the Ministry of Foreign Affairs.

Upon Melati's return to Jakarta, the Koreans wasted no time resuming contact. Kim Jong Min had already ended his tour and returned to Pyongyang; his new case officer was First Secretary Hwong Muong Su. Again, Melati was being handled by progressively more senior diplomats, which was further evidence that they saw strong eventual dividends from their investment.

Part of that investment involved inviting Melati back to Pyongyang. During a visit to Melati's house in January 1992, Hwong offered to send the student agent to North Korea in April to attend the eightieth birthday celebrations for Kim Il Sung. It was planned as a major extravaganza, with garish festivities and military parades.

Returning to his Bakin handlers, Melati outlined the trip proposal. Bakin, in turn, discussed the idea with three of its foreign counterparts that had an interest in North Korean developments. All three thought the trip worthwhile, if only to see who else attended.

Rendezvousing with Hwong in March, Melati confirmed his attendance. The Korean, visibly pleased, promised to make airline reservations. He also requested that the student compose a birthday letter for Kim Il Sung. Hwong said he would give Melati a large envelope of cash to go with the letter; once in Pyongyang, Melati was instructed to falsely claim that the money was a gift to the Korean dictator from the Indonesian people.

As Melati's April departure date drew near, Bakin's counterparts began to forward wish lists of questions. One foreign intelligence agency wanted to know details about North Korean immigration procedures, what other persons were in his group, and where he stayed. Another wanted to know about Kim Il Sung's health, about economic conditions, and whether reconciliation with South Korea was discussed. Still another offered to provide a video camera; Melati rejected this as too likely to draw suspicion because his case officer knew he did not own such equipment.

On 25 April, after taking a circuitous route via Beijing, Melati was in Pyongyang's reviewing stands. Kim Il Sung, who had been named "Great Marshal" two weeks earlier, made an appropriately grand appearance. His son and heir apparent, Kim Jong Il, who had been named "Marshal" that morning, also arrived to much pomp and circumstance.

Absorbing all the details, Melati was back in Jakarta by early May. Bakin spent hours debriefing its agent, the results of which were then passed to eager counterparts. While his insights were deemed of great value, Melati was apparently tiring of the espionage game. In March 1993, he informed his Bakin handler that he was unilaterally cutting ties with the North Koreans and leaving for an extended period of study overseas. He has yet to return to Indonesia.

Outside of the receding communist challenge, Bakin devoted part of its attention to potential threats from the Middle East. Highest on its list was Iran. For years, Bakin had been keeping track of diplomats from that country's revolutionary Islamic regime, usually through teltaps. The transcripts from these taps shed much light on the secluded, conservative lifestyle practiced by the Iranians, which sometimes rivaled even that of the idiosyncratic North Koreans. An example was Second Secretary Alireza Motevali Alamoti, who had arrived in August 1983 with his wife and two children. On the morning of 25 July 1986, his wife Azam, who was doubling as the embassy's receptionist, received a brief, rather innocuous call from an unidentified Iranian male (UIM):

UIM: Iranian embassy?
Azam: Greetings.
UIM: I want to buy basmati rice. Can it be found here?
Azam: Yes, at the [market].
UIM: Does it cook well?
Azam: Boiled, no. Steamed, yes.

Later that same day, Alireza called the embassy to speak with his wife. She dutifully reported the earlier exchange with the Iranian looking for rice, at which point her husband exploded:

Alireza: You should have asked who it was.
Azam: He came from Iran and asked about rice.
Alireza: You should have asked his name and where he came from.
Azam: He could say his name was Ali or some false name. He just asked about rice.
Alireza: He is an anti-revolutionary and he got the information he was after from you. You are so gullible.

Equally revealing (and inadvertently entertaining) was an October 1986 telephonic exchange between 39-year old First Secretary Ali Mohammad Bidarmaghz and his wife Manijeh:

Manijeh: I want to go to an aerobics class.
Ali: It is not a good idea. Somebody from the embassy might see you

and it would be embarrassing.

Manijeh: But I want to go to aerobics.

Ali: Go to French and Indian cooking class, and cake decorating.

But some of the calls seemed to be of a darker nature. One example was a cryptic 24 October 1986 conversation between Second Secretary Alireza and an Indonesian national named Ahmad Idrus:

Ahmad: I just returned from Europe and will be going around the ASEAN
          countries.

Alireza: ASEAN?

Ahmad: Yes, can I meet at your house?

Alireza: I am out until 3 PM.

Ahmad: The important thing is…about the books. They are ready now in
          Beirut. I want to know how many you would like.

Alireza: I see.

Ahmad: I plan to travel around ASEAN and then I'll go to Europe. There
          are matters not resolved yet.

Alireza: I see. If you want to see me, come at 3 PM.

Ahmad: Okay.

This dialogue was cause for angst in Bakin. The tone of their conversation – Alireza was noticeably hesitant to talk on the phone – and the mysterious reference to "books" seemed to be espionage doublespeak. But as with so much in intelligence work, subsequent surveillance of Alireza yielded no more light about the reference to materials from Beirut. Indeed, apart from sporadic attempts to cultivate local religious leaders – Alireza, for example, met on occasion with the head of the Muslim grassroots organization Muhammadiyah – by the end of the eighties Bakin had turned up no evidence of Iranian subversion on Indonesian soil.

   Among other Middle Eastern nations, Bakin also had its sights on Libya and one of the region's most radical regimes*. In the case of Libya, the Indonesian government had ample reason for concern. Ever since the mid-seventies, the Gadhafi regime had been tutoring a small but steady stream of

---

* *The second nation will not be named for security reasons.*

Indonesian radicals in paramilitary tactics. Initially, these extremists were drawn from various ethnic groups. But by the eighties, virtually all were ethnic Acehnese fighting a low-intensity separatist battle against the central authorities.[7]

Libya's constant, unprovoked meddling infuriated Jakarta. Back in the mid-seventies, the Indonesian government had severed diplomatic ties over this issue. But in May 1986, it looked like Tripoli might be extending an olive branch. Early that month, the Libyan embassy in Kuala Lumpur asked permission for a high-ranking government delegation to visit Jakarta to deliver a personal letter from Gadhafi to Suharto. Heading the delegation would be the secretary general of Islamic Call, an international Islamic organization sponsored by Libya. He would be joined by a second Islamic Call representative, as well as a pair of Libyan diplomats from the embassy in Malaysia.

Reviewing the request, the Indonesian government elected to admit the delegation. But together with a foreign counterpart, Bakin intended to keep track of the delegation by staging a technical surveillance operation. Codenamed *Puas* ("Satisfied"), it would last for the duration of their three day stay and focus on their rooms at the Borobudur Hotel.

As woodblocks were being installed, Bakin received background trace reports on the delegation members. The leader, it turned out, was a reputable figure within Islamic Call who had received a graduate degree from a U.S. university. His deputy, however, was actually a member of the Libyan intelligence service who had earlier served at the embassy in Gambia and had been cultivating an opposition candidate whom Libya was secretly bankrolling.[8]

On 20 May, the four Libyans arrived in Jakarta and were taken to their hotel. But after three days, Puas could only be rated a bust. None of the four did much talking, and their few phone calls were to the hotel's laundry service. And when they finally got their audience with Suharto to present Gadhafi's letter, it was not an appeal for rapprochement but rather an anti-American rant with accompanying photographs of damage inflicted by U.S. F-111 fighter-bombers against two Libyan cities the previous month.[9] Sans olive branch, the delegation returned to Libya with little fanfare.[10]

In the case of the second Middle Eastern nation, Bakin in 1987 had assigned its most promising foreign-trained officer with opening a new post at the Indonesian embassy in that country's capital. As had been the case with his foreign-trained colleagues, this officer was to aggressively monitor attitudes toward Indonesia using classic espionage techniques, not the more passive open source collection that had earlier been the norm for Bakin's overseas representatives.

This was easier said than done. While fluent in Arabic, the officer knew that that country's dictatorship, like many of the other Arab governments in the region, had little tolerance toward those that asked too many questions. Bakin had already learned this the hard way: when its station chief in Egypt attempted to make contact with a government critic in October 1985, he was summarily expelled.[11]

Despite this, Bakin's representative fared well. Networking among diplomats that had previously served in Jakarta – and thus harbored a soft spot for Indonesia – as well as dangling monetary incentives, he was able to cultivate sources in the president's press office, the foreign ministry, and army intelligence. And not without charm, he was able to hook a secretary in the ministry overseeing petroleum and other natural resources.

From these connections, classified documents began to make their way into Bakin's hands. Some had little direct bearing on Indonesia; for example, a confidential January 1988 memo from the petroleum ministry detailing recent events in Yemen. Others were outdated, like a top secret October 1973 report analyzing Indonesia's position in that month's Arab-Israeli War. But others contained valuable nuggets. A voluminous December 1988 report prepared by that country's embassy in Jakarta, for example, underscored the common perception that Indonesia was quietly cooperating with Israel. In addition, an army intelligence memo contained complete biographical data about the incoming PLO ambassador to Indonesia (the PLO gained permission to open an embassy in Jakarta during 1989). While perhaps not exactly the stuff of Ian Fleming, at least Bakin's spies were starting to operate like true intelligence operatives.

A final Middle Eastern target of special interest to Bakin was Iraq. As far back as 1969, the regime in Baghdad had generated an undercurrent of suspicion among Indonesia's spycatchers. But over the ensuing two decades, Iraqi diplomats in Jakarta, with rare exception, had generally been a benign crowd.

All that changed by the opening of 1991. Following Iraq's invasion of

Kuwait the previous August, the U.S. government, methodically building up its military forces in neighboring Saudi Arabia, made no secret it intended to lead a coalition to expel Iraq's occupation force. On 17 January, immediately after a final deadline from Washington expired, Operation Desert Storm kicked off with a spectacular nighttime aerial bombardment of Baghdad.

Given that U.S. preparations for war had been so publicly telegraphed, there was concern that Iraq had equally sufficient time to prepare overseas terrorist cells as a fifth column. To be sure, the Iraqi intelligence service had a sizable presence around the globe, erected the previous decade to support its protracted war with neighboring Iran. Because of this, CIA stations in most countries were keeping a close eye on known or suspected Iraqi intelligence officers.

In the Philippines, surveillance of the Iraqis had turned up an interesting lead. Iraqi Consul General Muwafak Ani, a known intelligence operative who had previously served in Washington, was seen meeting two burly countrymen who arrived in Manila during late December 1990. Despite their decidedly rough appearance, both claimed to be students on their immigration forms.

On 19 January 1991, a tail on the two alleged students watched them board a taxi to the Makati financial district. Exiting in front of the U.S.-funded Thomas Jefferson Cultural Center, one of the pair – later identified as Ahmad J. Ahmad – was seen removing his backpack and bending down under a tree near curbside.

Seconds later, an enormous fireball all but evaporated Ahmad. As the thunderclap subsided, leaves from the tree rained down along the block. Denuded of foliage, the tree now had chunks of flesh skewered on its branches. Ahmad had apparently intended to key the timer attached to an explosive in his backpack and lob it into the cultural center. Either through an error on his part – or more likely a calculated decision by their case officer to eliminate the bombers as well – the device had detonated instantaneously.[12]

Fortunately for the second student, his compatriot had absorbed the bulk of the bomb blast with his chest. Flung across the street, he was found in a bloody, unconscious heap, but otherwise alive.

Working together, the CIA and its Filipino counterparts were quickly able to make progress. Identification found on the second bomber led the authorities to their room, where they found passports and some interesting pocket litter. Based on these findings, Muwafak Ani and a second Iraqi diplomat were quickly deported to Malaysia (they could not return to their own country for the time being on account of the Gulf War).

The 19 January failed bomb attack confirmed the worst fears of Western intelligence agencies. Intuitively, they suspected the Iraqi intelligence service would have deployed other terrorists to Asia. But the second student in Manila – who was lucid despite his injuries – refused to talk about others that might have been concurrently deployed.[13]

At that point, barely a day after the Makati explosion, a CIA case officer working the assignment burst into the office of his superior. "Wanna hear something cool, boss?" His broad grin spoke volumes. "The passport numbers for the two bombers are sequential."[14]

As the implication of this sank in, his superior shared the smile. "I love it when the bad guys are dumb shits."

Within an hour, an ASAB – for "All Stations, All Bases" – telegram flashed to CIA posts around the world. Its officers were urged to liaise with their local counterparts to see if any Iraqi nationals had entered their respective countries with passports either ten numbers above or below the digits found in Manila.

Almost as quickly, embassies in Thailand, Malaysia, and Singapore reported back that pairs of Iraqi male "students" within that numerical range had arrived over the past three weeks. In all cases, they were tracked down and deported before they committed any acts of terrorism.[15]

In Indonesia, the situation was especially delicate. A small but vocal portion of Indonesian society had found it fashionable to declare Iraq underdogs worthy of support; hawkers selling plastic Saddam Hussein masks at traffic lights were doing a brisk business. Even worse, on the morning of 18 January, a time bomb containing two sticks of dynamite had been discovered in the bushes near the front veranda of the U.S. ambassador's residence; an alert gardener had spotted the device and it was removed by the police bomb squad before detonation. Scant details of this event had leaked to the press; the culprits had yet to be apprehended.[16]

Bearing Indonesian sensitivities in mind, the CIA had quietly passed Bakin the range of Iraqi passport numbers to investigate with their colleagues in the immigration service. They soon turned up two Iraqis fitting the bill – Ahmed F. Mohammed and Hasan Ali Hussein – who had arrived in Jakarta on 14 December 1990. The operation to find them, codenamed *Teluk* ("Gulf"), was given to UP 01.

Given the urgency in locating the two Iraqis, UP 01 spread itself across the capital to check hotel registers. They discovered the pair had changed addresses three times, but as of 21 December had been staying at the budget Hotel Menteng II. Establishing a stakeout at this venue, UP 01 operatives began following them over the remainder of January 1991. They found the Iraqis to be exhausting subjects to tail: accomplished playboys, on most nights, they frequented bars and discos until the early morning hours.

But other aspects of their schedule were cause for suspicion. The pair repeatedly visited the house of the Iraqi financial attaché and on several occasions took taxis past the U.S. embassy and the U.S. ambassador's residence. In addition, a bellboy reported that the Iraqis were hoarding empty coconut shells in their room; in a bit of a stretch, UP 01 noted there were coconut trees on the lawn of the U.S. ambassador's residence and the Iraqis might be planning to hide another explosive device in that compound.

Despite all this, Bakin was reluctant to order a deportation that might attract media attention. And like the earlier Yugoslavian assassin case, the Iraqis had not broken any Indonesian laws (it was suspected but never conclusively determined if they had planted the first bomb at the U.S. ambassador's residence). Opting to keep them under close watch (and coordinating with immigration officials to deny their application to extend their visas), UP 01 operatives shadowed them until the time they boarded a 2 February flight to Kuala Lumpur. One Bakin case officer, disguised as an airline representative, even entered the cabin to ensure they had taken their seats. On account of a job well done, Bakin chief Sudibyo later presented the surveillance team with generous cash bonuses.[17]

Despite the operational success of Operation Teluk, it proved to be the exception and not the rule. Continuing its organizational freefall, Bakin's slide toward irrelevance was dramatically demonstrated late the following year. That October, the police department had crafted a draft set of traffic rules, including some rather tame provisions mandating that motorcyclists wear helmets and drivers use seatbelts. While the legislation was set for immediate implementation, the government was preoccupied with a summit of the non-aligned movement it was to host in Jakarta the very next month.

Given that the summit was Suharto's opportunity to shine on the world stage, and given that the New Order was incredibly oversensitive when it came to domestic opposition, General Sudibyo received an emergency assignment. As a matter of urgency, he was to devote Bakin's analytical talent to determine whether or not the new traffic regulations would cause unsightly disruptions ahead of the non-aligned summit.

Bakin threw itself into the issue and, after much thoughtful consideration, set out its conclusions. Yes, they declared, the insistence on helmets and seatbelts would probably cause social problems. Thus advised, the government decided to postpone implementation for one full year. Sudibyo recalls this piece of analysis as one of the more important milestones during his tenure as Bakin chief.[18]

In hindsight, the traffic law episode was significant on a number of levels. For one thing, it underscored the fact that Indonesia at the time faced some of the most mundane of problems – in stark contrast to the multiple crises encountered later that decade. But more importantly, it highlighted that Bakin had become – as one journalist aptly described it – a "sleepy sinecure." Using a particularly colorless choice of words, Sudibyo reinforced this impression by describing his organization's mission as "strengthening national resilience."[19] And while this was a sad commentary as to the depths to which Indonesia's intelligence agency had sunk, the worst was yet to come.

1   Interview with Sudibyo, 23 March 2003.

2   *Buku I (Idiologi), Ensiklopedia Intelijen*, pp. 49-57, 89-119.

3   Ironically, the temporary location of the Chinese embassy was in the old Bakin headquarters on Jalan Senopati. Although Bakin was not overly suspicious of diplomats posted to the Chinese embassy, for decades it maintained dozens of detailed files on Indonesians of Chinese ethnic origin and those who had business dealings with China. Among these personalities were some of Indonesia's most prominent business leaders, such as Lippo Group's Mochtar Riady. To assist in collecting information on these targets, Hong Kong's Special Branch during the seventies and eighties regularly forwarded to Bakin details of Indonesian passport holders who crossed from Hong Kong to mainland China. But when Bakin showed interest in resuming this operation in June 1992, the Special Branch said

it was no longer possible because too many persons were making the crossing and they no longer maintained complete records.

4   By December 1989, there were five autonomous operational units answering directly to the Bakin chief. The first, UP 01, was the new name for the Satsus Intel spycatchers. The second, UP 02, was a signal intelligence formation intended as a miniature version of the U.S. National Security Agency; never provided with adequate equipment, UP 02 was effectively stillborn. UP 03 oversaw the administration of Bakin compounds, UP 04 was in charge of training and education, and UP 05 handled documentation.

5   *Melati* was a recycled call sign: in 1974, a leftist journalist recruited by Satsus Intel had used the same crypt for a short period.

6   Melati was given 250,000 rupiah to make the customized puppet. As this was a considerable amount of money in 1987, the North Koreans probably overpaid their agent with the intention that he would keep the balance in lieu of a stipend. Bakin Case File, "Ginseng."

7   As of 1987, nine Acehnese were training at the Anti-Imperialism Center in Tripoli. *Ensiklopedia Intelijen*, p. 27.

8   Bakin Case File, "Puas."

9   The April 1986 air strike against paramilitary sites in Tripoli and Benghazi was a reaction by the U.S. government after Libyan agents downed a Pan Am airliner over Scotland and bombed a West German discotheque, both resulting in American fatalities.

10 Despite providing decades of training for Acehnese separatists, Libya was given permission in 1991 to reopen its embassy in Jakarta; Tripoli was eager for this to take place so that it might have representation ahead of the 1992 summit of the non-aligned movement to be hosted by Indonesia.

11 This was the only case in which an undeclared Indonesian intelligence officer posing as a diplomat was declared *persona non grata*. In one other case during October 1987, a Bakin officer posted to Vietnam elected to return early from his tour following an aggressive (and unsuccessful) KGB attempt at recruitment. Interview with Effendi, 6 March 2003.

12 CIA officers in Manila showed no shortage of black humor when they framed a photograph of pieces of the ill-fated bomber in the denuded tree with the inscription: "Dear Guys, thanks for letting me hang around, Ahmad J. Ahmad."

13 The second student was kept in Filipino detention for eight months but refused to cooperate. He was then deported back to Iraq, but not before the CIA arranged

for sympathetic journalists in the Middle East to run stories that the had yielded under interrogation and revealed the names of his fellow terrorists in other Southeast Asian countries.

14 Interview with Davis Knowlton, 2 October 2002.

15 A reference to the Thai expulsions can be found in *Washington Post*, 25 January 1991, p. A25.

16 Although the ambassador's residence was surrounded by a three-meter fence, the time bomb had apparently been placed during the night of 17 January when the neighborhood had been plunged into darkness during a power outage. See *Pelita*, 19 January 1991; *Kompas*, 19 January 1991.

17 Interview with B.R., 22 April 2003; Bakin Case File, "Teluk."

18 Sudibyo interview.

19 "Spies Like Us," *Far Eastern Economic Review*, 27 January 1994, p. 16.

CHAPTER THIRTEEN

REVOLVING DOORS

I n April 1996, there was another passing of the torch at Bakin. Lieutenant General Sudibyo, after a seven-year run, turned over command to Lieutenant General Moetojib. The choice was curious, and arguably inappropriate. A cavalry cadet in the military academy's class of 1962, the gregarious Moetojib had diligently worked his way through the ranks but was never rated as a rising star. His career was dominated by administrative staff slots; at no point had he served in an intelligence assignment.

But Moetojib's lack of preparedness and ambition was perhaps what made him most qualified. Growing ever more sensitive to domestic challengers real or imagined, Suharto in 1994 had already downsized Bakin's formidable military rival, Bais.[1] Given that Bakin had been effectively defanged during the preceding years, Moetojib was the sort of non-threatening intelligence chief that made the president all the more comfortable.

Within Bakin, the new chief did not capture the imaginations of his subordinates. At best, Moetojib was said to have acted like an absentee landlord ("He spent most afternoons improving his golf game," sniffed one senior officer). At worst, he was accused of perpetuating the military mindset started by Sudibyo.

The result of all this was an intelligence agency that continued to border on irrelevance. As before, it was excluded from the most turbulent areas of the country, including Aceh, East Timor, and Irian Jaya.[2] Even within the critical political battleground of Jakarta, Bakin was barely a factor.[3]

To be fair, there were some accomplishments during Moetojib's tenure.

For one thing, he eventually made an effort to nurture promising younger talent among Bakin's civilian members. For another thing, he kept his spycatchers in UP 01 operating on a busy schedule.[4]

For UP 01, staying gainfully employed was not nearly as easy as it had been in the past. With the Soviet bloc a fast-fading memory, the unit had lost its mother lode of hard targets. Occasional stakeouts were still maintained against the North Korean embassy (a series of annual operations against Pyongyang's diplomats, initiated in 1993, were codenamed *Ginseng*). An effort was also made to recruit agents that had access to Iranian and Iraqi diplomats: two productive sources – *Kamboja* and *Bakung* ("Wild Lily") – were reporting on the Iranians by 1995; a female source close to the Iraqis – codenamed *Kenanga* ("Ylang-Ylang") – was nearly recruited in 1996, but dropped out at the last minute.[5]

But even with these residual ongoing operations, there was no denying that UP 01 had lost a good share of its raison d'être with the end of the Cold War. Following from this, interest from the unit's traditional patron – the CIA – was noticeably on the wane. In terms of training assistance, the flow of U.S. counter-intelligence instructors was cut sharply by the early nineties and ended completely by 1997.[6]

Picking up some of the slack was Great Britain. Aside from a single trainer dispatched in 1969, contact between that country's foreign intelligence service, MI6, and Indonesia's spycatchers had been sporadic, even contentious.[7] This was set to change in 1995, when plans were afoot to dispatch a single advisor to give a course on agent handling. While this was not exactly new territory for UP 01 – it had been practicing this craft for almost three decades and had received advice from no less than four counterparts – the course, which took place the following year, was well received. "We usually had theoretical case studies," recalled one participant, "but the British gave us relevant cases, like recruiting agents within the OPM [separatist movement] in Irian."[8]

The timing of the British help was not coincidental. In March 1996, Bakin began the first of six joint covert operations that would extend over the next two years. Three of these – codenamed *Oase* ("Oasis"), Oase II, and Oase III – were targeted against Iranians. The other three – *Onta* ("Camel"), Onta II, and *Kurma* ("Date") – were focused on Iraqis. In all six cases, UP 01 was tasked with conducting concerted surveillance of the targets in question. The benefit for Indonesia was to see if the diplomats were conducting intelligence activities, and, if so, whether they were in touch with Indonesians of Arab ethnic origins. MI6, by contrast, was looking to obtain lifestyle profiles for possible recruitment attempts.

The surveillance provided interesting dividends. In the case of one Iranian target, he and his family led ostensibly pious, conservative lives. But on most weekends, they would head outside the city to the discreet confines of the Imperial Country Club south of Jakarta. There, the UP 01 operatives were surprised to see the wife's traditional floor-length dress and veil give way to a t-shirt, jeans, and often a bathing suit.

The Iraqi operations were just as revealing. During the Kurma stakeouts in September 1998, the targeted Iraqi diplomat frequently used counter-surveillance techniques – but apparently not to conceal intelligence activities. The diplomat, it turned out, had a series of lady friends and was paranoid about getting caught. As compartmentalization is paramount in the world of espionage, Bakin never learned whether or not this information was useful to its British counterparts.

In hindsight, Kurma was the last joint operation conducted by UP 01. In May, Indonesia had been rocked by its greatest social upheaval since the failed 1965 coup. Pummeled by the sharp regional economic downturn, riots broke out in several Indonesian cities and fast-tracked a sharp, bloody end to Suharto's 33-year iron-fisted rule. Not surprising, given its lack of institutional influence, Bakin played no appreciable role in the New Order's final act.

Suharto was able to stage-manage his succession, however, by elevating Vice President B.J. Habibie to the top slot. A technocrat by training known for his slavish devotion to Suharto – as well as an eccentric manner that included a propensity to gesticulate wildly – Habibie was about as far from the reserved, circumspect Javanese stereotype as was humanly possible.

But if Habibie offered a clean break from the past in terms of personality, he still carried the baggage of the New Order and its Golkar political machine. With little legitimacy in the eyes of the public as a result, he also lacked support from the military and his own party, Golkar. Scrambling to patch together a powerbase in the face of all this, he exercised his prerogative in September 1998 to select his own man as chief of intelligence.[9]

Habibie's choice to head Bakin was no surprise. Zaini Azhar Maulani, 59, was born in South Kalimantan to Dayak parents. Graduating first in the military academy's class of 1961, he nurtured a reputation as an intellectual. This eventually earned him an assignment as the military attaché to London in the late seventies. Continuing upward, in 1988, he landed a three-year tour as commander of the West Kalimantan military region.

But despite his intellectual capacity, it was in West Kalimantan that Major General Maulani's military career peaked prior to a tailspin. Various reasons for this have been proferred. It might have been because of the glass ceiling that often blocks non-Javanese officers from further promotion; as a Dayak, Maulani was not of the preferred ethnic pedigree. Or it might have been due to his rumored falling out with the influential Benny Moerdani.Moreover, Maulani counted few friends among his military peers and was often derided for what they saw as his rank opportunism. For whatever reason, Maulani left the armed forces in 1991, ahead of mandatory retirement, to serve in the rather lackluster role as secretary general at the Ministry of Transmigration.

Four years later, however, Maulani's career rebounded after some prescient career choices. Taking up a pen, he made a name for himself as a prolific columnist on military topics for several media publications. He also took on a pious air and grew active in Islamic organizations, reversing the outwardly moderate religious views expressed during his military career. And snuggling close to Habibie, he served as an advisor when the latter was Minister for Research and Technology, then as secretary when Habibie became vice president.

By May 1998, Maulani – who had received an honorary promotion to lieutenant general the previous month – was perhaps Habibie's closest confidant among active and retired top brass. When Habibie was elevated to the presidency, he retained Maulani as his secretary. Given their mutual trust, and the need to select among officers with three stars, it was natural for the president to choose his loyal aide to helm Bakin.

The organization inherited by Maulani was in abysmal shape. For one thing, the collapse of the Indonesian economy left Bakin with little money coming from the national coffers. For another thing, Bakin, like many intelligence agencies in the West, was having trouble getting its bearings after the Cold War. "We no longer had a clear direction, a clear focus," waxed one UP 01 veteran. "It was like somebody saying they were hungry but not saying what they specifically wanted to eat. If you're hungry, you must tell me if you want fried rice."[10]

All of this paled, however, to the self-inflicted damage that followed. Consumed by increasingly conservative religious views, Maulani unceremoniously purged senior Catholics and Protestants (including one deputy and four directors) from the agency. He also spent an inordinate amount of time away from Bakin's headquarters to huddle with outside advisors and attend religious events. With their chief pursuing his own agenda, most of Bakin's upper echelon was ignored; many directorates were allowed to atrophy from lack of attention or assignments.

Maulani's preoccupation with religion also came to tinge Bakin's dealings with Western counterparts. In many cases, those links – such as with the CIA – were already on the decline after Washington's Cold War victory made Bakin's continued help in the fight against communism less than relevant. But Maulani took this further, insisting, for example, that UP 01 purge all of its donated U.S. surveillance hardware (this was replaced by a much smaller amount of British-made gear, which apparently was deemed more diplomatically palatable).

Not all foreign ties soured under Maulani's tenure. He pushed to have Bakin accepted as a member of the Islamic Intelligence Service Conference, a body comprised of intelligence representatives from Malaysia, Brunei, and five Middle Eastern nations which meets annually.[11] Maulani was also supportive of plans to expand the Multilateral Intelligence Exchange – annual seminars that brought together intelligence representatives from the original six ASEAN members – to include new ASEAN entrants Cambodia, Laos, Myanmar, and Vietnam. To help realize this, Bakin assumed responsibility for spearheading a liaison with the Vietnamese; Maulani himself ventured to Hanoi and initiated talks with their Ministry of Public Security.[12]

Irrevocably linked to Habibie, Maulani's tenure was destined to last only as long as that of his political guardian angel. On 20 October, that abruptly came to an end when blind cleric Abdurrahman Wahid – popularly known as Gus Dur – was sworn in as Indonesia's fourth president. As head of Indonesia's largest grassroots Muslim organization, Gus Dur's religious credentials were beyond reproach. But he was also a strident moderate and outspoken in his religious tolerance, traits noticeably absent in Maulani of late. Just as Habibie had done a year earlier, he intended to exercise his prerogative to select an intelligence chief that better meshed with his politics and personality.

For Gus Dur, the choice was not easy. During the final years of the New Order, the regime – and especially the military – had been suspicious of his harping for reform and public sniping at Suharto. Many generals were still leery of his provocative tongue and acid wit. The feeling was mutual, with the new president not particularly enamored with most of the top brass.

The president's eventual pick, confirmed on 18 November 1999, was vintage Gus Dur. Lieutenant General Arie Kumaat, who had previously served tours as Bais deputy chief and commander of the North Sumatra military region, had been marking time before retirement in a dead-end job at the Ministry of Defense. He was also a Catholic from North Sulawesi; many speculated Gus Dur was tweaking the collective nose of the armed forces by picking a Catholic as intelligence chief.

Gus Dur's controversial decisions did not end with the selection of Arie Kumaat. In 2000, he put his stamp on plans to revamp the country's entire intelligence apparatus. Central to the concept was the proposed creation of a new body known as the State Intelligence Institute (*Lembaga Institut Negara*, or LIN). Answering to the Minister of Defense – who was a close ally of the president – LIN would theoretically oversee the military's existing intelligence agency (in July 1999, BIA expanded and readopted its previous name, Bais). Significantly, all of Indonesia's overseas military attachés would now answer directly to LIN, not Bais.

LIN could only be interpreted as a direct swipe at the generals. The Ministry of Defense had earlier been gutted of true power; it had no authority over the armed forces commander, who enjoyed a direct line to the president. But by forcing Bais to answer to the Minister of Defense via LIN, the generals would be forfeiting hallowed intelligence turf to a civilian appointee. Worse, the military would also lose the right to manage its lucrative and prestigious attaché slots.

The president fired one more salvo against the army and its spies. In a decree signed by Gus Dur in October 2000, Bakin's budget was to be increased so that it might take on a larger domestic role at the expense of Bais. To flesh out this augmented mandate, Kumaat organized a working group comprised of the agency's top officers. Three months later, on 22 January 2001, the plan was finalized. On paper, Bakin now had five deputies. As before, Deputies 1, 2, and 3 handled foreign intelligence, domestic intelligence, and analysis, respectively.

Deputy 4, a new position, was responsible for security. An intentionally ambiguous title, this translated into oversight of five diverse directorates. Among them were the assets of UP 01, the country's veteran counter-espionage unit. UP 01 was now divided into two directorates under Deputy 4: Directorate 42 handled liaison with other government agencies, such as customs, immigration, and the post office; Directorate 43 absorbed UP 01's surveillance teams.

Deputy 5, another new position, intentionally took a page from the days of Ali Moertopo and was responsible for social conditioning. In practice, this meant the discreet lobbying of Islamic groups, the media, students, and other key community leaders.

Along with new deputies, Bakin also received a new name. As of January 2001, it was officially re-designated the State Intelligence Agency (*Badan Intelijen Negara*, or BIN). Signifying a break with the past, BIN's deputy chief slot would be filled by a civilian. Getting the nod was As'at Said, a career Bakin employee who had enjoyed several successful overseas assignments in the Middle East and most recently had been in charge of analysis. In reaching this level, As'at was the first civilian to attain the number two slot in the agency's history; previous deputy chiefs had almost exclusively been army major generals.

Although the transformation from Bakin to BIN consumed much of Kumaat's attention, the intelligence chief was being whipsawed by other pressing issues. For one thing, Gus Dur, not known for his diplomatic tact, was burning bridges faster than they could be built. Lining up against him was a growing legion of political opponents and suspicious generals; rumors that they were instigating public demonstrations against the president were probably grounded in truth. During some of the larger protests, Kumaat took it upon himself to tail the rallies with surveillance teams from UP 01.[13]

Then in October 2000, the BIN chief perceived a darker threat. That month, there was a series of demonstrations and robberies near the Sumatran fields where Caltex was pumping oil. Protests had also broken out on Sumbawa Island where Newmont was mining for gold. And on the last day of that month, an Exxon-Mobil storehouse in Aceh had been raided; the thieves had made off with a large quantity of explosives and detonation cords.

Not only was Kumaat convinced that the three cases were linked, but he was equally sure he saw the hand of extremists aligned against Western interests. To confirm this, he called on UP 01 to dispatch four operatives to Sumatra to conduct a discreet investigation around the Caltex oil fields. Their results, delivered to the BIN chief four weeks later, did not point to any extremist hand but rather to a poor community relations program on the part of the oil giant. A police investigation on Sumbawa arrived at the same conclusion, while the police suspected inside complicity in the Aceh theft.

Toward year's end, Kumaat had a new headache. On the night of 24 December, two dozen bomb blasts hit churches in nine cities across the country during Christmas Eve religious services. Nineteen persons were killed and more than one hundred were injured. No group claimed responsibility for the campaign of terror, but Gus Dur quickly described it as a bid to destabilize his embattled administration. Many in the media pointed their finger at the military, which was thought to be the only organization capable of synchronizing simultaneous strikes across the archipelago. Within BIN, there was also a gut feeling that elements of the military were close to the extreme religious right and could be behind the Christmas Eve bombings.[14]

In hindsight, these suspicions were all off base. The perpetrators behind the bombings were, in fact, linked to a transnational Islamic extremist network that had been slowly taking root across Southeast Asia for more than a decade. That network – which took as its name *Jemaah Islamiyah* (JI), Arabic for "Islamic Community" – had its roots in a small, outspoken cadre from the conservative Ngruki Islamic boarding school in Solo, Central Java, that had fled to Malaysia in April 1985 to escape re-arrest by the New Order authorities. Led by exiled Ngruki patriarch Abdullah Sungkar, JI was, in some respects, little more than a modern retooling of Darul Islam. Both, after all, shared the goal of a non-secular Indonesia ruled according to Islamic law.

But there were significant differences. Darul Islam at its height had devolved in ethnic pockets, most of which were deeply colored by local cultures and personalities. Sungkar, by contrast, had ventured to Saudi Arabia during

1985 in search of funds and came back to Malaysia inspired by the puritanical, intolerant Wahhabi strain of Islam common in that kingdom.

Sungkar was not the only Indonesian heading west. Also in 1985, the first Indonesian contingent – just five strong – ventured to the Pakistani frontier to participate in the jihad against Soviet occupation forces in neighboring Afghanistan. As was true with all subsequent contingents, several were Ngruki graduates; nearly all, too, had their travel coordinated by Sungkar and his Malaysian cabal. By that time, the war in Afghanistan had been raging for over half a decade. With the West channeling weapons and rich Arab sheiks helping foot the bill, some Arabs elected to do more than merely finance the operations. Led by Osama bin Laden, the scion of a wealthy Saudi conglomerate, a legion of non-Afghan volunteers – primarily Arabs, but including the Indonesian jihadists – entered the fray.

The jihad experience was pivotal for many of those involved. This was especially true for a member of the 1987 contingent, an ethnic Sundanese named Hambali (alias Nurjaman Riduan Isamuddin, alias Ecep). Born in 1966 to an ethnic Sundanese farming family in the devout Muslim community of Sukamanah, West Java, Hambali's great-grandfather had built one of the local Islamic schools, which Hambali later attended.[15]

Upon completion of high school, Hambali intended to continue his religious study. Because he considered Islam to be too restricted under the New Order government, he instead hoped to study in the more open environment of Malaysia. In 1985, at age nineteen, he applied for a scholarship in one of Malaysia's top Islamic schools. His application was rejected.

His plans for further study dashed, Hambali nevertheless departed for Malaysia. As the oldest son among thirteen children, for the next two years, he took menial jobs – selling medicine and cloth, for example, in order to repatriate money back to his family. But by 1987, with word of the Ngruki volunteers departing for Afghanistan, he too headed for that combat zone. Coming in contact with the Arab legion, he took a keen interest in the Wahhabi brand of Islam favored by the Saudis. He also met Osama bin Laden, the leader of the Arab volunteers.

Not until about 1990 did Hambali return to Malaysia. By then, he was a fiery advocate of the Wahhabi school, though his militancy was often concealed behind a calm persona.

At this time, he was destitute. In March 1991, Hambali ventured to the low-income Sungai Manggis neighborhood an hour's drive northeast of Kuala Lumpur and, together with a new wife, rented a small wooden shack. Desperate for work, for the next three years, he continued to hawk traditional medicines and food from a pushcart outside a local mosque.

It was during this period that Hambali came into contact with Sungkar and a second militant Ngruki cleric, Abu Bakar Ba'asyir. All three shared a common devotion to Wahhabi's puritanical take on Islam. Although he lacked the oratory skills of Sungkar, Hambali's Afghan experience served to get him noticed within the Indonesian diaspora and he soon began to teach short tutorials on jihad.

Others took notice of Hambali as well. Ever since 1988 – while Hambali was still in Afghanistan – Osama bin Laden had been scouting out new venues for jihad. During that year, he had co-founded an organization known as *al-Qaeda*, Arabic for "The Base." Intended as a means of better harnessing the diverse mujahidin bands mobilized for Afghanistan, one of bin Laden's first targets was the Philippines. Although his 1988 visit to the southern Philippines (where he is said to have made initial contact with Muslim separatists) remains unconfirmed, during that same year it is known that he dispatched his brother-in-law, Muhammad Jamal Khalifa, to Manila.

As would become common practice within al-Qaeda, Khalifa established a string of Muslim charities that at times performed legitimate humanitarian work, albeit to win sympathy and support. But much of their work involved channeling paramilitary assistance to Muslim rebels. As early as October 1991, Filipino officials tracked financial transactions between Khalifa and two armed separatist organizations, the Abu Sayyaf Group (ASG) and Moro Islamic Liberation Front (MILF).[16] By the mid-nineties, it is also believed that Khalifa was sponsoring the paramilitary training of foreign mujahidin from around the world at the MILF-controlled Camp Abubakar in central Mindinao.

As Khalifa was busy with these ventures, the Philippines suddenly took on new importance for brother-in-law Osama bin Laden. Having come to view the United States as his chief antagonist (largely because he was irate that the U.S. had stationed military units in Saudi Arabia during Desert Storm), bin Laden sponsored a 1993 operation to place a car bomb in the parking garage beneath the World Trade Center in New York City; six died and more than one thousand were injured in the resultant explosion.

The chief planner of that attack, Kuwaiti national Ramzi Ahmed Yousef, escaped a U.S. dragnet and fled to Manila and linked up with a local al-Qaeda cell. Almost immediately, they began plotting more terrorist plots against Western, and especially American, targets.

In doing so, the al-Qaeda cell members drew on help from another acquaintance from Afghanistan: Hambali. By about the first quarter of 1994, Hambali began to receive "Middle Eastern" visitors at his simple Sungai Manggis residence, a fact considered unusual for an erstwhile street merchant. With Hambali providing commercial cover and funneling funds through Malaysia, Yousef launched his next strike that December. Detonating a bomb aboard a Philippine Airlines jet en route to Japan, it killed a Japanese businessman but failed to bring down the plane.[17]

As it turned out, the December 1994 incident was intended as a trial run for a terrorist operation, the likes of which the world had never seen. Intending to simultaneously crash eleven U.S. jetliners in Asia – resulting in perhaps 4,000 deaths – their plot was codenamed *Bojinka*, the Serbo-Croatian word for "explosion."

As with the Philippine Airlines trial run, Hambali helped by channeling funds through Malaysia. But while the al-Qaeda cell in Manila was mixing explosives in January 1995, the mix accidentally caught fire. Police came on the scene, arresting two. Yousef managed to flee the scene; with Hambali allegedly providing cash and an escape route, he was able to make his way to Pakistan.

Although al-Qaeda's Manila cell had taken a hit, things were going well for Hambali. Neighbors noticed he was becoming a conspicuous consumer, though the source of his newfound wealth was never made clear. His contribution to al-Qaeda continued; he arranged, for example, to channel funds for nine Singaporean Muslims to attend paramilitary training in Pakistan and Afghanistan.

In late 1995, however, one of the fugitive members of the Manila al-Qaeda cell was arrested in Malaysia and extradited to the U.S. Not wanting to tempt fate, Hambali laid low for a time to focus on preaching and fund-raising. He also forged closer links to Sungkar and Ba'asyir, all three of whom lived in a small community, literally within sight of each other. By that time, Sungkar had expanded his goal to include the establishment of a singular Islamic super-state – *Daulah Islamiyah Raya* – that would encompass Indonesia, Malaysia, Singapore, and parts of the Philippines and Thailand.

While he preached this theme, Hambali would take aside select students to tutor them in the ways of jihad. In this, his Afghan experience served to give him greater credibility with his audience.

The result of this proselytizing was the establishment of radical JI cells across Southeast Asia. Patterned after al-Qaeda, the network was highly selective in membership and strictly compartmentalized. Sungkar was himself recognized as its *amir*, or senior religious leader. Hambali, who was named the head of the regional command (*mantiqi*) encompassing Malaysia, Singapore, southern Thailand, and Sumatra, was effectively its chief of operations.[18]

When Sungkar founded JI, Indonesia – and indeed most of Southeast Asia – was running at full economic speed. With much of Indonesian society satiated during the good economic times, the Malaysia-based radicals appealed only to the disillusioned fringe and attracted a scant following.

By late 1997, however, the situation had changed dramatically. With little forewarning, the economic crisis that started in Thailand quickly spread across Southeast Asia. Without question, Indonesia was hit the hardest. As social and political crises loomed, this collapse suddenly gave the radicals their best opportunity in decades. But while the fall of Suharto in May 1998 provided an opening for the Ngruki exiles to come home, they remained in Malaysia for the next year. Not until October 1999 did they venture back to Indonesian soil. For Sungkar, his homecoming was short-lived. On 23 October 1999, just three days after arrival, he passed away in Bogor.

Upon Sungkar's death, Ba'asyir suddenly was thrust in the spotlight. Ever since the establishment of Ngruki, Sungkar had been the more aggressive and media-friendly of the pair. Only now did Ba'asyir fully emerge from his partner's shadow. He did so during a period of intense religious discord across the archipelago. In places like the Malukus and Central Sulawesi, deadly sectarian violence had erupted; even in the capital, religious vigilantism was evident.

With the activities of armed religious militants growing commonplace by mid-2000, Ba'asyir oversaw the creation of an public umbrella for these various groups. Founded in Jogjakarta in August 2000, this front was labeled the Indonesian Mujahidin Council (*Majelis Mujahidin Indonesia*, or MMI). Those participating in the MMI's founding congress read like a history of Indonesia's religious radicals over the previous three decades. Among them, Ba'asyir was chosen as overall commander of the council's governing body.

Many of those present underscored their support for a regional pan-Islamic vision of the future.

While the MMI presented a public face for Indonesia's militants, Jemaah Islamiyah was active behind the scenes. In late 1999, Hambali had created a forum to foster greater cooperation among regional militant groups, not all of which were directly tied into the Jemaah Islamiyah network. Known as *Rabitah al-Mujahidin* (Arabic for "The Bond Among Mujahidin"), its first meeting, held in Selangor, Malaysia shortly before year's end, reportedly brought together Ba'asyir, Hambali, and representatives from Burma, Indonesia, the Philippines, Singapore, and Thailand. The Indonesians were the best represented in terms of numbers and included a member of an Acehnese secessionist group.

A second meeting in Kuala Lumpur during mid-2000, again reportedly led by Ba'asyir and Hambali, resulted in agreement to focus attention on Filipino interests; it is believed that the August 2000 attack on the Filipino ambassador in Jakarta was a direct result of this meeting. Jemaah Islamiyah footed the bill for the gathering, which included representatives from six nations (Burma, Indonesia, Malaysia, the Philippines, Singapore, and Thailand). Indonesia was again the best represented, including radicals from Aceh, Java, and Sulawesi.

The forum's third meeting, in the final quarter of 2000, was its most ambitious. Held at the Trolak Country Resort in Perak, Malaysia, it brought together fifteen representatives from across Southeast Asia for three days. Various terrorist plots were discussed, including the bombing of U.S. and Israeli targets in the region.[19]

Shortly after this third tryst, Hambali slipped into Indonesia. The reason, he told acquaintances, was to attend a small party. In reality, he had come to plan Project *Natal* ("Christmas"), Jemaah Islamiyah's church bombing spree set for Christmas Eve. Making his way to East Jakarta, he huddled with fellow militants and targeted seven Jakarta-based churches. Selected as the field coordinator was Edi Setiono (alias Abas, alias Usman), a former Afghan mujahidin who had met Hambali there in 1987. Others were recruited to help place the bombs, including at least one Malaysian who had illegally entered Indonesia earlier in the year to fight in Ambon.

With Setiono handling Jakarta operations, Hambali ventured to other cities. In Bandung, he recruited several bombers at a prayer group. They were to be paid $6,000 for their services.[20]

As planned, the bombs exploded within minutes of each other at two dozen churches in nine Indonesian cities. At all these locations, churchgoers were in the midst of Christmas Eve services. The casualties might have even been higher had it not been for a series of errors in Bandung. In that city, four would-be bombers were killed while making a device, while another died when the bomb on the back of his motorcycle went off en route to the target.

By the end of the first quarter of 2001, tips from BIN's intelligence net were increasingly pointing toward JI's involvement in the Christmas blasts. Delving into the world of such extremists was not exactly new territory for BIN. During the Opsus days, Ali Moertopo's operatives had astutely kept their finger on the pulse of Komando Jihad. During the eighties and nineties, new sources of information had been cultivated against the succeeding generation of religious radicals. Most of these sources were informants of varying degrees of reliability. One of them, who had run a business in Saudi Arabia, was recruited when his investment went sour and he needed emergency help from the local Bakin representative to flee the kingdom. Another was a cash-strapped Sundanese who had sought out Deputy Chief As'at at a mosque in search of handouts. Still another was an occasional separatist from Aceh who had been recruited by Kumaat when the latter was the military commander for North Sumatra.

One of BIN's best sources was not an informant, but a full-fledged penetration agent known as Dadang. As Islamic activist since his university days, he had approached Bakin in March 1985 and volunteered his services to the Republic. Embracing him, they encouraged his subsequent two-year studying stint in Saudi Arabia. By 1992, he had successfully ingratiated himself among aging Darul Islam veterans. The following year, he ventured to Malaysia for two months to meet fugitive clerics Sungkar and Ba'asyir. And in mid-2000, he attended the founding congress of the MMI.

Throughout this time, Dadang passed regular reports back to Bakin. For just as long, however, his information received scant attention. This changed by 2000, and especially during the second quarter of 2001, when the agent was attending an MMI gathering in Jogjakarta. Mingling among the attendees – many with JI links – Dadang heard fellow radicals commiserating that the Christmas Eve bombings had been an ineffective effort. This information, which seemed to corroborate the involvement of extremists in the attacks, was duly relayed to Bakin. "After that," recalled Dadang, "my reports were given more credence."

While JI seemed complicit, BIN's scanty knowledge about that network indicated it was an extremely large, and potentially fruitful, target to investigate. In the middle of that year, Kumaat tasked As'at with narrowing down the list of likely suspects. Intuitively, As'at knew where to look: the half a dozen contingents of would-be Indonesian jihadists who had ventured to Afghanistan since 1985 were surprisingly cohesive – they had even organized an alumni gathering in Solo in 1999 – and, given their exposure to demolitions and other martial skills, were exceedingly dangerous.

By late June, information from BIN's informants was starting to paint a more complete picture of Indonesia's Afghan ensemble. While the total number of veterans was unknown – a figure of about two hundred was considered realistic – As'at narrowed this down to a list of twelve top alumni. Of these, their de facto leader was Abu Rusdan (alias Abu Hamzah, alias Thoriqudin), a native of Kudus, Central Java, who had gone to Afghanistan in 1986.

BIN wanted to place all twelve under surveillance. But after years of negligence and shrinking budgets, the surveillance teams of Directorate 43 – the former UP 01 spycatchers – were woefully short of equipment and funds. Focusing solely on Abu Rusdan, the head of the directorate scrounged some operable teltaps, loaded three fellow members into a Kijang van, and on 5 July departed Jakarta for the two-day drive to Kudus. Their impending operation was codenamed *Jarum*, a reference to the famed Djarum brand of clove cigarettes manufactured in that city.

Their deployment proved timely. In April 2001, members of the Malaysian Mujahidin Group (*Kampulan Mujahidin Malaysia*, or KMM), a radical Islamic paramilitary organization founded in 1995 that was affiliated with JI, staged a botched bank robbery in a Kuala Lumpur suburb. Following a crackdown against militants by the Malaysian government, Hambali quietly left Malaysia and reappeared in Jakarta. Once inside the Indonesian capital, he rendezvoused with Imam Samudra, a young militant who had helped with the Christmas 2000 bombings.

Together again, Hambali and Samudra in July began planning for another bombing in Jakarta. In a repeat of their Christmas Eve formula, they set about recruiting field operatives who would assemble the device and plant it at the target. One of them was Edi Setiono, who had met Hambali in Afghanistan in 1987; he had previously been the Jakarta coordinator for the Christmas Eve bombings.

Also recruited was Taufik Abdul Halim, a KMM member who had illegally entered Indonesia in 2000 and was one of several KMM recruits who participated in sectarian battles that had been flaring in the Malukus. Like Setiono, he had also participated in the Christmas Eve bombings.

With explosives and detonators obtained by Samudra, Halim assembled a bomb and placed it inside a doughnut box. Then, on 1 August, Halim and a second operative visited Jakarta's Atrium Plaza on a reconnaissance mission. Though still open to speculation, it is believed that Atrium Plaza had earned the JI's wrath because a prominent charismatic Christian organization had offices at the locale.

Later on 1 August, Halim returned to the mall with the explosive device. While setting it, the bomb exploded prematurely; Halim lost his lower right leg but survived and was taken into custody. Others were soon detained in a police dragnet.

The Atrium bombing marked a turning point for Indonesia's security authorities. Not only did it force them to reevaluate the threat posed by domestic extremists, but it also forced them to seriously consider the possibility of a transnational Islamic threat in Southeast Asia.

Five days later, the Jarum team in Kudus intercepted some intriguing phone chatter. That morning, an unidentified Indonesian male called the Abu Rusdan household with bad news. A cell phone had been found on one of the Atrium suspects, said the caller, and its directory contained the names of mutual friends and organizations. Pausing to absorb the news, Abu Rusdan turned professorial. Inform those persons on the cell phone directory to be exceedingly careful, he said in an even tone. Every time they forge a contact, he added, it entails risks – even if the risks are not apparent immediately. While short of a smoking gun, the gist of this conversation (as well as those of additional calls recorded over the next two days) strongly indicated that Abu Rusdan's network was linked to the blast.

While the Jarum team was making progress, Arie Kumaat did not stay to see the operation's conclusion. Back on 23 July, Gus Dur had been sacked by the national assembly; the daughter of the country's first president, Vice President Megawati Sukarnoputri, was elevated in his place. Just as had happened during the two previous administrations, Kumaat went out the revolving door and the president went about short-listing her own pick as head of BIN.

Her eventual choice, confirmed on 10 August, took few by surprise. A.M. Hendropriyono, 56, had all the right credentials. A member of the military academy's class of 1967, he had spent his early career in either special forces or intelligence assignments. More than once he had proven his mettle in battle; his forearms and chest bore deep scars from a knife attack in West Kalimantan while combating communist guerrillas in the late sixties.

By 1986, Hendropriyono began to pull away from his academy peers. That year, while serving as intelligence chief for the Jakarta military region, he spearheaded the investigation into the JRA mortar attack on the Canadian, Japanese, and U.S. embassies. Acting as point man for liaison with Japanese police intelligence personnel, he managed to confirm the identity of the bomber through eyewitness reports and fingerprints.

Propelled by laudatory comments rolling in from the Japanese, Hendropriyono's career skyrocketed. Rated as one of the military's most promising rising stars by 1993, at just 48 years of age he became the youngest commander of a military region. What's more, that region was the Jakarta metropolitan area – arguably, the most sensitive in the country.

His subsequent term in Jakarta quickly proved Hendropriyono a regional commander like none to date. A staunch disciplinarian among his own soldiers – in May 1993 he began cracking down on tardiness and uniform violations, netting more than 100 violators a day – he was also genuinely liked by the public for his easy manner and effective public relations skills.

Unfortunately for him, Hendropriyono had not won over the one audience that truly counted. Suharto, a painfully dour orator, had for almost three decades turned the art of projecting an inscrutable Asian face into a science. In the president's eyes, any senior officer who projected serious charisma and cultivated a public following was committing career suicide, which is exactly what happened.

Abruptly derailed from the fast track, Hendropriyono was sent packing to Bandung in 1994 as head of an army training school. Then, in October 1996, he was shifted to a civilian post as chief of the military's development operations. While the military top brass tried to put a positive spin on this – the post answered to the president, they noted – few saw this as anything but a continued effort to keep the general humbled and sidelined.

While down, Hendropriyono was far from out. Through force of personality, he barely missed a beat after Suharto was thrown from office and managed to work his way into the Habibie cabinet as Minister of Transmigration. Back in the public eye, and promoted to lieutenant general, it looked like a strong comeback was in the works. But when Habibie lost his seat, the general was pensioned and faced life in the private sector.

Hendropriyono had one more ace. Just prior to becoming Jakarta military commander in 1993, he had been in charge of domestic operations at Bais. One of his assignments was to vet the application by Megawati to become head of the PDI. He had given her a clean bill of health, effectively allowing her to become party chairwoman. After his shabby treatment by Suharto, he continued to stay in touch with the future president. By the time of the Gus Dur administration, he had become perhaps her closest military confidant.

President Megawati, it turned out, did not just make Hendropriyono her intelligence chief. Taking this one step further, she gave him ministerial status. In doing so, this marked the first time an Indonesian head of intelligence had such clout since Sukarno had heaped ministerial positions on Subandrio.

While settling into his new government office, Hendropriyono faced a whirlwind of activity. For one thing, the Abu Rusdan teltaps seemed to confirm that a network of domestic religious extremists was committing acts of terrorism. For another thing, the U.S. embassy issued a strong travel warning the following week. This coincided with Indonesia's Independence Day celebration, and several politicians saw the warning as little more than an attempt by Washington to sour the first such celebrations presided over by Megawati in her capacity as president.

The truth was far more sinister. During the summer of 2001, U.S. intelligence officers in the Middle East had come upon a detailed hand-drawn sketch of the U.S. embassy in Jakarta. The sketch was attributed to members of al-Qaeda, the terrorist organization headed by Osama bin Laden that had already been linked to a pair of car bombings against U.S. embassies in East Africa and a kamikaze strike against the U.S.S. *Cole* while anchored off the coast of Yemen. At the time, it was not known who had made the sketch, or if an attack was imminent. There was some speculation that Yemeni nationals might have entered Indonesia for that purpose, but no further details were known.[21]

The U.S. embassy quickly arranged to give Hendropriyono a confidential briefing about the sketch; the gist was then passed to senior administration officials in an effort to soften the hard feelings generated by the embassy's warning. Most of those that received the briefing were not fully swayed. To that time, al-Qaeda was hardly a household term in Indonesia. Events on 11 September in New York and Washington would change that forever.

1   In 1993, Suharto dismissed Defense and Security Minister Benny Moerdani from the cabinet (apparently because Moerdani had the audacity to question the unchecked growth of the First Family's business empire). To reduce Moerdani's residual influence, especially within military intelligence circles, Suharto significantly downscaled the former minister's coddled Bais. Reduced in size and mandate, the agency was renamed the Intelligence Agency of the Armed Forces (*Badan Intelijen ABRI*, or BIA).

2   During the nineties, Bakin had almost no involvement in East Timor, with one exception of note. In May 1997, the agency formed a special team tasked with undercutting Portuguese diplomatic support for East Timorese separatists. Sugiyanto, the former Opsus officer who had been intimately involved in the Komodo operation during 1974-75, was brought back from retirement to advise the team. One of its initiatives was an effort to print a sympathetic English-language book written by a Portuguese academic. Despite its best efforts, the book was never published and the team scored no other appreciable successes.

3   During July 1996, Moetojib participated in a series of meetings with senior security officials to discuss the political affront posed by PDI supporters massing at their party headquarters in Menteng. Later that month, security forces orchestrated a raid to seize control of that building and expel the supporters; this sparked a weekend of bloody anti-government riots in the capital. Although Moetojib was questioned in November 2000 by a government inquiry board regarding his involvement in the raids, it was generally agreed that Bakin had little role, if any. In this case, Bakin's ineffectuality played in its favor.

4   By 1997, UP 01 had done away with the earlier indirect system of using *girah* handlers as middlemen between case officers and their agents. From that point forward, case officers met directly with their agents.

5   *Kamboja* was a recycled call sign: back in 1970, the same crypt had been briefly

assigned to an agent that had access to the Polish embassy.

6   During one memorable training session in 1986, the CIA arranged for a KGB defector to tutor UP 01 personnel in defeating Soviet counter-surveillance techniques. While being driven to one of Jakarta's museums for a weekend tour, the defector panicked when a car bearing Soviet diplomatic plates pulled alongside. While this was ultimately determined to be a coincidence, the ex-KGB officer from that point forward refused to venture outside the Cipayung training center. Benny S. interview.

7   Although relations had been strained in the early seventies, ties between MI6 and Bakin had improved somewhat by the eighties. In 1986, both agencies conducted a joint investigation of a British national living in Jakarta who was apparently targeted for recruitment by Soviet Third Secretary Alexei Andryuchin; the Soviet diplomat had been nurturing his potential recruit for over half a year at Hash House Harrier meets. Cooperation between the two services was also evident in 1992 during the Melati case. The following year, a British proposal to conduct joint operations against three embassies in Jakarta did not come to fruition. Bakin Case File, "Rex;" Bakin Case File, "CP 75."

8   In addition to U.S., British, and Israeli trainers, UP 01 in 1984 was given tradecraft instruction by an advisor dispatched from the West German intelligence service.

9   Moetojib did himself no favors when he became a magnet for criticism after callously commenting in August 1998 that there was no evidence that ethnic Chinese women were systematically raped during the May riots.

10 Benny S. interview.

11 Bakin had applied to join the Islamic Intelligence Service Conference during Moetojib's tenure, but it was stiff-armed because the agency's Deputy 1, in charge of foreign intelligence, was a Catholic. Bakin's reapplication during Maulani's term was given greater credence but had yet to see final approval. Not until 2002, with the global war on terrorism in the limelight, was Indonesia accepted as a full-fledged member of the forum.

12 To expand participation at the Multilateral Intelligence Exchange, Malaysia's intelligence service focused on bringing in the Cambodians, the Singaporeans approached Myanmar, Thailand concentrated on Laos, and Indonesia dealt with Vietnam. Not until the 2002 exchange, hosted by Indonesia, did all ten ASEAN members participate. Interview with Bom Suryanto, 27 August 2003; interview with Muaman, 27 August 2003.

13 Interview with Boche R., 19 April 2003.

14 "Year of Violence and Anarchy Ahead, Agency Warns Cabinet," *South China Morning Post*, 29 December 2000.

15 Hambali's date of birth is contested: Malaysian intelligence sources give an alternate date of April 1964. This second date, listed on his Malaysian permanent resident card, is probably fraudulent.

16 ASG was created in 1991 with some $6 million from bin Laden and Libya.

17 Yousef later called media outlets and claimed responsibility for the bombing in the name of the ASG.

18 Malaysian authorities believe that during 1997, Hambali was formally elevated by Sungkar to be the head of *Mantiqi Ula* (*Ula* is Arabic for "One"). On paper, Jemaah Islamiyah established four mantiqi across Southeast Asia and Australia, with each mantiqi controlling between two and thirteen branches (*wakalah*), and each branch controlling one or more cells (*fiah*). In practice, the Jemaah Islamiyah structure from the start has tended to be far more fluid than a wire diagram might suggest, with operatives taking on functional roles that vary in scope and responsibility from one operation to the next.

19 There are slightly conflicting dates for this third meeting, variously said to have taken place between September and November 2000. According to Faiz bin Abu Bakar Bafana, a key Jemaah Islamiyah operative now in Singaporean detention, the meeting took place in November.

20 According to debriefings of captured JI courier Marsan Arshad, Project Natal cost $50,000, of which $30,000 was al-Qaeda money couriered by Arshad from Pakistan to Hambali.

21 Said then-U.S. Ambassador Robert Gelbard: "…we knew from external sources, multiple sources, that an al-Qaeda team was coming into Jakarta to try and blow up the embassy." See "Moving Targets in a Strike Zone," *Sydney Morning Herald*, 23 November 2002. Later in 2001, media sources claimed that five Yemeni members of al-Qaeda had slipped into Indonesia and were living among a group of Arabs in Surabaya. This claim was never corroborated.

CHAPTER FOURTEEN

KONRO

O n the evening of 11 September, Hendropriyono was in his office on the top floor of BIN's Pejaten headquarters when aides interrupted with word of the terrorist attacks in the U.S. Coincidentally, the BIN chief was putting the final touches on briefing papers that he was to take with him when he joined President Megawati for a trip to the U.S. the following week, her first overseas junket as head of state. He was scheduled to present them during a meeting with CIA Director George Tenet.

Of all the briefing papers, one report stood out. Twenty-four pages long, it contained BIN's findings to date about Indonesia's Afghan alumni and assorted other domestic religious radicals. These included thumbnail sketches of JI and MMI, as well as brief biographies of 36 Indonesian militants (one of whom had died during the Christmas 2000 bombings and another of whom had been arrested in Malaysia).

Most intriguing was the report's specific mention of foreign militants operating on Indonesian soil. This passage reportedly included references to a Saudi "mujahidin instructor" named "Syeh Hussein," and "Umar Faruq," a Kuwaiti national. Faruq was mentioned three times in the report, including a reference to his frequent visits to Ambon as well as visits to Aceh and Sulawesi. Hussein, meanwhile, was said to have entered Indonesia in June 2000 and was allegedly living in Jakarta. This information had come largely from two BIN penetration agents, including Dadang, who overheard mention of the two at a MMI gathering during mid-year.

As planned, all of these details were presented to top CIA officials in

Washington on 19 September. By the time Hendropriyono returned to Jakarta the following week, intelligence organizations across the region were busy mobilizing against JI and its affiliates. In Singapore, the first indications of a local JI presence surfaced in late September when a Singaporean national told an acquaintance that he was going to Afghanistan ahead of a likely U.S.-led offensive against the Taliban regime. By the time he departed for Pakistan on 4 October, his movements were already being monitored. One month later, advancing Northern Alliance members captured the Singaporean, who soon gave details of his JI cell during an interrogation.

What this source revealed was shocking. Beginning in April 2001, he claimed JI members in Singapore had increased their surveillance of potential American targets. This source also revealed the names of others in his cell; initial arrests began on 9 December. As it turned out, the move came just in time. Back in May 2001, it was subsequently learned that a Canadian Arab and Fathur Rahman al-Ghozi, one of Indonesia's Afghan alumni who became a top JI operative in the Philippines, had arrived in Singapore to plan truck-bomb attacks against Australian, British, Israeli, and U.S. diplomatic targets. Coordinating the entire operation was senior JI officer Hambali.[1]

At the same time, JI's Singapore cell had initiated plans for a second attack in the city-state targeted against docked U.S. naval vessels as well as the shuttle bus used by American servicemen. Following the December arrests, however, both terrorist plans were thwarted. Although an additional five Singaporean cell members were thought to have fled to Indonesia, regional security officials were now (belatedly) aware of the extent of Hambali's regional role. Moreover, a clear picture of al-Ghozi was starting to emerge, which would lead to further arrests in the coming months.[2]

In Malaysia, the authorities were equally vigilant. Having already conducted arrests after the botched KMM bank robbery and the 1 August Atrium bombing in Jakarta, they made further arrests – some KMM, some JI – after 11 September (a total of 23 persons were in prison by the end of 2001).

In Indonesia, the reaction toward domestic militants was far different. During the second half of September and much of October, elements within the MMI announced plans to send Indonesian volunteers to fight against U.S.-supported forces in Afghanistan. Despite travel impediments placed by the Indonesian government, several hundred volunteers departed for South Asia, though they ultimately found themselves unable to progress beyond the

Pakistani frontier. At the same time, several paramilitary groups in Solo and Jakarta threatened to "sweep" American and other Western citizens from Indonesia. Sweeps were conducted in some Solo venues, though no foreigners were harmed.

In the face of these public outbursts, BIN busied itself, enhancing its understanding of the extremist threat. Part of its efforts revolved around technical operations by Directorate 43. While one team remained in Kudus, a second group of officers ventured to Solo in November for Operation *Bengawan* (named after the largest river in the vicinity). This group found the city a crowded place: a Bais team had arrived the previous week and already reserved several phone lines for taps. But with a wealth of targets – including the Ngruki boarding school and lines used by top MMI figures – Bais and the Bengawan team found more than enough to go around.

Part of BIN's efforts, too, involved recruiting more penetration agents. It was successful in roping in a Darul Islam veteran who had spent decades in Aceh, but was rebuffed when it attempted to attract an equally aged Darul Islam figurehead from South Sulawesi.

During November and December, three events elsewhere in the world focused attention on the potential for terrorist attacks in Indonesia. The first took place in Kabul, Afghanistan, which Taliban and al-Qaeda members had vacated in a rush as U.S.-supported Northern Alliance troops closed in. A check of one bombed-out house contained a detailed sketch of the U.S. embassy in Jakarta. This was the second such sketch linked to al-Qaeda that had been uncovered in less than half a year.

The second event took place in Spain, where flamboyant Spanish judge Balthasar Real Garzon, on 18 November, had spoken publicly about an extensive al-Qaeda presence in Spain. According to Garzon, an al-Qaeda cell had been operating in that country since 1994. He further revealed that a captured member of that cell, Yusuf Galan, was in close touch with Indonesian radicals and had trained on the island of Sulawesi. Hundreds of al-Qaeda members, he added, had gone to Sulawesi from Europe for such paramilitary instruction.

While there was reason to take Garzon's claims with a grain of salt – he was a showman known to relish the limelight and could well be prone to hyperbole – BIN knew there was proof of extensive radical activity in Sulawesi.[3] This had started in April 2000, when a chapter of the paramilitary Islamic Youth Front (*Front Pembela Islam*, or FPI) threatened to dispatch volunteers to Poso, Central Sulawesi, where sectarian violence had flared that same month. Fighting was centered on the backwater town of Poso, which was roughly split between Muslim and Christian communities.

In the end, no FPI militants ever arrived in Central Sulawesi – but others eventually did. These jihadists originated from neighboring South Sulawesi, where conservative Islamic groups were growing ever more vocal. Determined to implement Islamic law in their province, in May 2000 they had held the opening meeting of the Preparatory Committee for Upholding Islamic Law (known by its Indonesian initials, KPPSI).[4]

A key figure within the KPPSI was Agus Dwikarna. Born in 1964 and a civil engineer by training, Dwikarna was a longtime student activist (he had strongly opposed Pancasila as the national ideology) and divided his time between mainstream politics and more hard-line Islamic groups. He had attended the MMI's founding congress in 2000, and participated in two of the *Rabitah al-Mujahidin* forums in Malaysia. Reacting to the fighting in Poso, as well as sectarian bloodshed in the Malukus, he also played a prominent role in the creation of *Kompak* – the Indonesian abbreviation for Crisis Handling Committee – established as a forum for distributing aid from the Middle East to Muslim communities under hostile pressure.

In October 2000, Dwikarna made the jump from disbursing humanitarian assistance to paramilitary intervention when he helped establish *Laskar Jundullah* ("Army of God Force"). Publicly, Laskar Jundullah claimed to be the security wing of the KPPSI. In practice, it was an umbrella for hundreds, perhaps thousands, of young males from South and Central Sulawesi answering the call to jihad. It began its paramilitary campaign that December, when dozens of members destroyed a Makassar karaoke bar and café because it dared to operate during the Ramadhan fasting month.

More ambitious operations followed. In this, Dwikarna was assisted by Yasin Syawal, a Makassar-born, Afghan-trained militant who had spent time with the MILF and in Malaysia. While not a member of JI, he had taken the stepdaughter of Abdullah Sungkar as his second wife. With Syawal acting as paramilitary instructor, Laskar Jundullah deployed an estimated 2,000 combatants to Central Sulawesi. Although their weaponry (at least initially) was largely limited to bats and machetes, they made a significant impact when they sided with the Muslim community in the simmering sectarian violence around Poso.

On a parallel, but separate, track, an al-Qaeda cell took note of Poso from half a world away. This was largely the result of Parlindungan Siregar, an Indonesian national who had ventured to Spain's *Universidad Complutense de Madrid* in 1987. Remaining in Spain after his scholarship money ran out, Siregar supported himself by offering his services as a translator and teaching martial arts to children.

Siregar also happened to befriend Imad Eddris Barakat Yarkas (alias Abu Dahdah), the head of an al-Qaeda cell operating in Spain. In October 2000, Siregar returned to Indonesia but remained in contact with Yarkas. By now enamored with radical Islam, he ventured to Poso and met Omar Bandon, an older Indonesian who had fought in Afghanistan during the Soviet war and remained in contact with militants in the Middle East. To cement ties, Siregar soon married Bandon's sixteen-year old daughter.

With Bandon soon taking up arms against Christians around Poso, Siregar sent word to Yarkas about the unique opportunities available in Central Sulawesi. Not only was there an active jihad taking place, but the area around Poso was sufficiently isolated to allow for discreet paramilitary training.

In May 2001, Yarkas came to Indonesia to make his own assessment. Traveling on a false passport via Bangkok and Jakarta, he arrived at the town of Palu, linked up with Siregar, and then drove down to Poso. From there, they took a boat ten kilometers east along the coast.

For a terrorist organization like al-Qaeda, the locale was perfect. Situated near a jungle camp run by Omar Bandon, Yarkas and Siregar found an abandoned Christian settlement consisting of ten clusters of huts. Already present were a small mix of Filipinos, Malaysians, and even an Australian. It was estimated that the settlement could potentially house up to six hundred trainees. Siregar himself was tapped to act as a martial arts instructor.

Returning to Spain, Yarkas made arrangements to channel al-Qaeda money to Poso in order to make it a viable alternative to training facilities already available in Afghanistan and the Philippines. In July 2001, he dispatched a fellow cell member, Yusuf Galan (alias Luis Jose Galan Gonzalez) to bring cash to Siregar in order to properly bankroll what was now dubbed Camp

Mujahidin. Plans called for a facility to train thirty Filipinos, fifteen Malaysians, two dozen Europeans, and four Australians. Implementation of this plan was set to take place before year's end.

None of this was yet known to BIN when Judge Garzon made his comments in November. To investigate the Spanish judge's claims, an officer from Directorate 43 was rushed on 7 December to Central Sulawesi to search for Siregar (whose name appeared in Garzon's deposition). It was quickly determined, however, that its target had already fled to Java.

While the manhunt for Siregar was a bust, some compelling evidence came from eyes in the sky. Courtesy of a counterpart organization, satellite imagery of the Poso vicinity was shared with BIN; this showed what appeared to be an abandoned camp consistent with a training facility. Following from this, on 13 December, Hendropriyono announced the likely presence of an al-Qaeda training camp near Poso. The following day, he publicly stated that there had been foreigners in that vicinity.[5]

While his statements were met by derision by numerous prominent Islamic figures, more proof followed. On 23 December, BIN's deputy for foreign affairs rushed to Spain for meetings with police and defense officials. There, he was given the interrogation results of captured al-Qaeda terrorist Galan, as well as items found in his possession: airline ticket stubs to Indonesia, a passport (with immigration stamps from Indonesia), and two photographs of him in the Poso jungle. BIN subsequently determined that the Poso camp was probably abandoned shortly after the 11 September attacks, and certainly by the time the al-Qaeda cell was smashed in Spain.[6]

The third international event tied to Indonesia was the 22 December attempted downing of an American Airlines flight en route from Paris to Miami. Richard Reid, a British drifter and Muslim convert, had tried – and failed – to detonate a bomb hidden in his shoe; had he been successful, the damage to the aircraft's skin would have caused sufficiently rapid depressurization to tear apart the plane in flight.

After Reid was taken into custody in the U.S., investigators in several nations quickly began to piece together his links to al-Qaeda cells across Europe and the Middle East. In particular, he was thought connected to known

Egyptian members of al-Qaeda, as well as a Pakistani national named Muhammad Saad Iqbal Madni. It was further known that Madni had been in touch with al-Qaeda operatives in Kandahar, Afghanistan. Further investigation indicated Madni went on the run shortly before Reid was apprehended, and was believed to have fled to Indonesia.

During the final week of December 2001, BIN was alerted to the likely presence of Madni on Indonesian soil. He was thought to be using his real name, and had possibly sought refuge in East Jakarta. A copy of his passport details, obtained in Afghanistan, was eventually forwarded to Indonesia.

Based on this limited briefing, BIN initiated a search for Madni shortly before year's end. Because Directorate 43 was being whipsawed by targets in Kudus, Solo, and Sulawesi, the agency was given control over *Tim Alfa* ("Team Alpha"), drawn from the special warfare group within the army's elite special forces. Focusing on East Jakarta, the team eventually turned up information about a Middle Eastern individual who had recently rented a room in the vicinity. He was said to spend his time sequestered in his quarters and did not host visitors.

On 5 January 2002, intensive surveillance of the suspect's apartment was initiated. After a five-day stakeout – during which time no one was seen entering or exiting the apartment – Team Alpha moved in during the evening hours. As the team entered, it found the apartment empty; a check with the landlord revealed Madni had taken a trip to Solo.

Uncertain when Madni would return, the Alpha members maintained a vigil near the apartment. Their persistence paid off. At 0600 hours the following morning, an unidentified person of apparent Middle Eastern ethnic origin was observed approaching the building and entering the suspect's room. When confronted by Alpha, he did not resist. On his person was found a doctored Pakistani passport in Madni's name.

Over the next forty-eight hours, Madni remained in Indonesian police custody. During that period, he repeatedly attempted to bribe his way to freedom (his initial offer was one million rupiah, but this figure escalated sharply over the course of his confinement). Although he revealed little during questioning, he did admit that his father had earlier worked at the Saudi embassy in Jakarta for a decade and that he had visited the country several times in the past. Because of this connection, he had opted to flee to Indonesia.

After forty-eight hours, Madni was prepared for rendering to a third country.[7] On his way to the airport, he made one final attempt to bribe Indonesian authorities. This time, his offer stood at one hundred million rupiah. The amount was not accepted, and Madni was summarily expelled from Indonesian soil.

The new year brought additional arrests of JI terrorists across Southeast Asia. In many cases, the connection with Indonesia was glaring. Acting on a tip from Singaporean intelligence officials, for example, Filipino authorities arrested Indonesian national Fathur Rahman al-Ghozi on 15 January 2002 as he was preparing to leave on a commercial flight for Malaysia via Bangkok.

The al-Ghozi arrest laid out in stark detail the regional outreach of JI. As leader of a JI cell in the southern Philippines, he was often charged with procuring weapons and sending them to cells in other nations. He also revealed his links to an August 2000 van explosion at the Filipino ambassador's residence in Jakarta.[8] Additionally, he spoke of being in Singapore in late 2001 to plan for the aborted bombing campaign against Western targets. Back in the Philippines during December, he admitted to having procured a ton of explosives, four detonators, and six rolls of cables, which he stored in General Santos City with the intention of smuggling the load into Singapore.

Acting on al-Ghozi's information, Filipino police officers stormed his General Santos City safe house. Not only did they find the explosives bound for Singapore, but also seventeen M-16 rifles destined for militants in Indonesia. Four Filipino accomplices were arrested, though one managed to flee to MILF-controlled territory.

Additional arrests impacted other JI branches. Between December 2001 and July 2002, for example, a total of twenty-three persons were arrested in Malaysia, including four Indonesians and three Singaporeans.

Within Indonesia, BIN was still fixated on lingering questions about the Poso camp. Evidence pointed to at least one Australian national partaking in training at the site, with several sources indicating the person in question was 28-year old Jack Terrence Thomas (alias Jihad Thomas). Married to the daughter of a retired Indonesian police captain, Thomas was thought to have ventured to Afghanistan for paramilitary instruction in mid-2001. Assuming that his wife was still in Makassar – and that she would be in touch with her husband – Directorate 43 dispatched a team in January 2002 to place her residence under surveillance. The operation was codenamed *Konro*, the name of a spicy beef dish for which Makassar is famous.

After a couple of weeks of teltaps, it appeared Konro was a dead end. The wife and child of Jihad Thomas were not in the area, having apparently already departed Indonesia via Jakarta; their current whereabouts were not known.[9]

Without missing a beat, Konro found a new target. Over the preceding months, BIN had been amassing evidence that Agus Dwikarna was trying to bolster his Laskar Jundullah paramilitary force. Informants, for example, revealed he had obtained five AK-47 automatic rifles from jihadists in Ambon for use in Central Sulawesi. In addition, he had been heard boasting that two of his followers were dispatched to Afghanistan prior to 11 September in order to learn bombmaking techniques; both had been able to return via the southern Philippines. Another twelve Laskar Jundullah volunteers had been dispatched toward the Pakistani frontier to fight U.S. forces in Afghanistan. He had also established a paramilitary training camp along the banks of Lake Towuti near the border of South and Southeast Sulawesi, but this had been abandoned after the site was discovered by the authorities.[10]

The Konro teltap soon added more incriminating evidence. During a February 2002 conversation, Dwikarna was heard issuing instructions to two trusted subordinates. Both were ordered to act as local guides for a visiting Acehnese radical (who also happened to be a BIN informant). Significantly, Dwikarna told the pair not to speak to the Acehnese visitor about a contemplated cooperative venture between Laskar Jundullah and the Abu Sayyaf Group in the Philippines. Furthermore, the pair was not to speak about Faruq – apparently, the same Kuwaiti extremist mentioned in the September 2001 BIN report.

A second Konro intercept was equally revealing. In early March, Dwikarna was overheard telling his wife that he was going to General Santos City in the southern Philippines to meet with "Islamic brothers." That visit ultimately led to a short, but sharp, diplomatic incident. On 15 March, four foreign nationals – Dwikarna, two more Indonesians, and a Thai – were detained at Manila's international airport prior to taking a flight to Bangkok. The Thai, Prasand Sironord, was ultimately allowed to board the plane.[11] All three Indonesians, however, remained in police custody because explosives residue and detonation cords were found in their luggage.[12]

At that point, regional politics intervened. Because one of the Indonesians had political pull in Jakarta, the Filipino government was enticed into releasing him and a second Indonesian detainee. Dwikarna, however, did not have such good fortune. By that time, the captured al-Ghozi had revealed his ties with Dwikarna to the Filipino police. Confirming this, al-Ghozi's home phone number in Madiun was found in the memory of Dwikarna's cell phone. What's more, the Filipinos noted that General Santos City was a hotbed of MILF activity; they were convinced the Indonesians had come to meet MILF representatives and assess the damage done by al-Ghozi's arrest. Collectively damned by the evidence, Dwikarna was sentenced to 17 years in prison by a Filipino court.

Back in Indonesia, BIN remained busy chasing down reports about foreign terrorists on its soil. One such case involved Sheikh Ahmed Salim Swedan (alias Sheikh Ahmad Salem Suweidan, alias Ahmed the Tall). Born in Kenya in either 1969 or 1970, Swedan had managed a trucking business before being drawn into the al-Qaeda cell established in that East African nation. He was implicated in the August 1998 bombing of the U.S. embassy in Kenya; the U.S. government had posted a multi-million dollar reward for information leading to his apprehension or conviction.

On 7 March 2002, BIN was alerted to the probability that Swedan had sought refuge in Indonesia, possibly in Malang, East Java. Team Alpha rushed to Malang, but a raid conducted that same week revealed Swedan had boarded a flight out of Indonesia the previous day.[13]

Two months later, a counterpart organization notified BIN that a suspected Algerian terrorist using a French passport had entered Indonesia. Directorate 43 quickly located the suspect in Central Jakarta and tailed him for several days while he toured the city. As he prepared to board a flight for Europe on 24 May, he was detained and questioned. It turned out to be a case of mistaken identity: though he shared the same name as an Algerian on the worldwide terrorist watch list, he was actually a shoe salesman looking to expand into the Indonesian market. Before being allowed to board the next flight from Jakarta, the dejected salesman lamented that he was subjected to similar treatment at airports around the world.

But by far the most compelling case of a foreign radical on Indonesian soil was the long-rumored presence of Kuwaiti Umar Faruq. After the first brief mention of him in BIN's September 2001 report, the trail had gone cold for five months. Then in February 2002, the Konro teltap hinted the Kuwaiti had apparently been in South Sulawesi. BIN's Acehnese informant, who visited Dwikarna in Makassar that same month, was tipped by his handlers to send out feelers about the Kuwaiti. This netted results: a senior Laskar Jundullah member casually mentioned that Faruq was probably affiliated with al-Qaeda – and was now living near Jakarta. With senior Indonesian politicians publicly denying the presence of foreign terrorists within Indonesia's borders, BIN set its sights on Faruq to provide a smoking gun.[14]

1   Hambali had been exceptionally busy during the year. In February 2001, he ventured to Pakistan in order to plan operations in Southeast Asia later that year (he also wanted to leave the region because he feared he would be apprehended after the Christmas Eve bombings). During that same month, he allegedly talked up plans to identify four sympathetic pilots working for an Indonesian airline who would commandeer jets from Singapore and crash them into a U.S. aircraft carrier later in the year. After the 11 September attacks in the U.S., Hambali returned to Malaysia in December, then ventured across the Thai border in order to iron out the final details for the planned bombings in Singapore.

2   A total of 15 persons were arrested in Singapore during December 2001. Of them, thirteen were found to be members of JI. The other two were determined to be supporters of the MILF and were placed under restrictions.

3   This was the same judge who had secured former Chilean leader Pinochet's arrest in London in 1998, and he had later issued arrest warrants for all 48 members of Argentina's 1976-1983 dictatorship.

4   The KPPSI meeting was attended by an eclectic mix of paramilitary thugs, religious scholars from across Indonesia, romantics from the Darul Islam era, and the urban-based, university-educated Islamic activists for which Makassar is noted. In December 2001, the KPPSI was renamed the Committee for Upholding Islamic Law (known by the initials KPSI).

5   "Puluhan WNA Dimasukkan ke Poso," *Media Indonesia*, 14 December 2001.

6   Suryanto interview.

7   Media reports claim he was rendered to the Egyptian General Intelligence Service.

8   Al-Ghozi told Filipino interrogators that the assassination attempt was planned by himself and Hambali. In 2003, al-Ghozi escaped from a Filipino prison cell and later killed by Filipino security forces.

9   Jack Thomas was arrested in Pakistan in January 2003.

10   Dwikarna spoke of the AK-47 rifles from Ambon, the training in Afghanistan, and the camp at Towuti during a conversation at Masjid Darul Jalal in Jakarta on 24 December 2001; his comments were monitored by BIN. During that same month, Laskar Jundullah members were implicated in a Makassar bomb blast at a Kentucky Fried Chicken outlet.

11   Prasand Sironord, acting on behalf of a Thai-Italian company, allegedly was interested in investing in a coal mine near General Santos City. Regional intelligence agencies, who investigated Sironord's involvement, were convinced he was an unwitting dupe.

12   The Indonesian detainees insisted that the physical evidence against them had been planted in their luggage by BIN. This was categorically denied by both BIN and Filipino authorities.

13   During that same month, Team Alpha dispatched personnel to the island of Lombok. This came after an embassy in Jakarta relayed information from a longtime expatriate resident in Bali about an alleged suspicious residence in Lombok that was host to sixty Arab males. When Team Alpha arrived at the location, however, it found nothing.

14   Vice President Hamzah Haz, for one, repeated cast doubt on the possibility of foreign terrorists within the country. On 19 March 2002, he publicly stated, "I promise there are no terrorists in Indonesia." *Kompas Cyber Media*, 19 March 2002.

CHAPTER FIFTEEN

FARUQ

Had the stakes not been so deadly, Umar Faruq might best be described as a lanky, Arab version of Walter Mitty. Born in Kuwait to Iraqi parents in 1971, his conversion to jihadist had been especially spontaneous. After sitting through a fiery sermon from militant Kuwaiti cleric Abu Zeid just prior to the 1991 Gulf War, he abruptly agreed to follow the cleric on a forged Kuwaiti passport to Peshawar, Pakistan, and from there to the Afghan capital of Kabul. For the next two years, he divided his time between al-Qaeda's Khaldan training camp in Afghanistan and an uneventful spell alongside mujahidin in Tajikistan.

Faruq's time at Khaldan was particularly well-spent. Not only did he grow close to the camp commander, al-Mughira al-Gaza'iri, but also to senior bin Laden associate Abu Zubaydah. Lobbying them for permission to see action, he was sent by them to fight with Arab mujahidin in Bosnia. After just a brief spell, however, he was back in Afghanistan by 1995. Yet more al-Qaeda training followed, including classes on how to prepare invisible inks and write in codes.

Zubaydah, it seems, had big plans for him. Late that year, Faruq and al-Gaza'iri were dispatched to the Philippines with orders to enroll in flight school. Their ultimate goal was to become proficient enough to commandeer a passenger plane on a suicide mission, an al-Qaeda goal that came to deadly fruition in 2001. Failing to gain entry despite repeated applications, however, Faruq left Manila and headed south for a rendezvous with the MILF. He was no stranger to these Filipino militants, having earlier met several MILF extremists in Pakistan. Arriving at Camp Abu Bakar in Mindanao, Faruq was the second member of what ultimately became a 35-man Arab contingent (he eventually became leader). There, he trained for about a year, primarily in jungle warfare tactics.

Ironically, much of Faruq's time in the Philippines was spent not with Filipinos, but with Indonesians. This was because of palatable friction between the Arabs and Filipinos, with the latter claiming their pampered Middle Eastern guests stretched their limited financial resources. In addition, the MILF reportedly wanted the Arabs out of sight so as not to be accused of harboring foreign terrorists. As a result, Faruq was sequestered in one of three remote satellite camps populated exclusively by Indonesian JI trainees. Prominent among them was Fathur Rahman al-Ghozi, the Afghan alumnus who later became the head of the JI cell in Mindanao.

By 1998, Faruq was ready for a change. Indonesia held particular appeal for him for several reasons. First, there was a sense of chaos across much of the country after the end of the New Order in May; such chaos seemed to offer fertile ground for extremists. Second, Faruq had grown close to several Indonesians while training in Afghanistan and later at the MILF camp. In particular, he had re-established contact with Abu Jandal, an Indonesian JI member he had first met at Khaldan in 1991 and again at Camp Abu Bakar.[1] Now living in Sabah, Malaysia, Jandal originally came from Makassar and maintained a home in that city.

With Jandal acting as guide, Faruq took a boat from Mindanao to Borneo during August 1998. Because his forged Kuwaiti passport had since expired, he illegally entered East Kalimantan by boat and then made his way down to Makassar. Once there, Jandal provided introductions to several religious hardliners in his hometown, including Afghan veteran Hizbullah Rasyid and Agus Dwikarna.[2]

For the next few months, Faruq tried to establish a false identity with the help of Hizbullah. He had some initial success, arranging for a false Indonesian identity card and birth certificate to be issued in January 1999 under the assumed name Faruq Ahmad.[3] But when he ventured to the local immigration office to obtain a passport, the authorities grew suspicious because he could not speak Indonesian. Pressed by the officials, Faruq admitted to having entered the country illegally. Placed in a detention cell on 18 February, Faruq managed to escape after ten days. Again linking up with Hizbullah, he fled Makassar for Jakarta.

Once in the capital, Hizbullah took Faruq to meet like-minded

Indonesians. Among his new acquaintances was Abu Zejid (alias Haris Fadillah, alias Abu Dzar), a debt collector-*cum*-jihadist living in Bogor.[4] Shortly afterwards, Abu Zejid introduced Faruq to his daughter, Mira, who was enrolled in an Islamic school at the time.

To that time, Faruq had been singularly unlucky in love. For years, he had been trying in vain to find a Southeast Asian wife. Attempts in the Philippines had all fallen short. Upon arrival in Makassar in 1998, he had met a dean from a local Islamic university and asked to marry his sister; the dean's family rejected the proposal outright. After his introduction to Abu Zejid's daughter, he wasted no time asking for her hand. The debt collector scoffed at the first request, though he finally consented to a second plea in May.

With Faruq set to become family, Abu Zejid was quick to introduce his future son-in-law to a cast of militant friends from Indonesia and Malaysia. During the same month he became engaged, Faruq was taken by Zejid to a villa outside Jakarta for a planning session among extremists. Among other things, Faruq, Zejid, and his acquaintances talked up schemes to assassinate Megawati Sukarnoputri. At the time, Megawati's party was the front-runner in national assembly elections set for the following month. They hatched additional plots to assassinate retired General Benny Moerdani – not coincidentally a Catholic – and assorted other dignitaries.

To put the plan into action, Faruq agreed to act as a triggerman. He personally cased Moerdani's house in Jakarta, while others organized finances and the acquisition of a suitable rifle from either Malaysia or the Philippines. But when the weapon could not be delivered in time (Faruq suspected that the appointed cell member had absconded with the money), the plot fell by the wayside.

By July 1999, Faruq was a married man. Prone to ambitious, often fanciful schemes, he talked up destroying the U.S. embassy in Jakarta with a massive car bomb like the ones used in Africa during 1998. Faruq also cased tall buildings in the capital, which he intended to use as sniper perches in the event he could provoke a full-blown religious war.

When not talking tough, Faruq spent the rest of 1999 expanding his network of contacts. Because of the fact that he had spent almost two years in Indonesia, Faruq was considered a key conduit by his al-Qaeda seniors. By late that year, he was receiving frequent telephone calls from Abu Zeid – the militant cleric in Kuwait that originally inspired Faruq to become a jihadist –

with referrals of imminent arrivals from the Middle East. (Abu Zeid at one point suggested that Faruq might be able to find an unpopulated island in the Indonesian archipelago that could be used as an al-Qaeda base.) Other referrals were being phoned in by Ibnul al-Khattab, an Azerbaijan-based Chechen extremist with ties to al-Qaeda.[5] Typically, Faruq would meet these short-term visitors – including Algerians, Egyptians, and Yemenis – and brief them on the Indonesian situation.

Faruq also deepened his network of local contacts. This included Hambali, the JI operations officer based in Malaysia, and Agus Dwikarna, the Makassar native whom Faruq initially viewed as more of a businessman and politician than a militant. The three came together in mid-2000, when Hambali channeled funds to Faruq for the purpose of conducting a survey of Aceh.[6]

Aceh had been chosen with a purpose in mind. For much of the previous decade, the separatist campaign in that restive region had been simmering. But following the end of the New Order regime, it had shifted to a low boil. For several reasons, al-Qaeda viewed this expanded paramilitary activity with interest. First, the population generally sympathized with GAM, the rebel umbrella group that ostensibly supported a strict interpretation of Islamic law. Second, Aceh was readily accessible from neighboring Malaysia. Third, Gus Dur's administration was at the time supporting a tactical ceasefire, making the Aceh countryside surprisingly accessible. Fourth, GAM was a fragmented guerrilla movement perpetually in need of funds and arms; al-Qaeda could theoretically help with both.

To further explore this possibility, in June 2000 Faruq and Dwikarna acted as guides during an Aceh fact-finding trip by the Egyptian national, Ayman al-Zawahiri, the second most influential man in al-Qaeda, and Mohammed Atef, that organization's military chief.[7] Perhaps disenfranchised by the cultural and ethnic nuances that colored the insurgency, however, al-Qaeda interest in Aceh never progressed beyond this foray.

During this same timeframe, Faruq made two important Arab contacts. The first was Achmad al-Amoudi, a Saudi national who opened the Jakarta branch of the al-Haramain foundation in the summer of 2000. Al-Haramain traced its origins back to the eighties, when it was established by the Saudis to channel support for the jihad in Afghanistan. It was also widely seen as that kingdom's spearhead for spreading its Wahhabi precepts. Al-Amoudi was especially well prepared for his Indonesian assignment, having previously served in Pakistan, Bangladesh, and Azerbaijan.

The second contact was a Saudi named Rashid. Posing as an al-Haramain representative (though Faruq never conclusively determined whether his role in the organization was bona fide or implied), Rashid effectively became Faruq's handler and financier. Believed to have near-direct access to Osama bin Laden, Rashid used no less than eight aliases. One of these was Syeh Hussein – the same name that had appeared in the September 2001 BIN report.

During the second half of 2000, Rashid and Faruq both focused on the violence flaring in the southern Malukus. Since January 1999, the island of Ambon had been consumed by sectarian warfare. One year on, in January 2000, a paramilitary organization known as *Laskar Jihad* ("Holy War Legion") was founded in Jogjakarta. The leader of the legion, Jafar Umar Thalib, had studied in Pakistan in the eighties and fought in Afghanistan near the end of the anti-Soviet struggle (at which time he met Osama bin Laden). Two months after its creation, a Laskar Jihad spokesman in Jakarta announced what would become the group's focus for the next two years: its active participation in the Ambon conflict. In April, after several weeks of high-profile paramilitary exercises at a private compound in Bogor, some 3,000 members recruited from across Java departed for the Malukus. Their arrival ratcheted up fighting in Ambon several notches, with fatalities ultimately reaching the thousands.

The dispatch of Laskar Jihad to Ambon paved the way for the arrival of other extremists. Prominent in this regard was JI, which established its own safe house and weapons storeroom in the Air Kuning district of Ambon and coordinated the arrival both of its volunteers from Java (who collectively took the name *Laskar Mujahidin*) as well as jihadists from Malaysia's KMM.[8]

JI also helped coordinate the arrival of jihadists from South Sulawesi's Laskar Jundullah. Like the volunteers from Java, this Sulawesi contingent was locally known as *Laskar Mujahidin*, though the Ambonese sometimes referred to it as *Laskar Mujahidin Kompak*. The Laskar Jundullah contingent in Ambon remained secretive and aloof, often dressing in Indonesian military camouflage that made it difficult to differentiate its members from bona fide troops.

To channel assistance to the Ambon jihadists, Rashid developed two paramilitary projects. The first, initiated during the second half of 2000, was known as the "Special Program." The aim of this was to provide paramilitary and religious training to local (Ambonese) recruits, and to help procure weapons for them. Each period of instruction, lasting up to a month, would be provided to students free of charge.

As base for the Special Program, Faruq and Rashid oversaw construction of a modest, isolated training camp (including a wooden schoolhouse) in the southern part of Ambon's Hitu peninsula. They then began assembling a Middle Eastern cadre to act as recruiters and instructors. Between late 2000 and mid-2001, the program was supported by no less than twenty expatriates, including eight Saudis, four Yemenis, two Algerians, an Egyptian, and a Pakistani. Most of the foreign cadre remained in Indonesia for only a few months at a time.[9]

Rashid's second project was known as the "Cooperative Program," also known as "One Body." This was directly tied to JI and involved the provision of assistance for Javanese, South Sulawesi, and Malaysian volunteers. For this, Rashid and Faruq opened safe houses in Ambon and South Sulawesi, financed the establishment of JI jungle training camps on the nearby islands of Seram and Buru, purchased firearms, and even procured a twenty-foot boat for gunrunning missions.

Helping bankroll these projects was Sheik Bandar (alias Abu Abdullah), the head of the Al-Haramain branch in Damman, Saudi Arabia. Bandar was no stranger to Indonesia; one of his wives was an Indonesian from Surabaya, and the sheik had visited that city frequently since 1999. Bandar often carried bricks of cash to Indonesia during his visits, which were passed to either Rashid or Faruq for use in Ambon.

But despite this largesse, not all was well among the Ambon combatants. In particular, arguments frequently flared between the South Sulawesi and Javanese volunteers. Tension grew to such a degree that the Sulawesi group abandoned Rashid's Cooperative Program by mid-2001 and went home; that program all but collapsed soon afterwards.

With the effective end of the Cooperative Program, Faruq left Ambon and ventured back to Jakarta in order to manage Rashid's dwindling activities from the capital. There, he was joined by a newly-arrived Arab propagandist named Abu Daud (alias Seyam Reda). An Egyptian with a German passport, Daud had earlier lived an unremarkable, secular life in Germany. But after coming into contact with al-Qaeda operatives in Europe, he underwent a radical change. Making his way to war-torn Bosnia using a false German passport under the name Hans Walter Kreis, for a time he joined the "Afghan" contingent within the 3 Corps, an all-foreign unit accused of committing war crimes during its jihad in Central Bosnia in the mid-nineties. Helping produce propaganda videos to solicit donations from the Middle East, Daud reportedly received two awards from the Bosnian leadership.

Moving to Saudi Arabia, Daud allegedly forged contact with key al-Qaeda figures. Later shifting to Qatar in early 2001, he attempted to land a job as a photographer for a local television network. Unsuccessful, he moved to Indonesia by August, which he had visited several times in the past. There, he linked up with Rashid and, though he had no visible means of support, signed a two-year lease on a Jakarta house.

All three – Daud, Rashid, and Faruq – were in need of a new battlefield, and they soon found a good candidate in Poso. In late November, Faruq and Daud ventured to Makassar, then made their way north with Laskar Jundullah's Afghan-trained Yasin Syawal. On the evening of 1 December, a gathering consisting of an estimated fifty Laskar Jundullah guerrillas prayed and were then presented with firearms. A cameraman using night vision equipment – probably Daud – captured the event on film. Remarkable was the quantity and relatively good quality of their weapons, including M-16 assault rifles and Uzi submachine guns; Faruq was among those issued an M-16.

At 2232 hours that evening, the assault force closed on Sepe, a small village near Poso. Again captured on film, militants are seen setting numerous houses on fire and firing weapons. A total of two hundred homes were reportedly smoldering by dawn.

Before further attacks could be staged, squabbles undercut the momentum of the extremists. Some of this was internal: Dwikarna was prone to quarreling with several of his subordinates. But Dwikarna was also irate with the Arabs over the fact that they were videotaping their actions – which he deemed a security risk – and were not sufficiently generous with their donations.

Feeling unwanted in Sulawesi, Faruq retreated back to Bogor to live in a remote hamlet with his wife's extended family. He did not remain there long. During January 2002, at the urging of Rashid, he dispatched an Indonesian colleague named Nasir (alias Nafar) to make a survey of possible religious and military training sites on the island of Kalimantan. Rashid reasoned that

Kalimantan was a good locale because it was large and did not have a heavy concentration of security forces.

Nasir was a good pick to make the survey. Hailing from Kalimantan, he had trained in both Afghanistan and Pakistan during the early nineties. After a brief trip to the East Kalimantan city of Balikpapan, Nasir returned to Jakarta with a video of his survey. Before this could even be shown to Rashid, plans were forwarded in late January for Faruq and Nasir to lead a small group back to Balikpapan in order to conduct a month-long "Call to Jihad" course at the Hidayatullah boarding school. Joining them would be Yasin Syawal, the senior Laskar Jundullah operative who had fought alongside Faruq at Poso in December, as well as Aris Munandar, the head of the MMI's Department of Inter-Mujahidin Relations.

By late February, word of the militant proselytizing at Hidayatullah had reached BIN. A 25 February report from a foreign counterpart correctly listed the names of three persons dispatched to Kalimantan as Nasir, Yasin, and Abdul Hadi (an alias used by Faruq).[10] Nothing further resulted from this "Call to Jihad" session, though not for want of trying.

Upon his return to Jakarta, Faruq remained in frequent telephone contact with Abu Zubaydah, the al-Qaeda operations officer he had known since his time in Afghanistan, and Ibn al-Shaykh al-Libi, a Libyan who had headed an al-Qaeda training camp. Perhaps fearing his luck was due to run out because of the worldwide crackdown on terrorism, Faruq told them he was contemplating a return to Kuwait on an authentic Indonesian passport. His previous attempt to get a passport – in Makassar during 1999 – had resulted in a brief detention. This time around, he had managed to get another set of fake identity papers from corrupt bureaucrats in Ambon that listed his name as Mahmud bin Ahmad Assegaf, allegedly born in Ambon in 1971. With these papers, he successfully obtained an Indonesian passport on 27 February 2002.

There were problems, however. Faruq wanted to depart with his wife and two daughters, but the immigration office was dragging its feet on issuing the wife's passport. Meantime, Zubaydah was pressuring Faruq to make preliminary plans for large-scale car and truck bomb attacks against U.S. embassies in the region on or near the 11 September anniversary.

Though willing, Faruq could turn to few confederates. Rashid's Cooperative Program in Ambon and Sulawesi had already fallen apart due to infighting among the Indonesian JI counterparts. Likewise, Rashid's Special

Program – the unilateral effort to train an Ambonese paramilitary cadre – had also hit hard times. This was due in part to the fact that several of the Arabs that had ventured to Ambon as trainers (especially the Egyptians and Yemenis) had started bickering among each other, and several had returned to the Middle East after 11 September. Moreover, Indonesian security authorities in Ambon had belatedly started cracking down on foreign nationals arriving on that island; Faruq learned that at least one al-Qaeda instructor – an Algerian who went by the alias Huzaifa – was detained by Indonesian authorities during early 2002 and deported.[11]

But despite the shrinking cast, there were still some willing allies. Rashid, Daud, and al-Amoudi were all in the area. So was Gharib, a Somali who held a Bosnian passport.[12] In his early thirties, Gharib was director of Yayasan Aman, a front charity initially funded with 30 million rupiah provided by Faruq. Far from running a humanitarian operation, however, Gharib was fully responsive to Rashid and had been instrumental in sending Ambonese students from Rashid's Special Program for paramilitary training in Pakistan. Present in Jakarta, too, was Zein al-Din, an Egyptian who, for the past year, had been an instructor in Ambon for Rashid's Special Program.

From this number, Faruq delegated tasks for coordinated tasks to take place around 11 September. Zein al-Din, for one, was assigned with planning strikes against U.S. targets in East Timor. Other attacks were to take place against U.S. diplomatic posts in Jakarta, Surabaya, Manila, Singapore, Bangkok, Taipei, Hanoi, and Phnom Penh. Faruq himself made plans to conduct an eleven-day reconnaissance trip that would take him through Singapore, Malaysia, Thailand, Cambodia, Vietnam, Brunei, and Malaysia (Borneo) before returning to Jakarta.

Before he could depart, Faruq wanted to settle the issue of his wife's passport. To navigate through the bureaucracy, he had resorted to paying a hefty sum to a middleman who claimed close connections to immigration officials. Faruq obtained these funds from Gharib, the Somali who headed Yayasan Aman.

Faruq's attempts to obtain the passport opened up an opportunity for BIN. By that time, one of the agency's informants had gotten word that the Kuwaiti had married the daughter of a Bogor militant. He further learned that Yasin Syawal would likely know the location of his house.

With this information, BIN agent Dadang made an excuse to see Syawal at a meeting of Afghan alumni in Jakarta. From Syawal, he heard of Faruq's passport woes. Thinking quickly, he claimed to have good immigration contacts that could guarantee fast delivery at a discounted price. As it sounded like a good deal, Syawal escorted the agent to Faruq's residence in mid-April. Faruq quickly warmed to Dadang's offer and offered his cell phone number to expedite the process.

Immediately, BIN forwarded Faruq's cell phone number to regional and international counterparts. This led to several astonishing discoveries. First, Filipino intelligence sources informed BIN that Faruq's number was in the memory of Dwikarna's cell phone. And on 27 April, it was learned from Pakistani officials that Faruq's number was in the memory of a phone used by Abu Zubaydah, who had been arrested in Pakistan on 28 March.

Faruq, meanwhile, was proving to be a moving target. In late April, he had taken leave of Bogor to implement his latest terrorist scheme. Every year since 1995, the U.S. Navy's Pacific Fleet had sponsored a series of bilateral Cooperation Afloat Readiness and Training (abbreviated as "Carat") exercises in Southeast Asia. These exercises, designed to enhance regional cooperation, focused on humanitarian and disaster relief projects. Since 1996, a portion of the exercises were held in Indonesia. The 2002 Carat series was set to begin on 17 May in Surabaya with some 1,400 U.S. sailors, marines, and coastguardsmen arriving on four ships.

As the Carat exercises garnered significant publicity, Faruq had learned details from the press. Deciding that this was a target ripe for a suicide attack like that conducted against the U.S.S. *Cole* in Yemen, he began looking for extremists willing to partake in martyrdom. Thinking that suicide was a bit extreme for local tastes, he asked Gharib, the Somali heading Yayasan Aman, to find Middle Eastern volunteers. Gharib, however, was preparing to go back to Bosnia to renew his passport and could not spare time to assist. Unable to recruit on his own, Faruq quietly shelved the idea.

In the meantime, the incriminating evidence against Faruq continued to mount. During May, counterparts found a cell phone link between him and Ibnul al-Khattab, the late Chechen rebel commander who was tied to al-Qaeda. That same month, a photo of Faruq was shown to Abu Zubaydah, who was proving to be somewhat cooperative with interrogators; Zubaydah positively identified the photograph as that of his Kuwaiti al-Qaeda colleague trained in Afghanistan.[13]

Unaware that the dragnet was closing, Faruq was engrossed in eleventh-hour terrorist planning during late May. Claiming an interest in agriculture, he purchased a ton of urea fertilizer in Bogor. This was actually intended for use in an explosives package targeted against the U.S. embassy in Jakarta. Over the course of several shuttles, at least half a ton of the urea was picked up by a driver employed by a top JI lieutenant and stored at the lieutenant's house in Jakarta.

By that time, BIN became aware that Faruq's wife and children were in Sumatra and might be preparing to steal across the Malacca Strait without passports. Fearing that Faruq might be a flight risk, Team Alpha rushed to Bogor on the night of 4 June. Approaching the suspect's house, it entered at 0200 hours, 5 June.

What followed next was a case of déjà vu. As with the attempt to capture Madni, Faruq was not at home. Instead, it found eight members of his wife's extended family.

Team Alpha knew it was in trouble. In particular, it feared word would soon leak of its presence, especially since neighbors in the hamlet had undoubtedly seen it approach. Remaining huddled inside the house, it took pains to ensure that no members of the family attempted to alert Faruq or his wife via telephone.

Thinking fast, the Alpha commander, an especially competent lieutenant colonel from the army special forces, placed a call to Dadang. Shortly after sunrise, Dadang relayed a prepared message to Faruq. The wife's passport was ready, he told the Kuwaiti, and could be picked up later that morning. After several further calls to iron out the details, Faruq said he would be at a Bogor mosque at 1500 hours. In the event this was a ruse, BIN officials rushed photographs of Faruq (copied from passport photographs given to Dadang) to immigration officials at the Jakarta airport and seaport.

As promised, Faruq arrived at the mosque. Quickly surrounded by security officials, he resisted slightly before being taken to the Bogor immigration office. Over the next two days, immigration and police intelligence officers attempted to interrogate him. Though he spoke some Indonesian, he did not prove cooperative. Found in possession of a fraudulent passport, Faruq was deported on 8 June to a third country.[14]

While Faruq had been hustled out of the country, word had not yet leaked to the press. Without pause, BIN looked to move swiftly against his foreign colleagues thought to still be present in the capital. It had already gotten wind of frequent meetings at a house rented by Rashid in East Jakarta. These all-Arab trysts, BIN learned, regularly touched on terrorist plans and included such personalities as Gharib, al-Amoudi, and Abu Daud. Of these figures, Rashid was deemed the most pivotal.

Catching him was easier said than done. After weeks of discreet inquiries, the precise location of his house was not confirmed until 5 September. When Team Alpha entered the locale, however, it found that the Saudi was not there; it was later determined he had gone to ground and fled to Saudi Arabia in late September.

The search for Gharib was equally disappointing. A quick check showed that his Yayasan Aman had quietly closed its doors a week after Faruq was apprehended. Gharib, too, had probably skipped the country. As a silver lining, Yayasan Aman and al-Haramain stopped channeling funds to Ambon and Poso.

BIN next turned its attention to Abu Daud. Through sheer luck, this search proved fruitful. When Team Alpha conducted interviews among neighbors around Rashid's residence, it chanced upon a public transport driver who remembered moving household effects for a Middle Eastern man during August. BIN concluded that Daud had probably fled Indonesia soon after Faruq's disappearance, but had since returned to the country and shifted to a new home.

The public transport driver, it turned out, still remembered the Pasar Minggu address where he had delivered the items. BIN immediately placed this new locale under surveillance and was able to identify a foreigner of Arab ethnic origin frequenting the house. Faruq later positively identified the person surreptitiously photographed at the front gate as Abu Daud.

At that point, a bombshell hit Indonesia. On 15 September, the Asia edition of *Time* magazine published a front-page exposé about the capture of Faruq. Included in the article was mention of the al-Haramain connection. Also mentioned was sensitive information about the reported complicity of Abu Bakar Ba'asyir. Not only did the article start a political firestorm in Indonesia, but it alerted al-Qaeda that Faruq was talking; if any of its operatives were still in Indonesia, they would probably take additional evasive measures.

Realizing time was of the essence, Team Alpha personnel raided Abu Daud's house on the night of 17 September. Abu Daud, who insisted he was a German citizen, did not resist. Inside his house, they found eighteen videotapes.

Many contained footage of jihadists operating in Indonesia, which were apparently intended for fund-raising among rich sheikhs in the Middle East. The most damning of these was the December footage shot in Poso; not only did this include the day and date on the bottom of the frame, but it also featured Faruq and Yasin Syawal posing for the camera.

Further incriminating Abu Daud was his cell phone. Among the numbers in its memory was one known to be used for contacting JI operative Hambali. Another was for Agus Dwikarna, and yet another for the Wafa al-Igatha al-Islamaia organization, a Middle Eastern charity that, like al-Haramain, had been implicated in paramilitary activities.

As a result of the uproar caused over the extradition of previous terrorist suspects, BIN turned over Daud to the Indonesian police within twenty-four hours. Sentenced in January 2003 to ten months in prison for visa infractions, he was ultimately deported to Germany by mid-year.

During the weeks immediately after the detention of Abu Daud, BIN conducted a series of further operations. One was an attempt to locate al-Amoudi, the al-Haramain branch director. Although a BIN informant had spotted him soon after publication of the *Time* article, a visit to his residence revealed he had fled Indonesia at the close of September. Another was a search for Pakistani terrorists who had reportedly fled to West Java after killing eleven Frenchmen during a May bus bombing in Karachi. While Team Alpha investigated these claims for three weeks, it turned up no evidence that any of these terrorists were on Indonesian soil

BIN's top target, however, was senior JI member Hambali. Early in the second week of October, Team Alpha ventured to a small Arab community in East Java where an informant had reported the recent presence of a clean-shaven Hambali. Residents positively identified photographs of Hambali on 11 October, though the terrorist himself had apparently departed.

The following night, Indonesia suffered its greatest terrorist attack in history. Multiple explosions rocked Bali, destroying a pair of nightclubs. Two hundred and two individuals were killed, including 88 Australian nationals. The bombings had the hallmark of a JI, if not al-Qaeda, operation, and Hendropriyono said as much in the days after the event.

Immediately, Indonesia's security forces focused their energies on tracking the perpetrators. BIN, which in late October 2002 was given the responsibility for coordinating intelligence activity among all government bodies, played a significant role in compiling the dossiers of top suspects. Intuitively, the agency assumed the involvement of Hambali, especially as he was thought to have been near Bali shortly before the blasts. But since the trail had grown cold in East Java, BIN energies at the time were directed against other targets. Particularly promising were Team Alpha's efforts in West Java, where a teltap on the day after the Bali incident recorded an extremist boasting he had seen stockpiled explosives with a JI cell in the Central Java capital of Semarang.

On 28 October, Team Alpha moved against the West Java radical and turned him over to the police. But in a dramatic display of unhealthy inter-service rivalry, the police refused to use teltap transcripts and soon released the detainee. (Not until nine months later, in July 2003, did the police belatedly move against the JI's Semarang cell and uncover at least part of the demolitions cache.)

As 2002 came to a close, BIN resumed its search for Hambali. This came after an unsolicited letter from Medan arrived in December; the letter stated that an acquaintance of the writer, who had spent considerable time among the Ngruki exiles in Malaysia, spoke with Hambali at a market near Medan circa mid-2002. Team Alpha rushed to North Sumatra, located the writer, then found the acquaintance who reportedly met Hambali. The terrorist was now said to be clean-shaven, just as had been reported in East Java. But as the information was stale – it predated the East Java sighting – the lead went nowhere.

The search for Hambali was energized yet again in early 2003 following the March capture of top al-Qaeda operative Khalid Sheik Mohamad in Pakistan. A long-time acquaintance of Hambali, Khalid claimed that he had funneled $50,000 to the Indonesian after the Bali bombing. Khalid further stated he believed Hambali was in the final stages of a terrorist strike in Southeast Asia, though he was not sure of the target.[15]

In January 2003, BIN conducted an internal review of its ability to operate against religious extremists. While Directorate 43 was deemed fluent in wiretapping, there was a perceived need to establish a special team specialized in longterm agent penetrations of Islamic radical organizations. Canvassing the agency for Arabic linguists and religious experts, selection of the 25-man unit – whose name is still classified – was finalized by month's end. Its first operation proved a case of mistaken identity: based on information from a regional counterpart, the suspected bombers they tracked from Surabaya turned out to be a ring that smuggled illegal workers out of the country. But its second operation, a successful surveillance of extremists linked to the JI cell operating in Australia, proved the concept a success.[16]

While counter-terrorism had now become BIN's undisputed raison d'être, the regional war against terrorists was progressing in fits and starts. On a positive note, Hendropriyono received a call from the U.S. embassy in mid-August informing him that U.S. authorities would soon be moving against BIN's longtime nemesis, Hambali. As such calls were only placed after arrests were a done deal, the BIN chief instinctively knew Hambali was already in custody; a Thai newspaper confirmed as much the following day. But on a negative note, a JI suicide bomber blew up a van on 5 August in front of the J.W. Marriott hotel in Central Jakarta; ten were killed and one hundred wounded. BIN officials had been warning of such an imminent attack (Deputy Chief As'at made public comments to that effect the previous week), but had been unable to pinpoint a time or target.

Later that same month, on 22 August, BIN celebrated its thirty-seventh anniversary. There was no denying the agency had made significant, discernible gains over the previous year. Earlier in the quarter, for example, ground had been broken on two new intelligence schools – one undergraduate, the other graduate – that would be administered by BIN. At the same time, the agency had expanded to seven deputies – one new post for technology, another for research and planning – the largest number of top-echelon posts in its history. And in a country where impressions are everything, there was a widely-held public perception that the Hendropriyono team had not only reversed Bakin's decline of the previous two decades, but had significantly surpassed Bais in terms of output and profile.

But just as with other intelligence agencies around the world, its greatest gains were made in the shadows. Like Zulkifli Lubis had dictated back in 1946, Indonesia's spies were invisible soldiers engaged in a critical war of wits. Such was the case on 24 August, when Directorate 43 and BIN's special penetration team scored a trio of successes against foreign extremists on Indonesian soil, the full details of which are still classified. With no public kudos, no media platitudes, BIN's top officers briefly paused to offer a toast before setting their sights back on the target-rich environment that is Indonesia.

1   It is believed that Abu Jandal is an alias used by Yasin Syawal.

2   Hizbullah was one of the locals asked by Agus Dwikarna to guide BIN's Acehnese informant in February 2002; this conversation had been overheard by the Konro teltap.

3   Faruq's false identity card claimed he was born in Pakistan in 1966; it listed his occupation as a religious proselytizer. Prior to obtaining this false identify card, Faruq was sent a false Saudi passport from al-Qaeda's Abu Zubaydah. But when he tried to use this passport to leave Indonesia via East Kalimantan, it was seized by immigration officials because the entry seal was obviously forged.

4   Abu Zejid was allegedly a well-known *preman* (criminal thug) recruited into Darul Islam during the mid-nineties. *International Crisis Group*, "Jemaah Islamiyah in Southeast Asia: Damaged but Still Dangerous," 26 August 2003, p. 24.

5   Faruq had first met al-Khattab in Pakistan between training stints in Afghanistan.

6   *Tempo*, 4 November 2002, p. 23.

7   The June 2000 trip was first reported by CNN during its 9 July 2002 broadcast. Faruq had previously made a two-day visit to Aceh in early 1999 with Teungku Fauzi Hasbi, a member of a GAM splinter group.

8   Faruq's father-in-law, Abu Zejid, ventured to Ambon to fight in the Laskar Mujahidin contingent. In October 2000, he was killed in action. Given the fact that he was a generation older than most of his fellow Laskar Mujahidin volunteers, and the fact that there were few fatalities suffered by the contingent, his burial became a highly publicized affair. A fund-raising video for Kompak, which was produced by senior MMI official Aris Munandar, prominently featured the burial.

9   The Special Program eventually totaled four classes of twenty students apiece. Seven graduates from the first class were sent to Pakistan for advanced training.

10 Officials from the Hidayatullah *pesantren* admit that Aris Munandar and Yasin Syawal conducted self-defense instruction there in January, but deny Faruq was present. See *Tempo*, 2 December 2002, p. 22.

11   This deportation almost certainly corresponds to Shahni Farid, a 32-year old
      Algerian who was deported from Ambon on 27 March along with Hussein al-
      Zahrani, a 27-year old Saudi national.

12   Gharib had fought in Bosnia with the "Afghan" contingent under the 3 Corps; in
      appreciation, he was awarded a Bosnian passport.

13   On 17 May, it was learned that Faruq's old cell phone number (he changed numbers
      frequently) was found in the pocket litter of an al-Qaeda prisoner taken to U.S.
      detention facilities in Cuba.

14   Media reports indicate he was sent to a U.S.-run detention facility at Bagram
      airbase, Afghanistan.

15   Khalid noted that Hambali was obsessed with destroying the U.S. embassy in
      Jakarta. He also noted Hambali planned to hit a U.S. oil company in Indonesia
      prior to the September 11 attacks.

16   During this period, Team Alpha, fearing a repeat of the Iraqi terrorist deployments
      around Southeast Asia during the 1991 Gulf War, operated within Jakarta to
      guard against possible attacks during to the U.S.-led Operation Iraqi Freedom.

GLOSSARY

Al-Qaeda	Arabic for "The Base."
Apodeti	Portuguese acronym of the Timorese party advocating integration with Indonesia.
ASEAN	Association of Southeast Asian Nations
Bais	Indonesian acronym for *Badan Intelijen Strategis* (Strategic Intelligence Agency), Indonesia's military intelligence agency created in 1983.
Bakin	Indonesian acronym for *Badan Koordinasi Intelijen Negara* (State Intelligence Coordination Agency), Indonesia's civilian intelligence agency from 1967-2000.
BIA	Indonesian acronym for *Badan Intelijen ABRI* (Armed Forces Intelligence Agency), the name briefly adopted by Indonesia's military intelligence agency, Bais.
BIN	Indonesian acronym for *Badan Intelijen Negara* (State Intelligence Agency), Indonesia's civilian intelligence agency after January 2001; previously known as Bakin.
BISAP	Indonesian acronym for *Biro Informasi Staf Angkatan Prang* (Information Bureau for the War Forces), the name given to the military intelligence service in 1952.
BKI	Indonesian abbreviation for *Badan Koordinasi Intelijen* (Intelligence Coordination Agency), Indonesia's civilian intelligence service from 1958-1959.
BPI	Indonesian abbreviation for *Badan Pusat Intelijen* (Central Intelligence Agency), Indonesia's civilian intelligence agency from 1959-1966.
Brani	Indonesian acronym for *Badan Rahasia Negara Indonesia* (Secret Agency of the State of Indonesia), an umbrella intelligence organization created by republican forces in May 1946.
CAT	Civil Air Transport, a proprietary airline of the U.S. Central Intelligence Agency.
CIA	Central Intelligence Agency
Confrontation	The period of diplomatic tension and armed conflict, short of all-out war, between Indonesia and the Commonwealth forces defending Malaysia.

girah   Indonesian abbreviation for *kegiatan rahasia* (secret activity), the name given to agent handlers within Satsus Intel.

GAM   Indonesian acronym for *Gerakan Aceh Merdeka* (Free Aceh Movement).

GRU   The Russian abbreviation for Chief Intelligence Directorate, the Soviet military intelligence body.

JI   Abbreviation for *Jemaah Islamiyah*, Arabic for "Islamic Community."

JIEG   Joint Intelligence Estimates Group, the gathering of civilian and military intelligence chiefs who attended regular afterhours briefings coordinated by the BPI.

JRA   Japanese Red Army

KGB   The Russian abbreviation for Committee for State Security, the Soviet civilian intelligence agency.

KIN   Indonesian acronym for *Komando Intelijen Negara* (State Intelligence Command), Indonesia's civilian intelligence agency from 1966-1967.

KMM   Malay abbreviation for *Kampulan Mujahidin Malaysia* (Malaysian Mujahidin Group).

Kopkamtib   Indonesian acronym for *Komando Operasi Pemulihan Keamanan dan Kertiban* (Operational Command for the Restoration of Security and Order), which was the military's coordinating office initially created in 1965 for rooting out communists; by the seventies, the office was increasingly used for ensuring unwavering loyalty to the New Order.

LIN   Indonesian acronym for *Lembaga Intelijen Negara* (State Intelligence Institute), the name of a proposed intelligence agency under the Minister of Defense.

MILF   Moro Islamic Liberation Front

MI6   Britain's foreign intelligence service.

MMI   Indonesian abbreviation for *Majelis Mujahidin Indonesia* (Indonesian Mujahidin Council) the umbrella group created in August 2000 for Indonesia's jihadist and other radical religious groups.

NLF   National Liberation Front, the South Vietnamese revolutionary organization popularly known as the Viet Cong.

Opsus   Indonesian acronym for *Operasi Khusus* (Special Operations), the ad hoc body headed by Ali Moertopo that conducted discreet diplomatic, political, and military operations for the New Order.

Perti	Indonesian acronym for *Partai Tarbiyah Islamiyah Indonesia* (Indonesian Islamic Education Party).
Peta	Indonesian acronym for *Pembela Tanah Air* (Defenders of the Homeland), an Indonesian auxiliary home guard formed and controlled by the Imperial Japanese during World War II.
PDI	Indonesian abbreviation for *Partai Demokrasi Indonesia* (Indonesian Democratic Party).
PKI	Indonesian abbreviation for *Partai Komunis Indonesia* (Indonesian Communist Party).
PLO	Palestine Liberation Organization
rezident	The ranking KGB/GRU officer in a Soviet embassy; the equivalent of a CIA station chief.
Satsus Intel	Indonesian acronym for *Satuan Khusus Intelijen* (Special Intelligence Unit).
Satlak Bakin	Indonesian acronym for *Satuan Pelaksana* Bakin (Bakin Operational Unit). In 1976, Satsus Intel was renamed Satlak Bakin, signaling its full integration under Bakin administration.
STI	Indonesian abbreviation for *Satuan Tugas Intelijen* (Intelligence Task Force) the investigative arm within Kopkamtib.
UP 01	Indonesian abbreviation for *Unit Pelaksana* 01 (Operational Unit 01), Bakin's surveillance unit.

INDEX